CAI GUO

CHILLIDA

TUTTLE

RUSCHA

BASELITZ

GIACOMETTI

PICASSO

BOURGEOIS

BEUYS

NOGUCHI

VITAL

KIEFER

HIRST

PARR

KAPOOR

V&A

BLOOD ON PAPER

The art of the book

ILIAZD

CARO

LICHTENSTEIN

KOONS

BUREN

MATISSE

CLEMENTE

LEWITT

LECUIRE

McCARTHY

BACON

MOTHERWELL

REGO

DUBUFFET

ROTH

RAUSCHENBERG

TÀPIES

PHILLIPS

BUSTAMANTE

BALTHUS

MIRÓ

ANCIS

FREE ADMISSION
WWW.VAM.AC.UK
SOUTH KENSINGTON

ILLUSTRATION BY DAMIEN POULAIN

15 APRIL–
29 JUNE
2008

PRIL–
UNE
8

SPONSORED BY
Deutsche Bank

GRANTA

12 Addison Avenue, London W11 4QR
email editorial@granta.com
To subscribe go to www.granta.com or call 020 8955 7011

ISSUE 101

In the United States, *Granta* is published in association with Grove/Atlantic Inc,
841 Broadway, 4th Floor, New York, NY 10003, and distributed by PGW.

Granta is printed and bound in Italy by Legoprint.
This magazine has been printed on paper that has been certified by the Forest Stewardship Council (FSC).

Cover design: Graphic Thought Facility

ISBN 978-1-905881-01-7

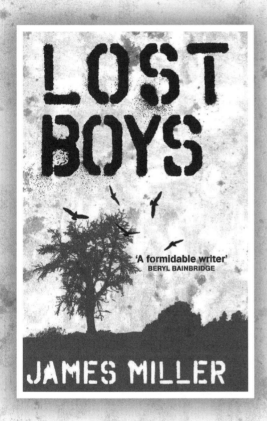

CONTENTS

Like a Rolling Stone

Last night I randomly chose an issue of *Granta* from my shelf to skim before going to sleep. As luck would have it, I picked up *Granta* 65 and discovered a remarkable thing in the Sergio Larrain piece, 'London Then'.

In the photograph captioned 'Party in a house in Archway', one sees a lantern-jawed visage on the left in the arms of an admiring woman [page 286]. This young man is without a doubt none other than Ian Stewart. He went on to become a founding member of the Rolling Stones, was shunted aside for his perceived lack of requisite girly good looks, but remained with the Stones thereafter as a much-loved and revered road manager/piano player and general aide-de-camp.

In this photo Ian Stewart must have been in his late teens and a few scant years short of meeting his history mates. Incredible that a roving Chilean photographer in London in 1958 would have chanced upon him.

James McCarthy, by email

The Complaints Department

It has been seven weeks since I placed my order and it has not yet been processed. I have had no response to my telephone enquiry as to why this has happened.

I have an existing subscription that I am strongly considering not renewing on the basis of this lack of response.

Alan Wenger, by email

GRANTA *has recently undergone a period of transition, involving a move to new premises and a change to a new subscriptions house. We regret that this has caused some disruption to our distribution operations and apologize to any subscribers who have experienced problems.*

Granta 100

I have signed up for the year and, from evidence of *Granta* 100, I'm glad that I did. Hope all later issues are of this high quality.

Michael Rowland, by email

SEND YOUR LETTERS TO GRANTA,
12 ADDISON AVENUE, LONDON W11 4QR
OR EMAIL EDITORIAL@GRANTA.COM.
WE RESERVE THE RIGHT TO EDIT LETTERS FOR LENGTH AND CLARITY.

Editor's Letter

I bought my first issue of *Granta* from a Waterstone's in London's West End towards the end of 1990. There was a small pile of the book-sized magazine next to the till, and I was attracted by its bright and witty cover image – a photomontage of Mikhail Gorbachev holding an unopened bottle of champagne. The previous year had been one of extraordinary convulsion and upheaval. From Beijing to Berlin, from Bucharest to Bradford, from Tehran to Hillsborough, Sheffield: 1989 was the year of the restless crowd. It was obvious that the world as I'd known it throughout my childhood and adolescence – the world of the Cold War – was changing irreversibly. So much seemed to be breaking apart, but as yet I had no idea as to how the pieces would be put back together and the shape and pattern they would form. I had recently graduated. I was feeling adrift and confused. I was looking for something that would help me make sense of what had been going on and what was to come. In retrospect, I was looking for something to read. And here was *Granta*, before me on a bookshop counter, with its bold, exclamatory title, 'New Europe!'

Rereading that issue recently, I feel about it now as I did then: that it had vitality and was engaging with the present moment in ways that so many other British publications were not. It had none of the parochialism, self-satisfaction and introversion one would have expected of a literary magazine. It looked outwards – to the whole world.

Nearly two decades later, I have the good fortune to be editor of *Granta*, and I want readers to feel about the magazine as I did when I first read it: that it is interested in everything, determined to witness the world.

Many assumptions have been

made about *Granta*: we don't publish writing about writing, we don't publish poetry and each issue is themed. In fact, if a ring-fence was ever erected around the content of the magazine, the posts have been pulled up. *Granta* has always succeeded when at its boldest and most unpredictable, when it has sought to challenge and confront as well as entertain and inform. Our intention, then, is to publish new writing in whichever form or genre we choose; to be more internationalist in outlook and ambition, to publish more literature in translation, more photography, more investigations and long-form reportage.

This issue has no theme: we wanted simply to showcase as many good and varied pieces as we could, without constraint. But we shall be theming occasional issues, starting with *Granta* 102, out in the summer.

We have refined the design, and introduced a new front section, which includes a letters page that will provide a forum for readers' views and opinions. We have reinvigorated our website, www.granta.com, with original content to be added daily. Our archive of articles will soon be available online, and subscribers will have free access to it. My expectation is that the site will become an important literary resource, and fun to visit and explore.

When I was asked to become editor last spring, I quickly realized that my first issue would be *Granta*'s 100th, and that my second would be its 101st. 101: an Orwellian number of doom! But my colleagues and I had no feelings of anxiety or dread as we worked on this latest issue; we felt only a sense of renewal and of possibility as *Granta* sails on into its second century.

Jason Cowley

www.granta.com
Listen to an interview with the editor

FIRST PERSON | RUTH FRANKLIN

Dreams of reason

We're on vacation somewhere in the country, by a lake. The light is hazy, green, as if I were looking at the sky from underwater; the lake, too, is green, surrounded by dense weeds and brambles. My husband and son are playing nearby, shouting to each other. Suddenly I realize – what have I been doing all this time? Why wasn't I watching? – that I can't see my little girl. And I know, with the certainty one has in dreams, that she has fallen in the lake. Shock has rooted me, but I scream for my husband. I know he will be able to do what I can't, to jump in and save her, if only he gets there in time.

For almost as long as I can remember, I've suffered from nightmares. Sometimes they strike regularly, once a week or so; or months of uneventful sleep will pass and then I'll have a blizzard of them, every night for weeks. The first one I recall, at the age of about five, was a single image: a bulldozer digging an enormous hole in the basement of our house, with a sign that read DANGER blocking the way in. I remember little of the precise circumstances around the dream: we were moving to a different house, and my parents' marriage was soon to break up, but I didn't know that at the time. What I do remember is the sickening dread, so overpowering that I could not bear to look down the basement stairs for fear of seeing that gaping hole.

We tend to dismiss dreams as unimportant – as no more than random misfirings of brain circuitry, meaningful only if we believe them to be. 'It was just a dream,' we tell children who awaken screaming in the night. As for the word 'nightmare', it has been debased through careless use, applied indiscriminately to long lines at the grocery store or packed subway cars. But for someone in the grip of a nightmare, it's not 'just a dream': he or she experiences the terror of the dream as if it were real.

'The person awakes panic-struck from some hideous vision,' wrote the nineteenth-century physician Robert Macnish, 'and even after reason returns and convinces him of the unreal nature of his apprehensions, the panic for some time continues, his heart throbs violently, he is covered with cold perspiration, and hides his head beneath the bedclothes, afraid to look around him.'

The terror of the nightmare, unlike the terror of a ghost story or a horror film, can be experienced only in isolation. Another person can appreciate that it must be frightening to dream of one's child drowning, but no one else can feel the waves of fear that reverberate long after one wakes to find the baby sleeping peacefully. We know that nightmares are unreal, yet they torment us all the same.

There have always been two theories about the interpretation of dreams: either they look forward or they look back. Before the age of psychoanalysis, the former was dominant. Dreams were commonly held to prefigure future events: in the Bible, Pharaoh's nightmares about the cows and ears of grain foretell the years of famine in Egypt. In Greek mythology, Hecuba, the mother of Paris, dreams of giving birth to a firebrand. Gustavus Hindman Miller's arcane 1901 manual *10,000 Dreams Interpreted* lists, encyclopedia-style, various dream symbols and their meaning in the cryptic, oracular language of fortune cookies: 'To see mosquitoes in your dreams [means that] you will strive in vain to remain impregnable to the sly attacks of secret enemies.'

Physician-philosophers from Robert Burton onward ('fearful

dreams' were among his symptoms of melancholy) have conducted investigations into the causes of nightmares, often inspired by their own suffering. Nightmares have been said to be a sign of a creative personality, of an elongated uvula, or of 'congestion in the brain'. They are brought on by eating any number of foods: cabbage, legumes, cucumbers. John Bond, the author of the first book written in English on the subject – *An Essay on the Incubus, or Nightmare* (1753) – believed that nightmares came from sleeping on one's back. His response was to sleep, miserably, in a chair in an attempt to ward off his 'attacks'. The Victorian physician John Waller thought that undigested food remaining in the stomach at bedtime produced 'impulses' in the nervous system 'which on reaching the brain are transformed into feelings of terror' (hence the modern-day injunction not to eat pizza before bed). Even so supremely rational a thinker as Kant had an original theory of nightmares: he believed they were the body's own built-in alarm system, designed to awaken a sleeper whose safety was compromised by poor circulation.

With the advent of psychoanalysis, nightmares came to be understood as a particularly perverse twist on Freud's famous theory of the dream as wish-fulfilment: namely, the nightmare expresses a repressed wish so taboo that even its distortion in the dream state suffices to terrify the dreamer. Ernest Jones, a follower of Freud who wrote a series of psychoanalytic studies of nightmares, argued that they are always 'an expression of a mental conflict over an incestuous desire'. This seems about as plausible as the ancient myth Jones finds at the root of his theory, which held that nightmares were brought on by a mythological being who sat on people's chests as they slept – hence the shortness of breath one often experiences on awakening. (In Old English, this creature was known as a *mare*.) A synonym for nightmare is 'incubus', the term for another supernatural nocturnal visitor said to have sex with women while they sleep. In Henry Fuseli's painting *The Nightmare* (1781), which Freud is said to have displayed in his study, a woman in a suggestively draping nightgown lies supine on a bed, eyes tightly shut and mouth agape, in what could be a vision of ecstasy were it not for the hairy demon crouched on her breast.

The psychological roots of my own dreams have always been so obvious as to render their analysis pointless, a puzzle so easy it's not worth the effort. My parents divorced when I was young: I dreamed of abandonment, of losing things, of becoming lost. (Did my bulldozer dream foretell the divorce? That would be the ancient interpretation; it seems more likely that my childhood self internalized some sign of the impending break – quarrels, coldness – and spun it into a fantasy of danger in the home.) When I was an adolescent, a close friend attempted suicide: for years afterwards my dreams killed off all the people close to me and, when the supply of loved ones ran out, my mind invented new ones. And, like all mothers, I dream about disaster befalling my children.

But what's common among my diverse nightmares – and I've come to understand that this is different from the way many people dream – is that they follow a classic narrative arc: beginning, middle, dénouement. They have resolution. My nightmares, over the years, have become my own private library of stories, with a roster of favourites that I return to in my waking thoughts from time to time, to see how well they've held up or whether I might be able to coax some new meaning out of them. I've come to treasure this secret storehouse of anxieties and disturbances. For nightmares, not unlike works of literature or indeed any art, are an investigation into the deepest, most primary forces that drive us. Not only that, but they even conform to one of the classic theories of literature: the defamiliarization of the familiar. Like ghost stories or Greek tragedies, nightmares allow us to confront our fears from a safe distance, and the catharsis that results is as powerful as any that I've experienced through literature. It seems no accident that the same word, 'haunting', is used for both nightmares and particularly affecting works of art. And so I've come to see my nightmares as less a burden than a gift, a private theatre for the safe staging of my personal melodramas, where the bombs detonated during the night won't shatter the peace of my waking life.

I've watched my children closely for signs of nightmares. My son, at age four, is a sound sleeper who rarely articulates his dreams. (Men are said to experience fewer nightmares than women.) But not long ago my little girl awoke during the night with a shriek unlike any I'd ever heard from her. I ran to her crib and found her sobbing.

'Did something happen?' I asked, and she nodded.

'What?'

She took a shuddering breath. 'Lion take me,' she said.

I rocked her, trying to imagine what she might have seen. The sleeping lions at the zoo she had visited that day, risen up, claws bared, to grab the toddler watching from above? The lion night light in her room, transformed by some trick of shadow or imagination into a live, frothing beast? 'To dream of a lion,' Gustavus Miller tells us with his typical combination of absurdity and gravitas, 'signifies that a great force is driving you' – a statement at which every parent of a two-year-old will nod knowingly. As she drowsed back to sleep, I imagined that lion standing at the gatepost of her own personal mythology, guarding the gulf that separates reality and imagination, and perhaps someday extending its paw to help her across. ■

VISUAL THINKING | DOUGLAS COUPLAND

Zulu Romeo Foxtrot

Last summer in Vancouver I attended a screening of the cult documentary *Helvetica* – a biography of the classic sans serif font designed in 1957. All 950 seats of the Ridge Theatre were filled, and I haven't felt as much energy in an audience since attending the 1993 taping of Nirvana's *MTV Unplugged* in Sony Studios in New York. Had it been possible to buy pennants and banners in the lobby, the air would have been filled with such graphic bursts as *Italics!* or **MEDIUM!** or Light!, and I'd have been holding one, too. Mine would have read: **Helvetica Neue (T1) 75 Bold**. The font is a rock star.

Directed by Gary Hustwit, the film richly rewarded an audience comprised almost entirely of designers, artists and architects. Afterwards, during a Q&A session, I asked a question that revealed that roughly eighty per cent of the audience used Macs, not PCs, and those who held up their hands as PC users received mild boos. It was a tough crowd.

This Mac dominance hardly came as a surprise to me. Last spring my New York publicist asked me who my reading audience was and I blurted out, 'Mac users.'

'Why is that?'

'Because Macs are used by visual thinkers.'

'I see.'

Silence.

No, he didn't see, because one is either a visual thinker or one is not. He was not. I'm beginning to think that being a visual thinker is like being right-handed or red-haired; it was all decided the moment the sperm hit the egg. And just to be clear, being a visual thinker isn't a preference like country and western music or a fondness for pugs. One has no choice in the matter. People who study the science of this stuff say that roughly one person in five thinks visually, which perhaps explains the four-to-one ratio of PC users to Mac users in the everyday world. My question here is, of course, if you don't see the world visually, then how exactly *are* you seeing it?

I came to realize this fundamental perceptual difference in humanity rather late in the day, perhaps a decade after I began writing novels. Before writing novels I worked as a visual artist and designer, and I naively and romantically assumed that writing precluded the making of visual art. Wrong. To illustrate the result of this assumption, let me provide a generic reconstruction of an interview with me in, say, 1999, just before I figured things out:

Interviewer: So, I read your book and, uh, you're a visual thinker, aren't you?

Me: Uh... yes.

Interviewer: (pained silence).

Me: (pained silence).

Interviewer: Yes, your work is so (insert loaded sigh here) visual.

Me (in my head): What is it with this person?

Me (out loud): Well, isn't everybody a visual thinker? We all have eyes and we all see. How can people not be visual thinkers?

Interviewer: (another sigh).

And there's the gist of it. I tried for a decade to be a part of the book universe, and the harder I tried, the more I encountered that same feeling that might have been experienced, say, by a black musician walking into a Baltimore country club *circa* 1955, sitting down at a dinner table and expecting to be served. *This is not a very good fit, is it?*

And so, around 2000, I began to rethink my relationship with words. I looked back on the origins of my relationship with text to the first time I ever remember getting an almost erotic charge from words. This would have been from reproductions of Pop art in elementary school encyclopedias: Roy Lichtenstein's *Whaam!* or Andy Warhol's *Campbell's Soup Cans*. They were words, but they were something else, too. It was those words that landed me in art school in 1980, where I received my next dose of words that made me warm and tingly: the work of US artist Jenny Holzer. Holzer came to prominence in New York in the late 1970s. She generated truisms wherein she went through the great classics and reduced them down to sentences or fragments of sentences, a body of work referred to as *Truisms*. For example, Machiavelli's *The Prince* boils down to ABUSE OF POWER COMES AS NO SURPRISE. These truisms were then collected together in extensive lists and wheat-pasted on to the hoarding boards surrounding SoHo construction sites. These lists were in turn ripped from the walls by classmates doing the art-student pilgrimage to New York and shown to me back in Vancouver. When I saw these ripped papers with their columns of hundreds of truisms, my brain popped like a popcorn kernel. Words were not simply what they connoted: they were art objects and art supplies in themselves.

There is a eureka moment that most visual artists have at some point early on in their career and, once the moment has happened, they take their first steps across the great divide between visual art and literary art, two camps to whom words mean totally different things.

Once sensitized to text as an art object, the visual artist must, in a way, learn his or her own language all over again from scratch. One looks at the shape of words and the texture of the paper they rest on. One looks not just at the book, but at its cover. Visual culture is a very free and permissive place; high culture, low culture, pop culture, all source material is permitted if it's a part of your world.

Literary students, however, don't relearn their language from a visual and material standpoint. They are, if anything, actively encouraged to consider the process *infra dig*, and are certainly never allowed to fetishize the physical, typographical form of a word. In France there exists the convention of standardized unemotional text-only book covers – basically, a Salinger-like belief that a book (excuse me, a *text*) ought to speak for itself and not be compromised by such vulgarities as cover art, non-standardized fonts or author photos. Words exist only inasmuch as they denote something individually and collectively, but that is *all* they are. They're merely little freight containers of meaning, devoid of any importance on their own. To see words as art on their own is heresy.

This inflexibility makes sense to a non-visual thinker, but to visual thinkers such dogma is depressing and sad, like forcing ballerinas to wear suits of armour.

Here's a personal anecdote. Someone recently asked me what the most beautiful word I know is. I thought about it and the answer came quickly: my father used to have a floatplane with those call letters on the tailfin, ZRF – Zulu Romeo Foxtrot. The way these words look on paper is gorgeous; the images they conjure are fleeting, rich, colourful and unexpected. To savour the look of Zulu Romeo Foxtrot on a page is almost the sound of one

hand clapping. The letterforms mean something beyond themselves, but the meaning is not empirical – and it's pretty hard for me to imagine discussing this at a literary festival. *Doug, there's no verb.*

Here's another question I was recently asked: when I see words in my mind, what font are they in? The answer: Helvetica. What font do you think in? It's a strange question, but you know what I'm getting at: how do you see actual words in your head as you think? Or do you see words at all? Is it a voice in your head? Do you see subtitles?

I think that an inevitable and necessary step for written culture over the next few decades is going to be the introduction of a *détente* between the visual and literary worlds – at the very least, an agreement to agree that they're not mutually exclusive and that each feeds the other. The notion that literary experimentation ended with the publication of *Finnegans Wake* doesn't leave much hope or inspiration for citizens on a digital planet a century later. Acknowledging the present and contemplating the future doesn't mean discarding the past, and to be interested in print's visual dimension isn't the same as being anti-literary. People in the art world do a spit-take when they hear that James Joyce is called modern. The literary world has the aura of a vast museum filled with floral watercolours and alpine landscapes, a space where pickled sharks will never be contemplated or allowed. Ten-year-olds now discuss fonts, leading and flush-righting paragraphs. Words are built of RGB pixels projected directly on to the retina for hours a day. Machines automatically translate spoken words into Japanese. Medium and message are melting into each other unlike ever before. Zulu Romeo Foxtrot. ■

WITNESS | LOUISE DEAN

I watched a man kill himself

The man lay naked on the marble of the Albert Memorial in Kensington Gardens and exposed his arsehole to the sky, his head resting over the lip of the ledge up high; quite, quite high. A dozen policemen paced beneath him, and told us, the crowd, to go home. We were not helping.

My husband and I had seen him half an hour earlier in Hyde Park. He might have lost his mind and come to his senses, binned the tie, dropped the suit and gone haywire… He had gambolled through the park, a naked Puck, he had cartwheeled in the grass, been fêted by young girls running behind him, been photographed by hundreds of strollers, been saluted, been hailed, had his share of attention. Perhaps all the attention he had never had before.

We had walked arm in arm towards the monument with our two children running ahead of us. We were separating and talking about the future, after a week of rage and tears. Hyde Park – the heart of the city, packed with people playing together, drinking wine, talking, happy for the most part – took us into its *tableau vivant* and we were less important there than in our house, beset with our problems.

To say goodbye kindly was hard. It seemed so important to be heartfelt and decent; it would never seem that crucial again. Our neighbours harangue each other every day in their anger and misery. I don't want to live like that, that's all I know for sure. I also know that we are all capable of being cruel when we lose interest, and that some sort of performance is better than nothing.

Our effort at decency took all of our attention that day and we failed to notice our blue-eyed boy, the seven-year-old, stumble into the pond. He was flailing around up to his waist in water by the time one of us saw that he was in trouble. We hauled him out, comforted and berated him, a note of real-life impatience intruding on the greater business of the future.

When we stood, as a family, before the Albert Memorial, we were staring up at the naked man as he sat at the feet of the statue of the adored consort. He had sores on his inner thighs revealed when he spread his legs and slapped his small penis.

'Sores,' my husband said, 'from piss. Homeless.'

'Go home,' said a policeman on a bicycle.

'Why?' we asked him.

He got annoyed. 'Because you are not helping.'

The police threw trousers up at the naked man, he at the end of sense: suffer in your home, kill yourself there if you must, but for God's sake put some clothes on in a public space.

The man rested his head a short while on the trousers, using them as a pillow, to enjoy the sunshine and the crowd. They fell away when he sat up to call the police 'cunts'.

There they were beneath him, the attendants of order. They could not climb up, it seemed, even if he had, and they wanted us to leave so we would not see what they would do next, which was nothing. We didn't leave. We had to have the ending. The man addressed us once or twice; it was hard to understand what he said. He beat his chest, spoke to the sky, ranted a little. We waited. He rolled back on to his shoulders, his legs apart, and then he tipped himself backwards.

He hit the concrete head first.

The crowd made no sound. The policeman on the bicycle dithered, his hands staying us, his head turning to look over his shoulder. Slowly the other policemen moved forward towards the dead man. Afterwards we moved away, feeling slightly ashamed. Without his audience he would perhaps have responded to an offer of a cup of tea and some hospital attention. He would have climbed down. Walking off in the sunshine, we took a piece of the man with us. Fielding the children's questions, trying to explain it, we ventured for their sake a spin on it all of luck and chance and happenstance. Then, further along the way, we got back to talking about our own lives.

My son, still damp, sulked on and on: 'When I was drowning, you didn't save me, you're a little bit mean, you were busy talking.'

'By the time I saw you, you were out,' I said, 'but I would have saved you. You can be sure of that.'

When I first saw the man larking about I said: 'Thank God for him, he's restored my faith in humankind.' We are uncontainable, unpredictable, one at a time! I didn't think that just a half-hour later his skull would be smashing on the concrete at the foot of London's most beautiful monument.

'Why was he naked?' asked my son.

'Because he wanted to be seen,' I said to him.

Moments of hiatus and truce, of reflection and grace are fleeting, and we gloat over them long after they are gone. I thought, that day last summer, that my husband and I might turn out to be kind in our letting go of each other. I thought peace was what we desired, but it wasn't. We strive for endings. We want the walk-out, the throwing down of keys, the cursing, the last scene. But there's always an afterwards, there's always something beyond the door.

My son, in bed at night, ponders, as did I at his age, what is beyond the end of the universe...

Continuity is what we dread, not The End. ■

LETTER FROM | AKASH KAPUR

The disappearing beach

Pondicherry, India

When I was growing up in Pondicherry, a former French colony on the south-east coast of India, I would go with my family each Sunday to the beach. Everything about the beach seemed perfect back then: warm waters, yellow sand, swaying coconut trees, and lines of soft white surf that stretched across a green-blue horizon. It was like something from a postcard.

Pondicherry didn't get too many tourists in those days; the beach was mostly empty. But now the tour buses drive up and down the coast, filled with pink men and women in white hats searching for a strip of sun and sand. The Pondicherry government advertises the city, on roadside billboards and in magazine spreads, as an idyllic retreat where 'time stands still'.

But time does not stand still. The beach as I once knew it does not exist any more. It began to die in the late 1980s, when the government built a new port to the south of Pondicherry. Politicians promised that the port would bring in investment and power economic development. Who could argue with that? Within a few years, however, as even a cursory environmental assessment would have predicted, the yellow sand started disappearing, carried away by new currents that swept around the port, starved of replenishment when natural sand flows were blocked. Today the beach I used to visit with my family is gone.

Beaches are fragile ecosystems; what starts on one stretch

continues along another. Over the years, the erosion has crept up the coast, eating away at the shoreline beyond Pondicherry, swallowing the homes and boats of fishermen. Villagers have been evacuated and livelihoods have been destroyed. The sandbars that used to absorb the shock of waves far out in the ocean have been flattened. In 2004, when the tsunami hit this stretch of the coast, there was nothing to stop the surge of water. Hundreds of villagers lost their lives, and thousands more their homes.

The latest victim of this man-made ecological disaster is the village of Chinnamudaliarchavadi, about ten kilometres north of Pondicherry. A few months ago, in an effort to halt the erosion, the government threw tons of rocks into the ocean just south of the village, and built three huge piers that were supposed to block the sand from flowing away. Although India has strict laws governing construction along the coast, the piers were built without environmental permission. The ecological consequences were simply overlooked. And so, as with the port that killed the Pondicherry beach, the piers have intensified the process of erosion. Over just a few months, Chinnamudaliarchavadi's beach has virtually disappeared and the village perches precariously over the advancing waters, slowly slipping away.

On a day of grey skies and summer heat I visit the beach. I know it well. I live about twenty minutes away. On the morning of the tsunami, I rushed here from my home, not understanding quite what had happened. It was only when I saw a dead boy on the sand, with distressed villagers gathered around him, and then noticed a coastguard plane buzzing overhead, searching for survivors, that I began to understand something of the scale of the disaster.

Today the village has a similar air of crisis. At least thirty metres of beach have been lost in just a few months. The narrow band of sand that remains drops quickly into the ocean, like a cliff, a sign of rapid erosion. Men and women walk up and down what is left of the beach, a vacant, perhaps incredulous, look in their eyes. The sea is crowded with empty boats. They used to lie on the sand, but now the fishermen have to row out to their craft in flimsy catamarans.

Outside a thatched hut, close to the ocean, M Valli, a single mother of two teenage boys, tells me that every night at high tide the waters advance into her hut, seeping into the single room where she tries to sleep with her sons. 'At night, the sound of waves is like an earthquake,' she says, in Tamil, her fingers pulling at her purple sari. 'My children want to move away, they want to go somewhere else. But where can I go?'

Valli lost nearly everything she owned in the tsunami. She almost lost her children, too. They were rescued by an auto-rickshaw driver who managed to pull them to safety before they were swept out to sea. For weeks after that, while the family camped in a ruined house, the children vomited and coughed blood. The headmaster at their school asked them to leave for six months, until they had recovered. When they returned, there was no place for them at the school. Now, aged thirteen and fifteen, they go fishing with their uncles.

Valli says several villagers have already lost their homes to the erosion. The week before I spoke with her, the electricity pole in front of her hut had fallen into the ocean. After the tsunami, the village was crowded with government welfare officers and representatives of international NGOs. They all promised help; they promised her a new home. Nothing came of those promises. In front of her hut, men are erecting a fence of palm-tree logs. Even as they work, the waters crash right through.

Outside Valli's hut, on the beach, there is a pile of discarded tyres. They were brought to the beach by a local organization that believed they would help to prevent the erosion; they were to be sunk out at sea, where they were supposed to collect sand. Now the tyres are abandoned; some have fallen off the sand cliff and will soon be swept away.

I walk along the beach, on the hot sand, until I reach one of the piers. Long and thin, it stretches into the ocean, like some menacing reptilian claw. The beach is chewed away here. I can see the hard red sediment that was once compressed several layers below the surface; centuries of beach have been washed away in a matter of months. The roots of coconut and palm trees poke through the sediment; some of these trees have already been uprooted.

In the distance, I can see the town of Pondicherry, its sea wall a dark blur through the heat waves. I can't see the port from where I'm standing, but I know that the Pondicherry government is talking about building a new and bigger one, just south of the existing site. Local environmentalists have warned that a new port risks destroying a hundred-mile stretch of the coast. But the government is insistent: India is developing, modernizing, and Pondicherry can't be left behind.

Before I leave the village, Valli invites me inside her hut. She seems to think I may be able to help her get a new home. I try to convince her otherwise, but she doesn't listen. The hut is small – no more than five metres by five metres – with torn thatched walls, and a low thatched roof interwoven with plastic bags to keep the rain out. There is a blackened kerosene stove in the corner of the room; a cardboard calendar with a picture of a deity hangs from the wall. It's midday, but her boys are asleep, lying on the cracked concrete floor. They each have a single pillow, no mattress.

Valli has nothing. And the future holds nothing for her. I ask how she makes a living and she says she used to buy fish from the fishermen and resell them in the market. But now, since the beach has been eroded, there are hardly any fish. She says her friends are suffering as well, but at least they have husbands to help. I don't want to ask about her absent husband, but she tells me anyway. She says they had another son. He went out one day into the ocean. It was a clear day, not at all stormy. But they never saw him again; they just found his empty boat. Her husband, she says, was destroyed by the loss of their son. They had to send him to an institution. 'Now I am all alone,' she says, and starts to cry. 'This is all I have, and this, too, I'm losing.'

In the dwindling sand outside Valli's hut, a woman in a green sari sits on her haunches. 'What will you do to help us?' she asks as I prepare to leave. 'Everyone comes here and talks, and asks us questions. What will you do? If this continues' – she gestures out towards the disappearing beach – 'we're all going to die.' ■

www.granta.com
Watch Akash Kapur's video of the disappearing beach

Album

Robin Robertson

I am almost never there, in these
old photographs: a hand
or shoulder, out of focus; a figure
in the background,
stepping from the frame.
I see myself, sometimes, in the restless
blur of a child, that flinch
in the eye, or the way
sun leaks its gold into the print;
or there, in that long white gash
across the face of the glass
on the wall behind. That
smear of light
the sign of me, leaving.

Look closely
at these snapshots, all this
Kodacolor going to blue, and you'll
start to notice. When you finally see me,
you'll see me everywhere – floating
over crocuses, sandcastles,
autumn leaves, on those
melting snowmen, their faces
drawn in coal; among all
the wedding guests,
the dinner guests, the birthday-
party guests – this smoke
in the emulsion: the flaw.
A ghost is there; the ghost gets up to go.

ROMAS FOORD

SUBJECT + OBJECT | HILARY MANTEL

You can taste the clay

I call it a travelling icon. It is slate, heavier than it looks: dull brown in colour, a little longer and wider than the palm of my hand. On one side, roughly incised, a crucifixion, and on the other a Madonna and Child. It is a triptych. On the fold-out doors are saints and patriarchs. They have big wobbly heads. They are all smiling, except for those at the foot of the cross.

When I first held the object in my hand, a few minutes before noon prayers on March 14, 1984, the feeling it communicated to me was one of hardship, near-desperation. You can pick out Christ's ribs, but I don't think this was the reason. The incised lines were filled with fine grains of sand, but I thought 'salt'. I have no idea why.

I bought it in a souk in Jiddah, Saudi Arabia, for almost no money at all. Later someone said to me, 'It's Coptic', so I took that to be true. Common object or rare, old or new? No idea. Sometimes I wish I were a collector – that I was avid in that way – but when I meet people who really are collectors, I stop wishing it. Ignorance of the history of the object means I've never endowed it with more meaning than it had at the moment when I picked it up; I prefer it that way.

I had been living in Jiddah for sixteen months with my husband, a geologist. A childless couple, bottom of the heap in the allocation of our company's property, we lived in the city centre in an apartment block known as Faulty Towers, because it had been comprehensively mis-wired. A common hall, floored with dusty marble, acted as no-man's-land. My Pakistani neighbour, so long as her head was covered, would flit like an exotic bird to ring my doorbell, fluttering in lapis or cerise, but my Saudi neighbour, who was nineteen and married to a man of conservative views, couldn't make the thirty-second journey downstairs unless she was fully veiled-up, black-kitted head-to-toe. It took so long unwinding her, while she laughed at her own daring. She had questions about my life. 'Where did you meet your husband? Was it an office romance?' The small change of a western marriage was gold dust to her. 'What do you talk about when you are by yourselves?'

On the day I bought the icon I was with the only friend I had in that city, a coltish American girl with a string of higher degrees and the human sensitivities of one of those machines with a steel maw that digs up pavements. She wore an *abaya*, but drifting from her shoulders it looked like a scholar's gown. 'Hey, look at this!' she called, every few seconds. There wasn't much to see. Snub-nosed coffee pots clustered together on balding carpets; Yemeni trinkets made of cheap salvaged beads and silvered metal that turned your skin black when you touched it. I can't remember bargaining for the icon. My neighbours had dressed me in an *abaya* properly pinned, and a veil that covered my hair. Though my face was uncovered, I was clearly a respectable woman, and the souk man treated me gently. When I got the icon in my hand at first, I knew enough to pretend I wasn't interested in it. I put it down and walked away, but the thought that anybody else might swan in and pick it up made my skin creep, made me cold, sick and weak.

It hadn't been easy to fix this trip. It was never easy to arrange to go out and, once out, I didn't want to go home, to rooms so dim that the overhead lights had to burn all day. They didn't get dim by chance; Saudi builders were suspicious of windows. Someone might look in; someone might look out.

Two years later, almost to the day, we left the kingdom. The icon has been travelling with me since, to five addresses, never more than fifteen miles from Heathrow: it's as if I were thinking of going somewhere. The triptych's wings are tied to the main panel with grubby purple thread, which I have never disturbed. But when I took it down to write about it, one of the threads frayed to nothing, and one door unhinged itself, and now it will have to be mended by me, in clean thread that won't match. It occurs to me that, though I care for it, I have no one to leave it to when I die. I asked my husband to confirm that it was made of slate, and he tasted it – geologists do this – and said, 'Yes, I can taste the clay.' ■

Stunning de
discover

Kei Miller

Rowan Somerville

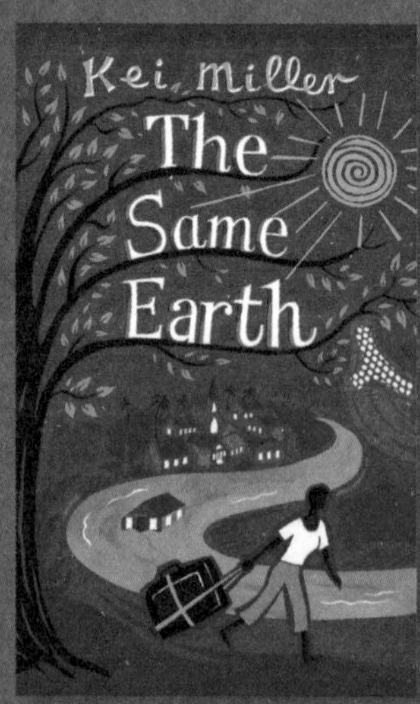

To read extracts from all these books and to find out more about the authors visit wwww.orionbooks.co.uk

THE PARIS INTIFADA

The Long War in the banlieue

Andrew Hussey

One cold evening in late November last year I left my flat in southern Paris, took the *métro* to Saint-Denis, a suburb to the north of the city, and then a bus to an outlying council estate, or *cité*, called Villiers-le-Bel. The journey took little more than an hour but marked a sharp transition between two worlds: the calm centre of the city and the troubled banlieue.

Banlieue is often mistranslated into English as 'suburb' but this conveys nothing of the fear and contempt that many middle-class French people invest in the word. It first became widely used in the late nineteenth and early twentieth centuries to describe the areas outside Paris, where city-dwellers came and settled and built houses with gardens on the English model. One of the paradoxes of life in the banlieue is that it was originally about hope and human dignity.

To understand the banlieue you should think of central Paris as an oval-shaped haven or fortress, ringed by motorways – the *boulevards périphériques* (or *le périph*) – that mark the frontier between the city and the suburbs or banlieue. To live in the centre of Paris (commonly

ALEXANDRA BOULAT/VII

described in language unchanged from the medieval period as *intra muros*, within the city walls) is to be privileged: even if you are not particularly well off you still have access to all the pleasures and amenities of a great metropolis. By contrast, the banlieue lies 'out there', on the other side of *le périph*. The area is *extra muros* – outside the city walls. Transport systems here are limited and confusing. Maps make no sense. No one goes there unless he or she has to. It's not uncommon for contemporary Parisians to talk about *la banlieue* in terms that make it seem as unknowable and terrifying as the forests that surrounded Paris in the Middle Ages.

The banlieue is made up of a population of more than a million immigrants, mostly but not exclusively from North and sub-Saharan Africa. To this extent, the banlieue is the very opposite of the bucolic *sub*-urban fantasy of the English imagination: indeed for most French people these days it means a very urban form of decay, a place of racial tensions and of deadly if not random violence.

In November 2005 the tensions and violence in the banlieue threatened for one spectacular moment to bring down the French government when, provoked by a series of confrontations between immigrant youth and the police in the Parisian banlieue of Clichy-sous-Bois, riots broke out in major cities across France. They were fuelled at least in part by the belligerence of Nicolas Sarkozy, then Minister of the Interior, who said that he would clean the streets of *racaille* ('scum'). Since then the troubles in the suburbs have been sporadic but have never gone away. The day before I set off for Villers-le-Bel, two teenagers of Arab origin had been killed at La Tolinette, one of the toughest parts of this tough neighbourhood, after their moped crashed into a police checkpoint. They had been on their way to do some rough motocross riding in an outlying field. No one in the area believed that this was an accident but rather a *bavure* – the kind of police cock-up that regularly ended with an innocent person dying or being injured. Within an hour gangs of youths closed their hoods, covered their faces with scarves and went on to the streets to hurl petrol bombs and stones at the police. A McDonald's and a library were burned down. Streetlights were smashed or taken out so that the only light came from the flames of burning cars. The mayor of Villiers-le-Bel, Didier Vaillant, had tried to negotiate with the gangs but retreated under a hail of stones. A car dealership was set alight. By daybreak as many as seventy policemen had been injured. President Sarkozy, in Beijing, was alerted to the fact that a small but significant part of French territory was beyond control.

By the time I arrived in the banlieue the next day, the scene was set for another confrontation. 'See, they treat us like fucking niggers,' said Ikram, a young man of Moroccan origin who lived nearby. He pointed at the police lines that were blocking all access to certain areas. Ikram didn't actually use the word 'nigger'. He used *bougnoule*, a racist French term to describe Arabs that dates back to the Algerian War of Independence, 1954–1962, when the French military used torture and terror against Algerian insurgents. The term *bavure* also comes from the same period. (The most infamous *bavure* was the so-called Battle of Paris, in October 1961, when a skirmish on the Pont de Neuilly between demonstrating Algerians and police led to a riot that ended with more than a hundred dead North Africans. Their bodies were thrown into the Seine by the police, under the orders of police chief Maurice Papon. Papon had previously been involved in the deportation of Jews during the German occupation of the early 1940s but was not accused of his crimes until the 1990s.)

As it was getting dark – at around five p.m. – the mood and atmosphere changed in Villiers-le-Bel. Drinkers in the café where I was sitting smoked harder. Civilians – that is to say non-rioters – were hurriedly leaving the scene and then, quite without warning, the area was entirely made up of the police and their opponents. I watched as the gangs moved in predatory packs around the road, the car parks and the shops. I had heard on many occasions their stated aim of shooting a policeman. The rumour was that this time the gangs were armed, with cheap hunting rifles and air pistols. But the only weapons I saw belonged to the police.

Later, on returning to the centre of the city and my flat, and then watching on television the surprisingly dispassionate coverage of what was going on in the banlieue, I reflected that Paris had become hardened to levels of violence that, in any other major European capital, would have threatened the survival of the government. The French were used to violence, to mini-riots and clashes between police and disaffected youth. Even in my own neighbourhood, the quiet district of Pernety, armed police regularly sealed off parts of the *cité* adjacent to the RER train lines running into central Paris (the RER is the fast commuter train that connects the banlieue with the city). Across the city, the Gare du Nord was a regular site for battles with police. It was there that an unnamed Algerian had recently been shot during another police *bavure* in the *métro*.

This past winter I set out to learn more about the banlieue. I started by visiting the area around Bagneux, to the south of the city. This was far from being the worst neighbourhood of the banlieue: Courneuve and Sarcelles to the north are much more run down and dangerous. These districts were portrayed in the 1995 film *La Haine*, in which a black, an Arab and a Jew, all from the banlieue, form an alliance against society. I found the film unconvincing, because I suspect that a Jew could never be friends with blacks and Arabs in this part of the city. Also, although I know plenty of Jews in Paris, I don't know a single Jew who lives in the banlieue. At one time the Jewish community flourished in the suburbs and there are still synagogues in Bagnolet and Montreuil that date from the 1930s. *La Haine* is an enjoyable thriller but no more true to Parisian life than *Amélie*, the fairy tale set in Paris that became an international hit in 2001.

Much more realistic, to my mind, were the intrigue and shocking violence of Michel Haneke's film *Caché* (2005). This is a story of murderous revenge in which a middle-class French intellectual is disturbed by memories from a deeply repressed and violent past. His fears are related both to his mistreatment of an Algerian child adopted by his parents and his complicity as a Frenchman in crimes committed by the French state against Algerians. *Caché* is set in the southern suburbs of Paris, not too far from Bagneux, the centre of which is much like any small French town. There is a church, a small market, cafés and green spaces. The architecture is not uniformly 1960s brutalism: there are cobbled streets and small, cottage-like houses.

The original meaning of banlieue dates back to the eleventh century, when the term *bannileuga* was used to denote an area beyond the legal jurisdiction of the city, where the poor lived. In the late fifteenth century, the poet and bandit François Villon described how Parisians feared and despised the *coquillards*, the army deserters and thieves who lived on the wrong side of the city wall. As the city grew larger through the eighteenth and nineteenth centuries, the original crumbling walls of the Old City, now marking the city limits, became known as *les fortifs* or the 'zone'. This was marginal territory, with its own folklore and customs, a world of vagabonds, rag-pickers, drunks and whores. This was also the fertile ground that later produced street singers such as Fréhel and Edith Piaf, who dreamed and sang of *le Grand Paris* or Paname (slang for Paris), of the rich city centre only a few miles away from where they lived but as distant and alien as America.

In the 1920s and 1930s, as France began to industrialize rapidly, the population of the banlieue swelled with immigrants, mainly from Italy and Spain. The banlieue rouge ('red suburbs'), usually led by a Communist council, were key driving forces in the Front Populaire ('the Popular Front'), the working-class movement that swept to power in May 1936. The first truly left-wing government in France since the days of the Commune of 1871 (when a rag-bag of anarchists and workers' groups held the city between March and

May), its success changed France forever with the introduction of paid holidays, a working week of forty hours and the sense that, for the first time, the workers were in control.

During the *trente glorieuses*, the period of rapid economic growth that occurred between the 1950s and 1970s, other major towns across France adopted the Parisian model of building estates far outside the centre. The first new developments in the banlieue were sources of pride to the Parisian, Lyonnais and Marseillais working class who were often grateful to be evacuated there from their slums in the central city. Once, long ago, the banlieue was the future.

I remarked on this to Kevin, a rangy black lad of twenty who, with his mate Ludovic (roughly the same age), was showing photographer Nick Danziger and me around the area. Both of them were obsessed with football, especially with the English Premier League. They were impressed that I had met and interviewed French footballers Lilian Thuram, who is black, and Zinédine Zidane, who is from an Algerian family. 'I can't imagine this as anyone's future,' Kevin said, gesturing at the car parks and boarded-up shops. 'All anybody wants to do here is to escape.'

Kevin himself is a footballer of average ability; he had a trial with Northampton Town in England. 'I hate France sometimes,' he told me. 'And, at other times, I just stop thinking about it. But the real thing is that here, when you are born into an area and you are black or Arab, then you will never leave that area. Except maybe through football and even that is shit in France.'

I asked him about his English name. 'I like England. And like everyone here, I don't feel French, so why should I pretend?'

Ludovic, who at least has a more conventionally Gallic name but is originally from Mauritius, joined in. 'They don't like us in Paris, so we don't have to pretend to be like them.' By 'them' he means white French natives – *Gaulois* or *fils de Clovis*, in the language of the banlieue.

It is this Anglophilia, transmitted via the universal tongues of rap

Graffiti in Bagneux are often in English. Here 'Made in Ghetto' is scrawled on the wall

NICK DANZIGER/NB PICTURES

music and football, which explains why so many kids in the banlieue are called *Steeve*, *Marky*, *Jenyfer*, *Britney* or even *Kevin*. They don't always get the spelling right, but the sentiment is straightforward: *we are not like other French people; we refuse to be like them.*

As we walked and talked we soon entered a dark labyrinth of grey crumbling concrete. This was 'Darfour City', a series of rectangular blocks of mostly boarded-up flats where the local drug dealers gathered. This was what the police called a *quartier orange*, largely a no-go area for the police themselves as well as for ordinary citizens. DARFOUR CITY was scrawled across a door at the entrance to a block of flats. As we wandered deeper into the estate, there was more graffiti, in fractured English: FUCK DA POLICE; MIGHTY GHETO. Halfway down the street we were hailed by a pack of lads, all black except for one white. They were all smoking spliffs.

These were the local dealers, a gang of mates who, according to

Kevin, could get you anything you wanted. They delighted in selling dope and coke at wildly inflated prices to wealthy Parisians. They were pleased to hear that I was English. 'We hate the French press,' said Charles, who is thin and tall and of Congolese origin. 'They just think we're animals.'

They looked at me with suspicion. 'No one comes here who isn't afraid of us,' said another of the gang, Majid. 'That's how it should be. That's how we want it.'

Then the gang tired of me and my questions; I understood it was time to go.

In January 2006 a twenty-three-year-old mobile phone salesman named Ilan Halimi was kidnapped in central Paris and driven out to Darfour City in Bagneux. Halimi, who was Jewish, had been invited out for a drink by a young Iranian woman named Yalda, whom he had met while selling phones. It turned out that it was her mission to trap him and lure him away from safety. Yalda later described how Ilan had been seized by thugs in balaclavas and bundled into a car: 'He screamed for two minutes with a high-pitched voice like a girl.'

Three weeks later, Ilan was found naked and tied to a tree near the RER station of Sainte-Geneviève-des-Bois. He died on the way to hospital. His body had been mutilated and burned. Since being kidnapped, he had been imprisoned in a flat in Bagneux, starved and tortured. Residents of the block had heard his screams and the laughter of those torturing him, but had done nothing. Fifteen youths from the Bagneux district were arrested. They were members of a gang called 'the Barbarians', a loose coalition of hard cases, dealers and their girls who shared a hatred of 'rich Jews'. The alleged leader of the Barbarians, Youssef Fofana, went on the run to the Ivory Coast to escape arrest. His trial began in Paris in February 2008.

Theories about motives for the crime were initially confused. Was it a bungled kidnap? A *Clockwork Orange*-style act of pure sadism? Or was it the work of hate-fuelled anti-Semitism? The police were, at first, reluctant to say that the crime was motivated by anti-Semitism. But Yalda, who turned out to be a member of the Barbarians, said in her testimony that she had been specifically told to entrap Jews by the gang. Her confession was widely reported, as was the fact that she called Fofana 'Osama', in homage to Bin Laden.

At the same time, out in the banlieue itself, the murder took on a skewed new meaning: the word was that what had begun as a heist and kidnap to extort a ransom from 'rich Jews' had become a form of revenge for crimes in Iraq and, in particular, the scenes from Abu Ghraib. Bizarrely, in the view of some, this made the torturers martyrs, soldiers in what is being called the Long War against the white Western powers. An ever-present slogan in the banlieue is '*Nique la France!*' ('Fuck France!'). The kids of Bagneux accordingly gloried in their own 'intifada'. They openly identified with the Palestinians, whom they saw as prisoners in their own land, like the dispossessed of the banlieue.

One afternoon I visited the rue des Rosiers, the Jewish quarter at the heart of the Marais. This is a little Tel Aviv in central Paris, a place where French-Israeli waitresses, dressed in combat fatigues, serve up beer and schwarma. It was from here, during the Occupation, that French Jews began the final journey to the death camps of eastern Europe or, closer at hand, to the Vél d'Hiv, the sports stadium to the south of Paris where thousands died because of squalid conditions. The cries of the dying in the stadium, like those of Ilan, were ignored by their Parisian neighbours.

In a coffee shop near the rue des Rosiers, a place owned by Moroccan Jews, I spoke to Myriam Bérrebi, herself a Tunisian Jew, about the killing of Ilan. 'I have never known such terror and anger in this neighbourhood,' she said, 'not since the shootings at Jo Goldenberg's Deli.'

She was referring to the massacre by Arab gunmen in 1982 of six diners at Goldenberg's Deli, just across the street from where we were sitting.

'But, you know,' she continued, 'there were other echoes too – especially of the Nazi period, when Jews died and everybody pretended everything was all right.'

After the murder of Ilan, to the anger of many Parisian Jews, the Chirac government dissembled about 'social problems' in the banlieue. Only Nicolas Sarkozy, then an ambitious Minister of the Interior and whose mother was a Sephardic Jew, denounced the murder of Ilan as 'an anti-Semitic crime'.

With Sarkozy's intervention the terms of the debate were changed. Was the killing of Ilan the isolated act of individuals, or was it a political murder in the largest sense: an act that expressed a collective hatred? Did it belong to individuals, or the whole community?

Good stuff happens in bad places. I said this to Hervé Mbuenguen as we sat in his flat in Vache Noire, in what is meant to be a less impoverished neighbourhood of Bagneux. 'That is a very quaint idea,' he replied. 'Nowadays the banlieue only means one thing: trouble.'

Hervé's family is originally from Cameroon but he has lived in the banlieue all his life. He is educated and articulate, a graduate of the elite École Normale Supérieure, and makes a living as a computer engineer. 'If you live here, if you speak with an accent *banlieusard*, you are condemned as an outsider in Paris and in fact all French cities. It is in fact a double exile – you are already an outsider because you are black or Arab. But then you are an outsider because you are *banlieusard*.'

Yet he has chosen to live here. 'The banlieue is my home. I cannot feel comfortable anywhere else.'

Hervé's block of flats was rotten; the walls of the lift-shaft were falling apart from the inside. But his apartment was tidy and organized. This was a place where a full, hard-working life was being lived. His flat is the headquarters of *Grioo*, a website devoted to the

African diaspora in France (*Grioo* is in fact a mild corruption of the West African term *griot*, meaning 'storyteller'). With Hervé, I was trying to talk through the idea that, in spite of the murders and the riots, good work is going on in the banlieue. The success of the *Grioo* website is testament to that. The only taboo subject between us was that of Jews in the banlieue. I had asked, innocently, why there were so few, if any, Jews left.

'They cannot live here,' Hervé said.

Hervé is not an anti-Semite but his remark reflected a shameful reality about the prevalence of anti-Semitism in the suburbs, a reality that makes even open-minded people such as him feel awkward. Through several weeks of my travels in Bagneux, I chatted casually to hip-hop kids, footballers, football fans and self-proclaimed *casseurs* ('wreckers' or 'rioters'). I met and talked to them in cafés, at bus stops, in shops and sports centres. It was mostly entertaining and enlightening; there is a lot of serious laughter and benign mischief going on in the banlieue. But the more time I spent there, the more, like a secret code being revealed, I began to pick up on the casual references to synagogues, Israelis and Jews. These references would be refracted through the slang of the banlieue. So phrases such as *sale juif*, *sale yid*, *sale feuj*, *youpin*, *youtre* (this last term dates from the 1940s and so, with its echoes of the Nazi deportations, contains a special poison), all racist epithets, were being widely used but also framed by irony. Yet for all I heard about the crimes of the Jews, it was hard to find anyone who had met a Jewish person. 'We don't need to meet Jews,' I was told by Grégory, a would-be rapper and Muslim from La Chapelle. 'We know what they're like.'

But that was the problem: nobody knew what 'they' were like. It seemed to me that hating Jews – like supporting Arsenal or listening to the rap band NTM – had become a defining motif of identity in the banlieue.

Hatred of the Jews: this was one of the oldest traditions in Paris, dating back like the very notion of the banlieue to the medieval period. In *Portrait of an Anti-Semite*, written in the wake of the German occupation of Paris, and searching for an explanation for his compatriots' complicity in anti-Semitic crimes, Jean-Paul Sartre describes the typical French anti-Semite as driven by his own sense of 'inauthenticity'. By this he means a sense of existential and psychological unreality which at once challenges and undermines the anti-Semite's identity as a middle-class Frenchman. Unconvinced of his own true place in society, the anti-Semite nonetheless finds comfort in the reality of his Jew-hatred.

Anti-Semitism in France is a phenomenon of the political Left as well as of the Right, of the underclass as well as of the ruling elite. This in part explains, if it does not justify, the writings of Louis-Ferdinand Céline, the great chronicler of Parisian working-class life in the twentieth century. Céline hated Sartre. In response to Sartre's accusation that he had been paid by the Nazis to write anti-Jewish propaganda, Céline retorted with fury that he did not need to be paid to feel hatred for Jews: his hatred was authentic enough. Rather, it was his identity as a petit-bourgeois, a member of a class forged in the late nineteenth century and already sinking into history, that felt most unreal.

Céline describes the banlieue to the north of city as a kind of inferno. His description of the imagined banlieue called Rancy in his 1932 novel *Journey to the End of the Night* is as dank and polluted as the Wigan described by George Orwell in *The Road to Wigan Pier*. But Céline's banlieue is infected by a particular kind of metaphysical misery:

> The sky in Rancy is a smoky soup that bathes the plain all the way down to Levallois. Cast-off buildings bogged down in black muck. From a distance, big ones and little ones look like the fat stakes that rise out of the filthy beach at the seaside. And inside it's us!

Céline was a pessimist, obsessed by disease and filth. He saw no hope for the poor of the banlieue. In the end, he blamed nearly everything

Night-time in Bagneux, which is midway between Orly airport and the Eiffel Tower

NICK DANZIGER/NB PICTURES

on the Jews. 'War in the name of the bourgeoisie was shitty enough,' he wrote in one of his pamphlets, 'but now war for the Jews!...half negroid, half Asiatic, mongrel pastiches of the human race whose only aim is to destroy France!'

In recent years, Céline has become an inspiration of rappers in the banlieue, who admire his use of stylized slang and street language. The rapper Abd al Malik has devoted a song on his latest album to Céline. 'Céline revolutionized literature because he was very close to real people, like us rappers today,' he said in an interview on his blog. 'That's generally a good thing, but there's a danger about being so close to the people; you can start to embrace all the things that are wrong with society.'

Today the literary heir to Céline as the chronicler of the Parisian underclass is novelist Michel Houellebecq. His vision of the banlieue is of a failed utopia, a district that has now reverted to wilderness.

Houellebecq gives voice to this view in the novel *Platform* as the businessman Jean-Yves Espitalier muses on the rape of a female colleague by Arab and black youths on a 'dangerous railway line' between Paris and the banlieue.

> As he was stepping out of his office, Jean-Yves looked out over the chaotic landscape of houses, shopping centres, tower blocks and motorway interchanges. Far away, on the horizon, a layer of pollution lent the sunset strange tints of mauve and green. 'It's strange,' he said, 'here we are inside the company like well-fed beasts of burden. And outside are the predators, the savage world.

One afternoon I visited Jean-Claude Tchicaya, a black official in the *mairie*, the local town administration. I had read an interview with him in which he had spoken of knowing the murderers of Ilan Halimi. Tchicaya was dressed in a smart suit with a black leather *gilet* draped over his back. In his office, amid old copies of *Jeune-Afrique* and *Libération*, there were portraits of Martin Luther King and Nelson Mandela. Wasn't it a contradiction to admire these 'heroes of peace' when the reality of the struggle for racial equality had also involved so much death and conflict?

'Struggle doesn't just mean violence,' Tchicaya said. 'It also means dignity.'

I asked him how he knew the murderers of Halimi.

'This is not my milieu,' he said, 'but everyone in Bagneux knows everyone.'

Then I asked him if he knew the Tribu Ka, a group of black militants, resident in Bagneux, who openly declared that they hated Jews and had issued messages in support of the Barbarians who had killed Ilan Halimi. Tchicaya was becoming agitated. 'Look,' he said, 'all extreme situations create extremists. It's the pattern of history. But I don't want to know about those people.'

Out on the street, the Tribu Ka is in fact a hard-core political movement of black supremacists led by Kémi Seba, whose real name is Stellio Capo Robert Chichi. He was born in Strasbourg in 1981 into a first-generation immigrant family from Benin. Kémi was a clever, restless and angry young man who, at the age of eighteen, began his apprenticeship in radical politics with Nation of Islam's Parisian chapter, based in Belleville, the traditionally working-class district in the north-east of the city. Founded by Elijah Muhammad in the 1930s and now led by Louis Farrakhan, Nation of Islam has only a tangential relationship with 'authentic' Islam. It preaches that the black races are descendants of the Tribe of Shabazz, the lost tribe of Asia.

Nation of Islam gave Kémi a cause and philosophy, but he was determined to lead his own political group. He travelled to Egypt in his twenties, and there he began to construct his own worldview, a mix of Islam, black power and revolutionary politics. Kémites are the chosen race of God, or Allah, and will lead the black race out of slavery to their rightful position as masters of the world. The non-violent methods of Martin Luther King (a betrayer of the black race, according to Kémi) and Gandhi (an enemy of Muslims and agent of the British crown) are denounced as ineffectual.

'Only if you are black or Arab in France can you understand the contempt people feel for you ...'

Even when Kémi was imprisoned for five months, in 2007, for inciting racial hatred, he placed his faith in Allah and called himself a martyr. During his time in the jail of Bois d'Arcy, to the west of Versailles, until his release at the end of last year, Kémi's blog was regularly updated on his website and his supporters spoke of his being *embastillé*, locked up in the Bastille.

The Tribu Ka are regarded as the real masters of Bagneux. 'Those guys are mad fuckers,' I was told by Kevin, my guide through the suburbs.

Kémi has a variety of modes of dress, ranging from Afro-centric gear to suits in the style of Afro-American intellectuals of the Black Panther generation. Tribu Ka are having a discernible impact on France: if you are hassled by tough black kids in the shopping centre at Les Halles in central Paris, they will often be wearing the Tribu Ka's colours of black, red and yellow, or the insignia GKS (Génération Kémi Seba). This happens less than half a mile away from the rue des Rosiers where, in May 2006, the Tribu Ka marched, chanting anti-Semitic slogans, and launched 'a declaration of war against Jews' while attacking anyone in their path with baseball bats. Two months later, they launched a raid to 'take back African treasures' from the new museum of colonial history at Quai Branly.

Tribu Ka are now banned on the orders of President Sarkozy, but they are set to return to the political front line with 'Génération Kémi Seba'. This new group is effectively the Tribu Ka, reinvented and well organized, but with a new media-friendly profile; support is professed on their website by rappers such as ragga star Princess Erika, and Orosko Racim of Ghetto Fabulous Gang. One of Kémi's defenders is the mainstream black comedian Dieudonné, who was once as mild and inoffensive, and as popular, as the black British comic Lenny Henry. Now, Dieudonné has become widely known for his virulent anti-Semitism.

Kémi's website is still publishing his speeches on the end of the white and Jewish races. He remains an accomplished public speaker and a master of double-talk. His interviews and speeches on YouTube are models of chilling self-righteousness, and he is seldom seen without two menacing guards at his side. For several weeks I tried to arrange a meeting with him. I was told by an intermediary that 'Kémi will speak soon. But he doesn't want to speak to the white press you represent. His time will come later. This will be when the white press is no more.'

I was then told that they knew who I was and it might be wise to leave them alone. Or stay out of Bagneux.

This cité in Bagneux is characteristic of much of the banlieue and its bleakness has contributed to the marginalization and frustration of its inhabitants

NICK DANZIGER/NB PICTURES

'I understand Kémi,' I was told by a friend, a young black woman. She has a degree, a good job in publishing and a white boyfriend who is a lawyer. 'Only if you are black or Arab in France can you understand the contempt people feel for you, and the hate and desire for revenge that this inspires in you. Kémi is nasty but I understand his appeal. He is about war and violence. What angry young man in the banlieue doesn't feel the same at some point? It's the same for the Taliban as the youth in the banlieue: they are fighting to let us know that they exist and that they hate society as it is. They feel that the Jews rule the world, and from one point of view it can look that way. They see Iraq and Gaza and Rwanda and Kenya and the Jews of Paris or New York who have profited from their pain. To them, it all makes sense.'

It would naturally be foolish to describe everyone in the banlieue as an anti-Semite. But there is a prevailing anti-Semitic, and indeed anti-European, mentality there, the anguish and prejudice of the truly lost. From the most moderate voices to the extremists of Tribu Ka, anti-Semitism is a binding cultural force, a singular bigotry in which genuine and complex historical grievances and pan-Arab sympathies cohere in disfigured form.

What makes the events there so troubling is that they don't conform to any previously established pattern of revolt. French historians have written of *le passage à l'acte*, of the moment when a society passes into revolutionary violence, which is precipitated by a confluence of negative forces: bad government, poverty and hunger.

But what is happening in the banlieue is different – which may explain why French intellectuals have been so notably silent on the subject. What is happening there is perhaps best understood in the language of psychoanalysis, because the violence seems more and more to be an expression of post-colonial trauma, the kind of 'motherless rage' that Frantz Fanon diagnosed so acutely as the defining condition of post-independence Algeria.

France may be in Europe but many of its fears and nightmares began during the brutal Algerian War of Independence. It was during this conflict that many horrors of our new century – asymmetric war against Muslim terror groups, the systematic use of torture in the name of democracy – were first deployed. France may be unique among Western European nations in refusing to recognize its colonial crimes: deeply embedded in the psyche of political parties of the Left and Right is the idea that the French colonial empire performed a *mission civilatrice*, a 'civilising mission', imposing universal republican values on the 'uncivilized' world. This 'mission' was less about capital and commodity than an explicitly political task of exporting 'Frenchness'. The loss of Algeria was, following this logic, less like losing a dependent colony than the sudden death of a family member. The bereavement continues to affect both colonizer and colonized.

France is far from coming to terms with the repressed memories of its colonial past. Like the dead Algerians who were thrown into the

Seine in 1961, and whose bloated corpses shocked ordinary Parisians when they were found in the days after the massacre on the Pont de Neuilly, these memories are once more resurfacing to provoke new and fresh anxieties.

Back in the banlieue the rioters, wreckers, even the killers of Ilan Halimi, are not looking for reform or revolution. They are looking for revenge. Their rage is often expressed symbolically: the appropriation of the language of the Intifada, which, at its origin, was a spontaneous and legitimate uprising against oppression, the speaking of Arabic slang, the waving of the Algerian flag and the provocative wearing of the veil. These are all acts directed at subverting the French Republic. For many Parisians, the banlieue represents 'otherness' – the otherness of exclusion, of the repressed, of the fearful and despised. Until this ceases to be the case, the unacknowledged civil war between Paris and its disturbed suburbs will go on. The positions and tactics of the immigrants of the banlieue – their identification with Palestine, their hatred of France – reveal the struggle to be part of the Long War every bit as much as those caught up in the conflicts in Iraq and Afghanistan.

In the nineteenth century, Charles Baudelaire wrote of Paris being haunted by its past, by 'ghosts in daylight'. In the early twenty-first century, the ghosts of colonial and anti-colonial assassins, from Algeria to Beirut, from Congo to Rwanda, continue to be visible in the daylight of the banlieue. It may be that what France needs is not hard-headed political solutions or even psychiatry, but an exorcist. ■

FICTION

VIDEOS OF THE DEAD

Rick Moody

In this one you see only the lower extremities of the protagonist. The brand of tennis shoe is known as the Chuck Taylor. Her blue jeans are tapered. There's a small expanse of pink sock. The shot that we have here is silent but for the murmuring from the next room – partygoers. If my interpretation is correct, these murmurings concern a chandelier and whether one portion of this fixture is intentionally lopsided. Meanwhile, on a linoleum floor, before floral wallpaper, the feet, once parallel, splay themselves into a classic V-shape. And then they are parallel, anew, facing oppositely. One sneakered foot balances on its toe, as if the protagonist of the video intends to pursue ballet. In the room adjacent, a voice audibly remarks, 'Is he just shooting feet?' 'Yep, he's just shooting feet.'

Mirth follows.

The feet appear heedless of aesthetic controversies raging in the next room. And yet perhaps they are *not* heedless. They attempt a few tentative dance steps – foxtrot, cha-cha – each with a certain earnestness. After which, they come to a halt. Becoming again:

sneakers – and metatarsals, toenails, warts, bunions.

As with all the materials in our collection, the subject died not long after the filming of this document.

Welcome to our interactive brochure.

The footage of the young African-American boy amounts to a mere ninety-one seconds, and the submission letter from his family apologizes for the brevity of the sample, noting that the long-term storage techniques used were not archival. I have supplied a tentative date of 1984 mainly because of some of the popular music that brays through the public address system towards the conclusion of the sequence. The space in which the contest takes place is an ill-lit assembly hall in a common American elementary or middle school, and as usual the microphone on the video camera is better at picking up the ambient noise than the action onstage. As music fades, a squeaky-clean educator, fully buttoned-down, intones the word 'syzygy'. There is consternation in the back row of the auditorium, where videotapers are practising their craft. The cinematographer of the recording then remarks, on camera, 'What the heck he say?' An acquaintance: 'I think he said "Saturday".' 'He did *not*. The hell he did.' The exchange all but interrupts the exposition, during which the boy ambles to the podium without a hint of nervousness. The protagonist is wearing a pressed white shirt and a plaid tie. Flannel trousers. There's a stain on the right breast of his shirt, the nature of which some have disputed. A consensus has recently emerged, however, which asserts that the stain is from a frequent cafeteria menu item from those days: American chop suey.

The young man, as I've pointed out myself, is unnaturally serene as he repeats the word. Then, as per the rules of engagement, he begins to spell, 's-y-z-y-g-y', after which he repeats the word. 'Correct!' cries the judge. The room erupts. It's as if this is the World Cup or Super Bowl. Did they ask him to define it later? How on earth did he know this word? I couldn't have spelled it myself! The boy *won*, this is undeniable. We also know that on leaving the school in an Olds Cutlass Supreme (he occupied the front passenger seat) he was, along with the relative behind the wheel, struck and killed by a drunk driver.

There's a developing etiquette here at Videos of the Dead. The more you look at these videos, the more you realize that everyone has a story along these lines – if they don't yet they're going to – and in the process of combing through their lives they are likely to find that there are varieties of mnemonic material that best suggest the qualities of their lost loved ones. Not toasts at a wedding (although we have some), or trips to DisneyWorld, but the instants of life, the insignificant gestures or turns of phrase, the awkward outfits, the effusions of self belonging to a person now gone.

Lev Chandler of St Louis, MO, observes, in a commentary posted last February, 'Why was my father not wearing a shirt during the footage from the camping trip of 4/5/93? Inexplicable! The man always wore a shirt! He was the kind of person who wouldn't even consider a cotton T-shirt. Still, here he is in this excerpt posted by my cousin, hefting up a large piece of dried brush over a bonfire. For a second the shrub, or whatever it is, blazes, as it catches fire, and you can see my father's naked torso. Not a slim man, my father. My God, the size of that gut! The point is that I thought I knew him well. I thought that when he died I was in a position to let him go, because there was so little unfinished business between us. And yet he never seemed more of an enigma to me than when I first watched this video. In the last moment of the film, he waves his flannel shirt at the camera, as though attempting to smoke signal. However improbably, it's through this footage that I feel I have come to know my father entirely. Thank you, Videos of the Dead.'

This is exactly the kind of post that generates engaged responses at our Web portal (which is itself a spin-off of the Videos of the Dead Exhibition Hall in Waterbury, CT), and it is exactly why our Web traffic averages in the tens of thousands of hits a month. Some of the traffic is devoted to answering how-to types of questions. (From the FAQ: 'Make *certain* to file the appropriate paperwork with the local authorities.') But more often one finds, on the site, expressions of grief. In bulk. Though part of our mission includes policing the bulletin board to eliminate posts that are considered mischievous, in bad taste, or which somehow attempt to market services that we do not endorse, I can't be bothered. Life, self-evidently, is short.

'This note is for my sister, Audie,' says the suicide in advance of his deed. Standing at the front door of a two-bedroom flat. Traffic rumbling in the street below. 'Audie, I know you've tried for a while to make sure this moment doesn't come. I guess I wish it didn't have to. *(Long pause.)* But let's try to face facts. I've been doing everything that everyone said to do. *(Long pause.)* I went to the doctors when everyone said to go. I cooperated. I let them load me up with medications, which didn't do anything at all. Audie, these drugs don't work for everyone. I haven't been able to work, I haven't been able to sleep for weeks, maybe months. I can't even think about eating. *(Extremely long pause.)* You can have my stuff, my books, and everything. I paid down the credit cards. You'll only have to deal with the apartment. *(Long pause.)* I'm sorry that you are the one who has to manage it. But try to remember that no one's responsible. I'm responsible.'

The protagonist moves out of frame. A rustling behind the camera and then silence. Followed by a dread commotion on the street below. The cry of a woman. Swerve and screech of tyres. Within minutes, there are sirens, and then, not long after, the tonalities of the neighbourhood revert to a former pace and rhythm. The camera is free to run. And so it does. If we assume that Barry G bought the shortest available digital cassette he would have as yet about forty-five minutes. And this is borne out in what follows. A long shot of the front door of his apartment, a composite hollow-core door, cheaply manufactured. Half-hearted renovations in the building were overseen by the landlord, looking to maximize his take.

Forty-five minutes of videotape of an inexpensive door in an apartment in Detroit, MI. Light moving imperceptibly across the edges of things, light ephemeral and elegiac. You will not be surprised to learn that many viewers are dry-eyed through the remarks quoted above. In fact, people speed through the suicide note to concentrate instead on the video of the door. There is the symbolism of the door, I suppose. There is the tendency to think of a door as a mystical passageway. Such an interpretation is more likely because of the singular and expressive way in which the particular shot of the door is framed. Though deceased at the time the sequence was filmed, Barry G, cinematic documentarian, was possessed of vision enough to foresee the striking possibilities of autumn light in a posthumous composition. Doors are hung badly every day by contractors who are no longer personally attached to the task. Why such immense feeling about a door? As executive director of the Videos of the Dead Exhibition Hall, library and Web archive, it's my responsibility to celebrate these little things around us: a Coke bottle rolling in the empty parking lot, a leak in the roof spilling into a plastic bucket, or the sunlight on an apartment door.

The mayor of Waterbury, before going off to serve three to seven for racketeering, showed considerable interest in our project – at least while there was an election to be won. He would not discuss which dot.com potentate was responsible for financing the Videos of the Dead multi-purpose Retreat Centre, and this was perhaps owing to the sensitivity of campaign finance in these troubled times. Nevertheless, builders were promised the permits necessary to renovate a certain ramshackle factory, once part of the shoe manufacturing infrastructure of Waterbury. Our interior design was by a fashionable architectural theorist from the Baltics. (No ninety-degree angles in the interior.) Cranes, cement mixers, and dump trucks flooded into the vacated industrial district around Maple

Avenue. Union guys who'd been furloughed for weeks were suddenly bringing home the big pay cheque.

Our mayor was squat, and his nose had been multiply broken during his period as a middleweight. His blue eyes looked like dollar-store replacements. There were remaining only a few tufts of hair that he brushed forward. A generous helping of front teeth had been knocked out at some point and replaced in such a way as to suggest the tentativeness of modern dentistry. He was a bully who enlisted political friends and threatened them when they failed to cooperate, and yet for a while he did considerable good. We had a new mall, we had a sparsely attended books festival, outdoor silent films in July, a sequence of street fairs in the warmer months, and then we had the Videos of the Dead Archive and Retreat Centre. There weren't a lot of museums in Waterbury. There had once been a chance for a sports hall of fame. That organization went elsewhere. The mayor, according to public avowals on the subject, would not allow this to happen again. He was going to hook this fish, and then he was going to land it on the deck and club it insensate.

Meanwhile, federal agents were impounding the mayor's campaign finance records. They began promising immunity to organized crime figures from Worcester and Hartford. The mayor knew all about it. He had friends who were well situated. And perhaps this constituted another reason why, when he saw the members of our executive committee driving into town in their Saabs and Volvos, he said a big resounding yes to a national archive that memorialized the lost. This two-fisted drinker, this cheater at cards, this informant, this compulsive gambler, said *yes*.

Not long after his conviction, the mayor's son enlisted in the military. This son, a layabout who'd been frequently disciplined in the Waterbury school system, and whose brutal play as a defensive lineman on the high-school football team was legendary, darkened the doorway of the local recruiting station, tearful and inebriate. Len was his name, and immediately he was shipped to Fort Dix for basic training, and from there, after a visit to the penitentiary to let his father know, Len was flown to a sandy and dangerous country at the crossroads of monotheism.

This son's unit convoyed out one afternoon to assist when a hospital in one of the restive neighbourhoods was emptied. The hospital, which had taken one too many hits from allied ordnance, was to be demolished, its beds relocated to a facility in a less dangerous sector. The roads on the way, as the story goes, were lined with the usual poorly wired fireworks. A demolitions expert was out by the tarmac, trying to dismantle yet another IED, a decoy, when a hail of automatic weapons fire rained down upon him. Snipers. The mayor's boy disembarked from the Humvee in order to give aid. It was the mayor who sent along the tape. And it was the mayor who filed the supporting materials with Videos of the Dead, from his cell at the federal minimum-security facility. 'Marcus,' he wrote in blocky and uninflected capital letters, 'I don't know if this will be up to your standards. It would please me, though, if you would have a look and tell me what you think. Maybe my misfortune can benefit *someone*.'

The Videos of the Dead Archive frowns upon slow-motion footage, or footage that has been manipulated with the special-effects editing suites that are available these days. But we are not so wedded to our rules that we don't know poetry when we see it. For example, coins falling out of the sky into the upturned service helmet of an American GI somewhere in the Green Zone. The length of time that it takes you to read this sentence? That's the length of time that it takes one of Len Gionfriddo's coins to fall an inch in the arid Middle Eastern sky. Twenty-five legal-tender cents! And then there is another, two quarters hovering above the service headgear. A drab camouflage helmet, such as any American enlisted man or woman might have. The upturned helmet is an emblem of military sacrifice or futility. However, the infantrymen in question were off duty, relaxing, and thus they imagined they did little more than memorialize a contest with which they passed their tedious afternoons. The person or persons who managed to land the most quarters in the helmet took possession of the spoils. The game was known as Baghdad Horseshoes.

Quarters multiply. First there are two, and then there are three, and the footage labours on, and then there are four, and then there are a dozen or more coins in the sky over the helmet, the slightly beat-up headgear of whichever enlistee it was who convened the men. There is a truck in the rear of the shot, a personnel carrier. The truck is moving imperceptibly – because the coins are *not* moving, because gravity has been slowed to inconsequentiality, because the war, ephemerally, has come to a halt.

The footage arrived *after* the news of the boy's sacrifice. In this way, even the most hardened politico in the most crooked town in the state of Connecticut is driven to his knees.

Initially, we were just a physical display in the city of Waterbury. It's no surprise that we didn't get much foot traffic. Waterbury, unlike other cities in the state, hadn't undertaken one of those stylish makeovers in its industrial district – the sort that brings in musicians, sculptors, and multi-media artists in search of cheap rent and a quiet work environment. Maple Avenue remained the unvisited and somewhat sinister neighbourhood it had always been. Gradually, however, road signs for the museum began to appear at major intersections. If we didn't manage to secure a 'location of interest' sign on I-84, groups of misplaced tourists and Goth kids did nonetheless amble through our door occasionally. I worked the first few months in a lonely thrall, accompanied only by bag lunches and evening glasses of cognac. I worked as if each piece of video that materialized, in some heavily fortified Jiffy bag, was holy.

The films of Sheryl Goldfarb have been indexed and collected by a number of international curators. They appeared sporadically on the Web over the course of her not terribly long life. Goldfarb, the daughter of a Hollywood studio executive who disavowed her, was an aspiring gallery owner when she began making what might be described as living dioramas in the privacy of her modest one-bedroom apartment. She used materials at hand – usually mismatched collectable dolls that she picked up at tag sales on the stoops of her Brooklyn neighbourhood. She'd pull a head off Wolverine and glue it on to a Joey Ramone action figure, and this pop-cultural hybrid would, in a glass fish tank filled with home-made backdrops, fight to the death against a Barbie doll whose lower half had been replaced with an egg beater. The soundtracks to these pieces consisted of unearthly drones and sheets of metal screaking against one another. The Goldfarb films, according to certain online publications, date to the onset of the directrix's agoraphobia. At the end of her tenure as associate director of a gallery in Williamsburg, Brooklyn, you see, she began to refuse to leave her apartment.

Her sad narrative, in abbreviated form, is herewith. Goldfarb, as directed by her mother, and in an attempt to find relief from her psychiatric symptoms, decided to take a cruise on one of those liners known chiefly for their ability to spread Norwalk virus among passengers. Goldfarb, according to news accounts, came out of her stateroom only under cover of night. In her rambles, she attempted to avoid the blackjack tables, where she otherwise lost money at an awesome clip. It's hard to imagine an agoraphobic standing on the deck of a ship looking out at the Caribbean Sea, but you can't make this stuff up. Goldfarb was heavily medicated. She liked to hang around the upper decks smoking and mapping the stars. On one occasion, she spoke with a young gentleman about her former career as an actress. She had no such career. Whether Goldfarb jumped or fell, who can say?

The Goldfarb films, I am ashamed to observe, have left us open to charges of professionalism. They are, many believe, simply too good. Sparks flew at the board meeting at which I announced my decision to collect the entirety of the Goldfarb oeuvre. My friendship with board treasurer Kate McClanahan, the paper-towel heiress, was effectively terminated by reason of salty language.

Answering to my own conscience, therefore, I spent some time selecting among the Goldfarb films. Because I believed in them. We have a number of large-screen viewing theatres at Videos of the Dead, for the most worthy artefacts. Goldfarb was looped in Screening Room A. My favourite piece featured bobble-headed dolls of celebrated local athletes, and simulated colonoscopy. In the footage, the brutality favoured by the directrix begins to seem like something else entirely, something quite beautiful, almost as if this were an existentialist drama filmed by the Ingmar Bergman of *The Seventh Seal*. If I regret the Goldfarb exhibition a little bit now, for the expenditure of political capital required to mount it, that doesn't mean that I don't love the films.

Our first intern at Videos of the Dead was August Morse. He happened to be an orphan. August applied for an internship when we offered no internships, when I hadn't yet addressed the need for better grant writing, a decent filing system, names of companies that could help us preserve the tapes, bookkeepers, and so forth. August had a memory like a virgin hard drive. He became invaluable immediately. The poor kid never mentioned his family – I can't even remember how I found out about the tornado – but soon enough I learned that he found himself without the kind of footage that he might have submitted to his place of employment for consideration among its holdings. Which means, I suppose, that we gave August Morse memories he didn't have.

He was also a very fine computer programmer. August, to whom I rarely offered explicit directions, would head off into the mostly neglected Tuttle Exhibit Hall, where we had collated the videos that depicted people blowing out candles, and there, on a laptop, in the dark, he began creating a database of funding entities and a system for tracking video submissions. Yet it wasn't until he brought me a proposal for the Videos of the Dead Web portal, and showed me the kind of elegant, understated banner advertising that we could include on the site, that I truly understood how lucky I was. Before that fateful morning meeting six months ago, Videos of the Dead was hanging on by the barest of threads.

Let me describe this morning's haul: Anne R, who died of an inoperable brain tumour last May, juggling lemons with her three kids; Ronnie D, who lived to eighty-two and who was still skydiving well into his seventies; Deborah W, who had Aspberger's, cataloguing major-league ballplayers who appeared in only one game; Mike S, the poet and unremitting alcoholic, taping an instructional video on how to use a juicer; Paula S, a florist, on a security cam, complaining about a teller at her bank; Norbert U, a painter of houses, who died of one too many cigars; Malachi N, who was in the Department of Health and Human Services, doing his weekly drag show at the gay bar; Regina G, myocardial infarction; Brian G, struck by lightning; Louis R, renal cancer; Barclay L, who took pills; Dave D, who tried to help his colleagues from the Murrah Federal Building; Emma P, who went through a guard rail; Jonette E, dead of natural causes, displaying her collection of locusts. Someone loved each enough to send along the videotape or the CD-R or the DVD or the flash drive. Think of it this way: this morning, yet again, grief pooled in the catchments available, and then it overspilled the walls, travelling downhill into the larger reservoir of lost things, viz., Waterbury, CT.

We had a fourteen per cent increase in hits on the site in the second year of operation, largely due to August Morse, and an increase of nearly one hundred per cent in advertising. For these reasons, we began offering our own compilations of various films housed in the archive. After which, we conceived of an even more promising revenue stream. In certain cases, donor families have allowed reproduction of footage of their loved ones for commercial purposes. Naturally, these requests need to be handled with sensitivity. But consider the possibilities. Ricardo F died of ALS two years ago. His family felt that any monies accruing to his estate should be donated to ALS-related charities. Indeed, the family was eager to have a philanthropic presence. They therefore generously allowed footage of Ricardo F's fumbling attempts at the steel drum to appear in a nationally broadcast automobile advertisement, as long as the commercial was not exploitative. We secured a finder's fee and commission.

Through this kind of creativity, a budget line for a second assistant appeared. She was an acquaintance of August's, Carrie Preston, who had an energetic demeanour that reminded me of, perhaps, a vole, but in a good way. Carrie Preston was exceptional at palindromes. She wore thrift-store dresses. Her enthusiasm attracted others. Soon there were other part-time staff who joined our enterprise. I'm not going to mention all their names now, but they know who they are. This new larger staff was noteworthy for its team spirit and kindness. We were tolerant of the days when people had to get away. I had a counsellor on retainer who was able to talk to salaried staff, or interns, when they felt they couldn't continue. The counsellor agreed to work for free, as long as I would allow him to conduct an inquiry into PTSD among our employees.

Some video footage of people kissing – and I have seen a great many kissers since I agreed to take this job – is of such intimacy that I find it difficult to watch, even for the purposes of cataloguing. When I say 'intimacy', I do not mean the provocative soft-core intimacy that is everywhere evident in movies or on television programmes. Far from it. What I mean is that the kissing of the dead does not assure romantic escape. It's just sad. No matter the comeliness of the participants or the fervour of their romantic longueurs, I wish they would stop, because I know how it will turn out.

Let me then, with mixed emotions, hasten to the item I mean to describe today. The camera is held astonishingly close to two faces, a teenage boy and girl. Off-camera, a voice announces, 'Hi, everyone! This is Geoff, and this is Carla, and I'm your host for the Arlington Cable Access programme, *Pete's Friends*! Today on *Pete's Friends*, Geoff and Carla tell us about how they met, what they like about each other, how long they've been together, that type of thing! Then they agree to kiss on camera for the first time, so that you at home can rate the hotness of their *brand fricking new relationship*!' Carla trembles with suppressed embarrassment at the introduction, and while as a matter of policy I disagree with that commonplace which locates emotion in the human eyes, it could be said in this case that Carla's eyes do smile a bit. They are green, and she brings out their greenness with an orangey lipstick shade. Her ringlets, which are mostly blue, are somewhat disarranged. She sports a torn black T-shirt that hangs off the shoulder nearer the camera. Geoff, her counterpart, wears big black-framed eyeglasses that may be surgically attached to his nose. His expression is intent, even humourless. One of his teeth is badly discoloured, and his flannel shirt has burn holes in it, likely self-administered.

These two young lovers look into each other's eyes, and then they move imperceptibly closer. And closer still. Eventually, after an uncomfortable pause, their chapped lips mutually caress. It's a slow kiss. I for one find it all rather humiliating, especially for Geoff, who seems palpably uncomfortable in the lens of the camera. The sound of the lip smacking follows, that wet, fleshy sound that reminds me of sodden washcloths flung upon a tile floor. Carla contracted non-Hodgkin's lymphoma the year after filming and quickly lost most of her hair from chemotherapy. She was frequently nauseated and physically exhausted. She threw up often. She bruised easily. Because of her illness, she dropped out of high school. Geoff writes in his essay on why this video kiss should be included in our display: 'I wasn't her boyfriend for very long. But I went over to her place all during her treatments, right up until the bone-marrow transplant. I'd read a book to her or play games with her when her sister and her parents needed a break. They let me stay over a few nights. Carla got weak towards the end. You could tell she had no energy, even though she didn't really complain. She told everyone she knew that she loved them. She gave away her stuffed animals, including Red Teddy. I know she was frustrated that she just never really got to do much with her high school years. I don't think she ever smoked any pot or got drunk or anything. She just had time to get through puberty and die.'

The staff in our research department report that no public access programme entitled *Pete's Friends* was ever broadcast.

Yes, non-profit organizations in recent years have suffered mightily, especially as people have donated the better part of their earnings to the alleviation of natural catastrophes and genocide. People imagine that a non-profit exclusively devoted to preserving video mementos of the dead would not have a problem fund-raising. And yet it's through this kind of thinking that non-profits often come up short, at least the sorts of non-profits that are not splashy, that don't command the Hollywood board members, that don't manage big benefit dinners where limousines queue up, or where the gentry leave in possession of the much sought-after goody bags.

Despite the revenue enhancements I've already described to you, last year we began dipping into the endowment to the tune of eleven per cent. We had deferred maintenance issues relating to flooding in one of the apartments in the loft above us. There was a mould problem that grew worse over the course of a wet spring.

Which is why we'd like to hear from you.

If someone you know or love has died and has left behind footage of herself, footage in which she teaches her daughter about the propulsion of the common American tricycle, or in which a gaggle of urchins in Halloween costumes learn to assemble the dessert known as *s'mores*, please contact us. We don't care if your videos are sentimental. We don't believe in the concept of sentimentality. There is no video we will *not* take, as long as the documentary impulse is preservationist. We are the museum that turns away no party. We like boring things, things that lack focus. We like people who irritate and who waste your time.

And, let me assure you, I too know what loss is. Long ago, for example, I was a student film-maker. As an ambition, I'll warrant, it's almost preposterously arrogant. I was a kid from north-eastern Connecticut whose parents operated a failing travel agency. It takes a lot of drive to become a film-maker when your origins are this modest. I am forced to confess I didn't have what it takes. When I didn't get the scholarship money to go to one of the big film programs, when no one wanted my script, when I couldn't even get work as a production assistant, I started looking around for a more reliable vocation. My first stop was a graduate program in social work.

This was in Storrs, thirteen years ago. We were living off campus in urban housing stock, just outside the beleaguered downtown section of the capital city. My suitemate, Jenny Hobart, came from New Hampshire. She was studying hotel management. Karl, Department of Mathematics, and I found Jenny through an advertisement in the free paper.

She was a tidy woman who disliked masculine carelessness. She tried to persuade Karl and myself to do the laundry more frequently. She preferred organic and locally grown produce, which was not as much available then as now. She was not a classical beauty. Although I should hasten to admit that I was not terribly experienced in the matter of beauty, nor with the feminine things of life. It didn't occur to me to be troubled by Jenny's crooked front teeth or chipped incisor. She had curls that headed off in many directions, as though she had given up on several hairstyles at once. She was skinny above the waist, more generous below. She wore sweatshirts and ironed her blue jeans. There was never a sign of make-up. Most days, she seemed exasperated. This was among her many unforgettable qualities.

In the course of things, it occurred to me that it was pleasant to have coffee in the morning with another human being. Karl would pop a couple of coffee beans into his mouth, along with a multivitamin, and he would leave for school. Contact with people made him uncomfortable. Jenny was just the opposite. We sat in the kitchen during this and subsequent conversations. We fired up the old-fashioned percolator I'd purchased at a tag sale in town. We heated a little milk, because warm milk made all the difference. I always felt a little bereft when heading off to class.

Among the things Jenny and I never discussed were: politics, religion, our unhappy childhoods, our mutual interests in music and film, love, degradation of the environment, the Middle East, overpopulation, baseball, the weather, our dreams, the weaknesses of our fellow men, high prices of electronic gadgets, the fastest routes between any two points, our most uncomfortable medical experiences. I didn't even know what television programmes she liked.

Friends came and went. Karl kept vampire hours. Jenny had a female friend who telephoned on the common-room handset. She dropped by now and again. There were things I came to wonder about Jenny. Did she know how to ride horseback? Had she ever consulted a financial adviser? What were her hobbies? Did she have a recipe for peach cobbler? Were the books on her bookshelves alphabetized? There were, it seemed, a number of topics yet to be covered.

Eventually, I got the idea that I might *film* Jenny. As a failed film director, I had a few mostly unused digital storage devices in my bedroom that were intended for compilations of the facts of my life. I had a Dictaphone, for example, with which I occasionally recorded my dreams. I used a herky-jerky webcam on my computer to talk to online acquaintances. I had an old, beat-up DV camera. My whim with regard to filming Jenny slowly acquired the opalescent exterior of purpose. I was ashamed to broach the idea at first, because I didn't really know if I had a story to tell. I suppose I knew only that I wanted my film to feature Jenny, because in performing she would be in my company a while longer.

One morning over coffee I did at last manage to ask if she would perhaps do a brief screen test for a feature I wanted to make. It's possible that I exaggerated the budget of this film or the financial commitments I had from investors. I can't remember the conversation precisely. It *is* likely, however, that I said something about the innocence of sock puppets, how sock puppets, in their way, concealed reservoirs of longing, the longing in whose grip, I might have added, we commit endless gaffes and misapprehensions, ever desiring and failing to articulate desire. The sock puppet, I may have said, in which one stuck a hand into an extra-large athletic sock and with the other drew a smile upon the sock with a Sharpie, was genuine and human and innocent, and, I told Jenny, making it up as I went along, she had the perfect voice for a sock puppet film. Maybe we could just film a few minutes of her wearing a sock puppet, saying a few lines. It didn't matter all that much. It was just a screen test. The balcony scene would do, you know, from *Romeo and Juliet*. Was she familiar with the play? I was.

Jenny giggled nervously, and regrettably I don't have that giggle on film, nor do I possess her expression in the moment when she realized that I already had a sock puppet on my person, secreted in the pouch of my hooded sweatshirt. What I do have on tape, however, is a very energetic sock puppet hovering above the footlocker table in our living room. The sock puppet, in this close-up, dances as if no screen actor were ever more innocent nor more committed, with its jaunty Elizabethan smile, with its bleeding, magic-markered eyes, with its glued-on strands of yellow string serving as a wig. This was Juliet, with a squeaky soprano, octaves above Jenny's normal speaking voice: *Three words, dear Romeo, and good night indeed. /If that thy bent of love be honourable, /Thy purpose marriage, send me word tomorrow, /By one that I'll procure to come to thee, /Where and what time thou wilt perform the rite;/And all my fortunes at thy foot I'll lay/And follow thee my lord throughout the world.*

Perhaps it was too much. The sock puppet strove for iambs that were well out of reach for it. The sock puppet was a bit histrionic. And therefore the sock puppet flattened the bard of Stratford-upon-Avon. At the completion of filming, Jenny was not unhappy to get the sock off her perfect hand. She had to go to class. There were some obligations with friends in the evening. In fact, Jenny said, she was embarking on a field trip to a convention centre in the Springfield area, during which she was going to learn about marketing strategies for trade shows. There might also be a side trip to one of the restored colonial villages nearby. This I do remember clearly. She'd be back late. While going about her business, she remarked that she would consider the possibilities of the film.

The city of Hartford is among the most violent in the state of Connecticut, among the most violent in New England. What was she doing *walking* there? After dark? When she was supposed to be in Springfield? Why didn't she ask Karl or myself to pick her up downtown? I could go on and on. After the shock wore off, of course, the regrets flooded in. For example, there were any number of remarks I might have made earlier in the day. I catalogued and replayed these remarks, the flights of rhetoric in which I unfurled my vision of the sock puppet epic, holding Jenny's rapt attention in the living room so that when the time came she would elect *not* to go into the dangerous night. I suppose what I mean, at this late date, is this: I may be an effective, ambitious philanthropic professional, but I am also a person with regrets.

I still have the footage. Her family may have her clothing, her diaries, her to-do lists, her gymnastic trophies and her complete collection of soft-rock favourites on cassette, but I treasure the footage of the sock puppet.

In the upcoming giving season, please consider Videos of the Dead. ■

BLITZED BEIJING

Why the Olympic city is set on abolishing its past

The Beijing National Stadium (The Bird's Nest)

Robert Macfarlane

When I first came to Beijing, seven years ago, I lived next to a building site. When I returned a year later, I lived next to a building site. This time round, I'm living next to a building site, in an apartment on the seventeenth floor of an eighteen-floor development. My tower block doesn't have a fourth floor, or a thirteenth floor, or a fourteenth floor, because four is an inauspicious number to the Chinese (it rhymes with death) and the management is also worried about putting off Western triskaidekaphobes. So the lift ticks superstitiously up past floors 3, 5, 5A…12, 12A, 15, 15A…

Just east of us, a residential skyscraper is being built: one of the hundreds under construction across the city. I'm woken each day around six a.m. by the gong strokes of hammer on girder. This is the

CORBIS

new dawn chorus of Beijing – the peal of hit steel, the crump of the piston hammer, the high song of the drill. Bicycle bells, jackdaws and the wind in the ginkgos have lost out in the decibel competition. The hammering rings on until ten or eleven p.m. as men smite metal with quota-filling diligence.

But I am relatively lucky. The bigger projects are attended to 24/7, with the workers toiling in a permanent halogen daylight. To entertain them, site managers erect speaker banks that would shame the Rolling Stones, and blast out Chinese radio. Nearby apartments cop the sonic backwash.

Right now, Beijing is probably the biggest building site on earth, with the possible exceptions of Shanghai and Dubai. Urban re-engineering has taken place on a greater scale, perhaps – Haussmann's Paris, Lutyens's New Delhi – but never so rapidly. Since Beijing was awarded the Olympic Games in 2001, the city has been pelting itself into modernity. By the opening of the Games, it will have added five new subway lines, 300 kilometres of road, thirty-seven new sports venues, and uncounted millions of square metres of retail, residence and office space. Hundreds of skyscrapers have been built in the past fifteen years. The dark and low-rise capital of the 1980s has become leggy and gaudied with neon.

Cranes have long been considered sacred in China, cherished by Buddhists, Taoists and the Manchu: black-necked, sandhill, red-crowned. Now a different type of crane dominates Beijing's skyline: Positech, Manitowoc, Pegasus. Over half of the world's construction cranes are presently in China. I can count thirty-four of them from the windows of my apartment alone, each with a red People's Republic of China flag fluttering from its spire.

Human labour is so abundant here, planning restrictions so loose and safety regulations so scant that buildings can be knocked down and thrown up in astonishing times. Beijing's population of migrant workers is estimated at five million; thousands more migrants arrive from the countryside every week. The majority are employed in the construction industry. You pass groups of them – yellow helmets, luminous tabards – smiling despite the hours, the distance from their families and the dangerous nature of the labour. Injuries are countless in the sense of unrecorded. The first year I came here, four men working on the building site next to my room were killed. Each was holding a corner of a sheet of safety netting. A gust of wind turned the netting into a sail, bellied it out and spinnakered the men into the air. Then the matting folded and they fell fifteen floors.

All cities are continually remaking themselves, but in Beijing there is an urgency to the task that approaches mania. In the older sections of the city, estate agents begin by telling clients a neighbourhood's life expectancy instead of its price. Taxi drivers rarely know a destination, because the city's fabric shifts so quickly. Opportunist real estate agents spring up overnight like pound shops: tack up a lintel sign, get going, get gone. Downtown, every tenth or twelfth building is framed in scaffold or wrapped Christo-like in green mesh. An economic journalist recently calculated that a Beijinger presently experiences as much environmental change in a year as a Londoner would in four years and a Malawian would in a generation (poor Malawi, too often the butt end of these comparative surveys). Yanjingli Middle Road, the potholed *hutong* or alley on which my apartment block rises, is among the hundreds of areas undergoing Olympic regeneration. Chaoyang Park to its north will be the beach volleyball venue, so Olympic cavalcades will have to pass up Yanjingli. Over two months, I have watched it being transformed from an alleyway into a highway. It has been tripled in width. Hundreds of people have been compulsorily evicted from their homes and paid a one-off per-square-metre relocation fee. The market where we buy fruit and vegetables and the concrete tin-topped shacks where we buy breakfast will all soon be destroyed. None of the stallholders knows where he or she will go once the bulldozers arrive. On the wall of each condemned building, the Chinese character for 'demolish' (see over) has been spray-painted in pinks, like trees ring-marked for felling.

拆

Two months before coming out to Beijing, I had spent a day with the writer Iain Sinclair, walking the perimeter of London's 'Olympic Park': the 500-acre site in the Lower Lea Valley that has been requisitioned, fenced off and depopulated in preparation for its 2012 Olympic future. The idea for the walk had been Sinclair's. For years now, he has been working on a book about Hackney: a deep history or mapping of that borough, whose final chapters will detail the damage done to it by the coming of the Games. Our circumambulation of the park was a part of this survey – a ritual pacing-off of London's new Empty Quarter.

From London, I had come out to Beijing, another Olympic city. Soon after I arrived, I began looking for a way to walk Beijing: a route-logic that would take me under the city's skin, or at least through some of its contrasts. A few weeks after arrival, I found the answer.

Take a street map of Beijing, a ruler and a pencil. Draw a line running north–south down the city, and bisecting Tiananmen Square, so that you have given Beijing a central axis. You will see that many of the city's most significant structures align along this meridian. The Bell Tower and the Drum Tower in the north. Coal Hill, on which the last Ming Emperor hanged himself in 1644. The Forbidden City. The Monument to the People's Heroes, China's answer to the Iwo Jima memorial. And south of that, the 'Maosoleum', as it is locally known: the vast pseudo-classical building, inside which is a bullet-proof sarcophagus of angled glass, inside which is the embalmed corpse of Chairman Mao, lying precisely along the axis, his head to the south. Mao, smart in his long coat, aloof even in death, orange from the formaldehyde used to preserve him: a great proto-Hirstian shark, mandarin in three senses.

The meridian alignment of these sites is not accidental. For Beijing is a creased city, originally designed about a centrefold.

During the first main pulse of Beijing's construction, in the Yuan Dynasty (1260–1368), the city planners embedded a lateral symmetry into their blueprint. A four-mile axis or ridgeway was to run down the city's centre from north to south. Fishbone streets were to run orthogonally out from this spine, within which courtyard houses were to make a chequerboard pattern, and important buildings were to be constructed equidistantly to the east and west of the spine. The symmetry was intended to connote and to embody harmony: metropolis as Rorschach print for the balanced mind.

This axial conceit thrived throughout the imperial centuries, and even beyond them. For after the Communists came to power in 1949, they extended the idea of the axis. Tiananmen Square – a Communist construction – was oriented along it, and Mao's portrait was hung perfectly astride it, in the centre of the Gate of Heavenly Peace, the Forbidden City's great southern portal. The portrait remains there, sentinel and vast: Mao's head twenty feet high and the wart on his chin big as a bowling ball.

Then, in 2002, Beijing held an open competition for a redesign of the city in advance of the Olympics. Starchitects from around the world submitted proposals. And the winner was none other than Albert Speer, the son of Hitler's own architect, Albert Speer.

Speer Senior became the Nazi Party architect in 1934. He designed and built the Nuremberg parade grounds, the new Reich Chancellery and the German Pavilion for the 1937 International Exposition in Paris. He helped to plan the stadiums for the Aryan Games, a proposed replacement for the Olympic Games. He oversaw the construction of the Olympic Stadium for the 1936 Berlin Games, which were filmed by Leni Riefenstahl. He devised the theory of 'ruin value', the idea that buildings should be constructed with a view to their future dilapidation. And he drew up plans for a widespread redesign of Berlin, to celebrate its status as the capital of Germania – the Greater Germany. Speer's new Berlin was to be organized along a three-mile central avenue, running

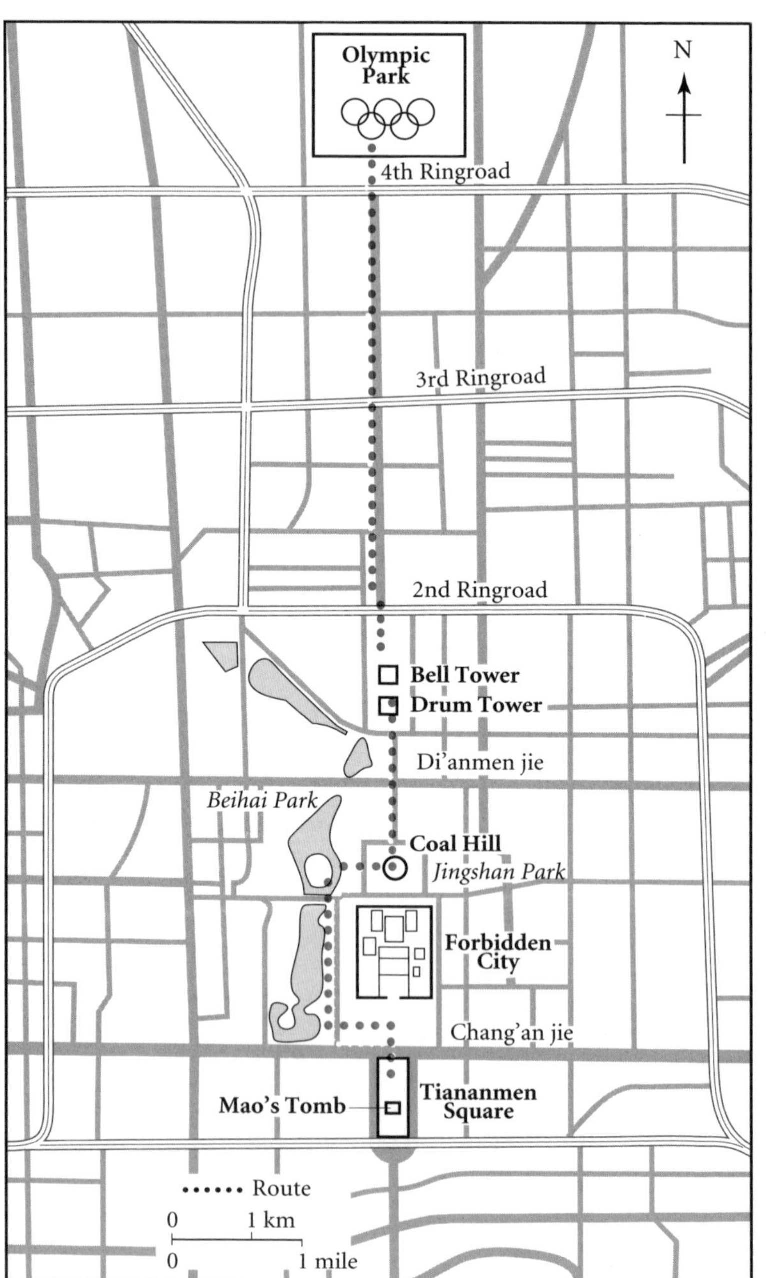

Olympic Park
N
4th Ringroad
3rd Ringroad
2nd Ringroad
Bell Tower
Drum Tower
Di'anmen jie
Beihai Park
Coal Hill
Jingshan Park
Forbidden City
Chang'an jie
Tiananmen Square
Mao's Tomb
Route
0
1 km
0
1 mile
JOHN GILKES

north–south through the city: an axis for the Axis. At the north end would be the huge domed Volkshalle; at the south a triumphal arch and a railway station. An estimated 80,000 houses would be demolished to accommodate the avenue.

Speer's plans for Berlin were abandoned on the outbreak of war in 1939. But they found a curious reprise in Speer Junior's winning vision for the redesign of Beijing. For his plans involved a radical widening and lengthening of Beijing's central axis. A vast avenue would run south from the new Olympic stadiums in the north (the Bird's Nest and the Water Cube), down to the Bell Tower. Then south of Tiananmen, the avenue would resume: another four miles to a new rail terminal and an eco-park.

Affinities were, of course, quickly pointed out between Speer Junior's Beijing and Speer Senior's Berlin. Speer Junior rejected the comparisons as invidious and ignorant. His design was, he said, indigenous to Beijing: 'My philosophy is to find something related to the situation, to the climate, to the history, to the people who are there.' He explained that he took his inspiration partly from the city's own pre-existing axis and partly from the Chinese ideogram for 'middle', *zhong*, which is also the first character of China – *Zhongguo*, meaning the Middle Kingdom. The character *zhong* resembles a cube of meat pushed on to a skewer. It is my second favourite Chinese character, after that for kebab, *chuan*, which resembles two cubes of meat pushed on to a skewer (see below).

The day I set out to walk Beijing's axis – its skewer, its meridian – was bright and high. A steady northerly was blowing down the city, dispersing the pollution haze: a rare 'blue-sky day' in the phrase of SEPA, China's environment agency. Cold and sharp; good conditions for a middle-distance walk. I reckoned the line – starting from Mao's body in the south and ending at the new Olympic stadiums in the north – to be eight or so miles as a crow would fly it. Ten or twelve allowing for diversions and getting lost.

So I started walking. Out and past one of the six hairdresser's on my street: as I approached, the coiffeur left the perm he was working on, walked out on to the street, cleared each nostril with an efficient clamp and a snort, shook his hands by way of washing them, then went back in to continue his work. Past the local restaurant specializing in Five Fragrance Donkey, and past its competitor, whose window-blazons were pushing a Dog Special for twenty-eight *yuan*: warming winter chow. Then south for a mile, down into the skyscraper-lined roads of the Central Business District: Beijing's steel-and-glass canyonlands. Hundreds of feet up, plastic bags looped the loop and zoomed in the wind shears set up by the tall buildings. At Dawanglu, I caught the underground and surfaced at Tiananmen Square, to begin the meridian proper.

Tiananmen Square is an open space that induces claustrophobia. It masquerades as a gathering place for the people, but the Party's suspicion of unauthorized groups means that surveillance there is of an exceptional density. Closed-circuit camera sight lines mesh invisibly. Public Security Bureau officers carry out stop-and-searches on people entering the square. Soldiers goose-step down its flanks. Blacked-out police vans park up in rows, ready for trouble. Plain-clothed PSB men mingle with the crowds. And there is not a single bench or seat in this, the largest civic plaza in the world. Moated by busy roads, cut across by the wind, and seatless: the square is designed to control presence and to thwart loitering.

So I didn't dawdle. I walked up past supine Mao in his death hall – banking round the tat sellers who had locked on to intercept courses with me – past the friezes of the People's Heroes, and then by the pedestrian underpass beneath Chang'an jie: the great avenue that runs east–west through central Beijing and cleaves Tiananmen Square from the Forbidden City.

In his book *Seeing Like a State*, James Scott discusses the fondness of absolute regimes for city-centre avenues. Why? Because, wide and penetrating, the avenue allows for the rapid deployment of tanks. Rangoon in 1996, Beijing in 1989: it was along avenues that tanks reached the protesters quickly and crushingly – another reason why Speer's vision of a north–south avenue might have winningly appealed to the Party planners.

I chose the road that runs up the west flank of the Forbidden City and walked north along it for a mile. It was cold out of the sun, in the shade of buildings and trees: ginkgos on the turn from green to gold, acacias, poplars. For every tree I passed I saw two or more stumps, chainsawed off an inch above ground level. Beijing, a city once renowned for its tree cover, has been steadily deforesting itself for street-widening and parking.

Labourers were at work every few yards: smashing down, mixing up, cementing over. Men in shabby suit jackets – pinstripe, single-breasted – and battered canvas plimsolls. Some stopped their work and leaned on their long-handled spades to watch me pass. No one stares at you in Britain or America now, since eye contact is a potential precursor to assault. In China, however, staring remains standard issue. Three men walked down the pavement towards me, the two outside men each with an arm flung round the shoulder of the one in the middle. They looked tired, but were smiling. They wore blue boiler suits spattered with white paint as thick as candle wax. Together, they made a Jackson Pollock triptych. Another man, spanner in hand, was bent over the innards of a Maoist-era tractor, its side panels gone and its body rusted horseback-brown. Further up the street, a cement lorry was piping its load into the foundations of a future building. I stood and watched the tube down which the liquid cement was spating, juddering with the force of the flow.

China now consumes more than half of the world's cement. This is one of the reasons why air pollution in its cities is so notoriously bad. Fragments of particulate matter – 'fines', as they are called – hang in the air: soil dust, coal dust and above all cement dust. The

Friday before my walk, I had woken to find visibility down to a hundred yards at most. A yellow smog, thick and diceable as tofu, filled the streets. Most flights were cancelled. A health warning was issued advising the old and the young to stay indoors.

It's at night that you really notice the dust, because artificial light suddenly makes the fines visible. Car headlights show as swirling cones. Each neon sign gains a smoggish halo or projection of itself. *This is what I am breathing*, you think. Air that is raw against the eyeball and silty in the larynx. Recently, a new term was coined to describe the polluted air: *wumai* (see characters below), a portmanteau of fog (*wu*) and haze (*mai*), a derivation that makes the smog sound considerably more benevolent than it is.

污埋

Due north of the Forbidden City, at the foot of Coal Hill, I met a French couple with a motorbike and sidecar. They had bumped the bike up on to the pavement. She was sitting in the sidecar. He was trying the starter pedal with regular patient stamps, as though working a lathe's treadle. He had a handlebar moustache (Great War General) and a soft blue felt beret (onion seller). She had dark glasses (Jackie Onassis) and a mulberry silk scarf (perfume advert). He answered my questions, as the bike coughed and hawked and refused to start. The bike itself: 1960s, I guessed, and painted a gleaming black. A single wide headlight mounted above its thin front wheel, and the sidecar plump as a thorax.

'She is a beautiful machine,' I said.

'He is a beast.'

'A French design?'

'No. Chinese manufacture from a German pre-war design. A CJ 750.'

'Have you travelled far on it?'

'Not today.'

'More generally, then?'

'We have been on the road for two years now. The present leg of the journey has taken us from Kashgar to Beijing. From here we go due north, to the ice. Harbin.'

The woman looked off into the middle distance, waiting for the conversation to end. Another stamp and the bike gunned. He tweaked the choke until the engine roared, pulled his goggles down into place, smiled a farewell. Then the bike trundled forwards, the back wheels thumped off the kerb and on to the road, and they sailed off northwards with a blast, her hair and scarf flying out behind them.

A CJ 750: a Chang Jiang 750. A strange link back to the Third Reich; an unforeseen ghost of Speer's line. For much of the 1930s, Germany was forbidden under the terms of the Treaty of Versailles from any form of military vehicle production, including motorcycles and sidecars. But with the signing of the Molotov-Ribbentrop Pact in 1939, three years before Speer became Minister of Armaments, Hitler circumvented this proscription. Manufacturing became a joint venture: Germany supplied the designs and Russia the labour. Among the technological rake-offs for the Russians was the original BMW design for a high-capacity motorbike and sidecar, with superb off-road abilities. After the war, the Russians sold on the basic design of the motorbike to their new allies the Chinese, who quickly began large-scale production. The CJ 750 became the People's Liberation Army standard issue from 1957 and over the course of forty years, more than 1.5 million of the bikes were produced in China.

I left the road to the motorbikes and the cars and climbed Coal Hill. The hill – flat Beijing's only high point – is artificial: made from the heaped-up rubble excavated during the building of the Forbidden City. Five pavilions are erected on its crest: the highest and biggest stands on the meridian line; two lesser temples align to the east and two to the west.

Up in the highest temple, in the full strength of the northerly wind, the city's symmetry became visible. To the south, I could see the axis bisecting the seven great central roofs of the Forbidden City. Northwards, it led to the squat shape of the Drum Tower and proceeded, vanishingly, into the pink-and-yellow granite hills that shield Beijing.

But in every other direction, disrupting the symmetry, were buildings: plazas, trade towers, hotels, banks. Beijing is not a brutalist city, because it is so various in its styles. There is no architectural vernacular, only competitive idiosyncrasy. Single superstar buildings stand aloof, like models in a fashion parade. Scanning the skyline, I could see pseudo-air-con towers (chalk-white in memory of modernism), a 300-foot-high steel coil (the city's technology museum), a gigantic 'buckyball', office towers like vertical chocolate bars and dozens of the undistinguished slabs of glass and steel that embody the Stalinist architectural logic of grandiose intimidation: Engulf the Pedestrian, Turn Visitor to Supplicant.

Spread between these buildings was the city's architectural understorey: five-floor Maoist-era work units and a few relict areas of *hutong*, with their four-sided courtyards, or *siheyuan*. The courtyard was the cell of the old imperial city, a domestic space designed to encourage harmonious family living. But rampant land speculation, uneven development and corruption have now brought the *hutong* to the cusp of extinction.

I came down the steep northern side of Coal Hill and walked out through the wood of conifers at its base. The air was fresh and resin-scented. Black-capped corvids with jouncy tails bickered in the branches. I passed four elderly Chinese women in smart brocade jackets singing Peking opera to the backing of a crackly tape-player, their high voices carrying far between the trees. Further on I found a glade of sorts, in which thirty or forty women in tracksuits were dancing in time to what sounded like a Chinese version of do-si-do. They beckoned me to join their hoedown, but for their good as well as mine I shook my head, and walked on. I'd cleared too many dance floors in my time.

It was north of Coal Hill that the destruction really began. It was as if I had walked into a bombsite. On either side of the road were cratered acres of rubble, twenty or thirty metres across. Fields of demolished *hutong*, smashed by the wrecking ball and the hand hammer, presumably to permit the widening of road into avenue. The debris had spilled on to the pavement, which was strewn with shattered slabs, broken bricks and slip-heaps of scree.

Some of the buildings had been left part standing, so you could see into rooms designed to see out of: half a bathroom, with its flush tank still standing on iron struts. A ripped-back bedroom, flowered and stained wallpaper leaning out from one of its walls. Sheaves of tin roofing and collapsed sheets of corrugated asbestos. I thought of the blitzed Vienna of *The Third Man*, with Harry Lime fleeing over the rubble, or Rose Macaulay's adventures – described in *The World My Wilderness* – exploring the bombed-out buildings of London: 'the vaults and the cellars and caves, the wrecked guildhalls, the broken office stairways that spiralled steeply past empty doorways and rubbled closets into the sky…'

'An estimated 300,000 people have been displaced to make way for the Olympic developments.'

Scavengers were picking over the remnants, looking for fragments of scrap metal and other trophies, lashing their finds on to pedal carts. I stepped up on to one of the rubble fields and wandered across it, the bricks sharp underfoot. The scavengers shot me curious stares: *What are you doing*? Hints of lives previously lived were depressingly visible: a shred of curtain here, a doll's arm there. I recalled Eugène Atget, the photographer who had chronicled Paris following the years of Haussmann's overhaul. His walks had turned into acts of elegy: photography as a loving salvage. To some of his images – of alleyways, bars, street corners – he gave the caption '*Cela aura été*': This will have been.

Further north, welders were at work, squatting on the pavement, orange sparks flurrying off the white-hot centre of the weld. An old man on a bench held a T-shaped perch on which two magpies sat, one on either arm of the T, each tethered by a wire halter about its head and neck. Just south of the Drum Tower, two men came past me in the opposite direction, carrying a mirror four feet by four feet. They had tilted it upwards, so that from where I stood it seemed as though they were carrying a slice of the cold winter sky.

A mile on, I stopped at a small park. At its gate, an old man dipped a long-handled brush into a paintpot filled with water. Then he began to write on the paving slabs, with the water serving as ink. He used the brush confidently, producing large, full-form Chinese characters with dynamic strokes and tapering tails. A character per paving slab, more or less, descending vertically, to make a line of text. A classical poem, I guessed, like the start of one pictured below, but didn't have the Chinese to ask him. By the time he had reached the bottom of his long line, the topmost characters had begun to evaporate into Beijing's super-dry air.

In a corner of the park was a weight-training area. I wandered over and watched a Chinese man with a long beard stained a nicotine yellow. He looked as though he was in his seventies, was wearing grubby linen trousers and was bench-pressing enormous weights. He saw me watching, stopped lifting and came over. When he smiled, I saw that he had three top teeth and a full bottom row of false teeth, each gold-capped. Through the fog of my poor Mandarin, I gleaned that his name was Ban Yue, that he was eighty-two years old and that he was a park regular. At one point, I seemed to supply him with a sequence of baffling answers, at which he laughed extensively. I later reconstructed the conversation with a bilingual speaker, and it appears to have gone something like this:

BY: How old are you?

RM: Three o'clock.

BY: What's the nature of your work here in Beijing?

RM: Old man literature.

BY: Where are you living?

RM: Also Fruit Nursery.

We might have been two spies verifying each other's pass codes. But it didn't matter. Following an affectionate handshake that lasted twenty seconds and jellied my fingers, we parted company: me to continue my ascent of the city, Ban Yue to continue bench-pressing the equivalent of a small family car.

So my legs kept me walking forwards, crossing Beijing's third ringroad (it now has six in total). I passed scores of men at work on the embankments: trimming, planting, digging, potting. Millions of *yuan* are being spent on the city's so-called 'greenification' campaign in advance of the Olympic Games, whose manifestations range from printing litter bins with messages exhorting people to KEEP ENVIRONMENT BEAUTIFIED to the establishment of thousands of box-hedged flower beds – peonies, roses – lining the major routes in and out of the city. The aim is Potemkinist: municipal legerdemain, a floral distraction from the otherwise wrecked state of Beijing's natural environment.

The nearer I got to the Olympic Park area itself, the denser the Olympic signage became. Every bus stop and hoarding carried images of China's sporting heroes – Yao Ming, the seven-foot basketball star, and Liu Xiang, the gold-medal hurdler – or the five Olympic mascots, primary-colour sprites who already have their own hit cartoon series.

North of the fourth ringroad, the upper surfaces of the Bird's Nest Stadium, Beijing's flagship venue, rose into view: undeniably fabulous in their ribboned swoops and curves. And there, too, was the blue corrugated fence marking the perimeter of the Olympic Park itself.

In 2005, a huge area of northern Beijing was requisitioned, cleared of its inhabitants and fenced off. Human Rights Watch estimates 300,000 people to have been displaced in order to make way for the Olympic developments: BOCOG, the Party committee in charge of the Games, puts the figure at 6,000 households. Either way, the Chinese Olympic Park – like London's – has now become an exclusion zone: cleared and enclosed and accessible only to apparatchiks and constructors. Beijing's new Forbidden City.

I tried to cadge or bluff my way into it several times: the confident stroll past the barrier, the feigned incomprehension... But access was repeatedly denied. Teenage security men in oversize greatcoats were only too pleased to tell a foreigner to turn back. So on the south-western corner of the zone, I gave up. I had followed the axis as far north as I could go: walking a 700-year-old line through a city that was set on abolishing its own past. I looked back across the park. Tens of miles of razed ground, scores of emptied buildings, thousands of men at work.

On the pavement a few yards from me, a middle-aged woman wearing a blue serge Mao jacket was flying a kite. She controlled the kite with a wooden reel a foot across – big enough to play a marlin – and on her left hand she wore a white glove, to save her from friction burns. The line was as taut as piano wire, and I could hear it humming quietly in the wind. The kite – eagle-shaped, sharp-beaked – hung perhaps 800 feet up, gazing down on to the Olympic Park. Higher still an aeroplane was flying due south, and its contrail lay white in the sky: a surveyor's chalk stroke, running the length of the city. ■

The young Rod Hall at a party

INVESTIGATION

THE JUDGEMENT OF LUT

A murder story

Tim Lott

The last time I saw Rod Hall, he bought me lunch at a Chinese restaurant in a basement just behind Oxford Street in the West End of London. This was early in 2004. He was my film agent and wanted me to write some pitches for him to sell to Hollywood. He was tetchy in the restaurant, although not with me. The service was poor and he apologized to me several times, explaining how much better the place was as a rule.

I can't recall much about the projects we discussed. I didn't want to write film pitches anyway. All I can remember about the meal is that when we'd finished patiently waiting for, and then swiftly eating, the stir-fry and silver cod and drinking the champagne, Rod had hurried to get his coat, while I went to the bathroom. He was rushing to make it to yet another of his meetings. He was a busy agent, and a good one: tough, shrewd and charming. He represented successful film writers such as Lee Hall (*Billy Elliot*), Jeremy Brock (*Mrs Brown*) and Simon Beaufoy (*The Full Monty*).

When I joined him at the desk in the cloakroom I found I had no more conversation, so I resorted to asking him about his socks. I said that I liked them, and asked where they were from. This wasn't an entirely serious question. I knew style was important to him, and I enjoyed teasing him about it from time to time. I didn't really like his socks all that much. They were just ordinary socks. I merely wanted to find out how much he was prepared to pay for a pair from Yohji Yamamoto or Margaret Howell or whatever exorbitantly expensive shop he was bound to have bought them from. I shared the popular idea that gay men had inside knowledge about the minutiae of style. I knew nothing else about Rod's personal life then. The only reason I knew he was gay was because one of the executives producing the film of my first novel, which I was adapting for the BBC, had branded him a 'hysterical old queen' after he pursued my interests with his usual determination and brio. In fact, he had never struck me as hysterical, queeny or old.

As his coat arrived, he told me that he'd bought his socks at Marks & Spencer. They had cost £3.99. He waved goodbye and headed towards the steps. He was tall – six foot four – and skinny. Jeremy Brock accurately observed that he resembled someone who had escaped from a Quentin Blake drawing, 'stalk-thin, with the ears of the Big Friendly Giant'.

I watched Rod leave the basement restaurant, up the green marble steps spectrally lit at ankle level by glowing red panels. I waited for my coat. The service at the cloakroom wasn't that much better than in the restaurant. The blue fluorescent light made everything look elegant, but unfriendly.

I'd enjoyed the meal, but the conversation with Rod had been stilted. I'd had a dispute with him some months previously about the dating of a particular contract, during which we'd had several terse telephone calls and email exchanges. I had no strong feelings for him. We simply had a professional relationship. My younger brother, Jack, on the other hand, who cut Rod's hair at his salon in Soho and knew him better, described him as a 'lovely, kind man'.

It was a description of him I was to hear many times later that year. Something similar is carved on his gravestone at the St Thomas à Becket churchyard in Framfield, East Sussex, a few miles from the sixteenth-century cottage where he grew up. He is buried a few yards away from his father, Tom, who had died ten years previously. Rod's headstone reads:

RODERICK THOMAS BERRINGER HALL
'ROD'
27.4.51 – 22.05.04
A KIND AND GENTLE MAN
REMEMBERED WITH LOVE

Rod would most likely have been seeing Ozzy, as he called him, around the same time as we had lunch, but no one is sure when they first met. Charlotte Mann, Rod's business partner and close friend, received an email from him on December 13, 2003 headed 'Mnnnnnnnn!' which said: 'Just got home from a mega raunchy meal (fun/dinner/fun)... Rest and relax this weekend. Next year is going to be wonderful! Love – Rod.'

Charlotte is convinced that the 'mega raunchy meal' was with Ozzy. There was no one else in his life as the year drew to a close, though by the beginning of 2004 Rod was having frequent romantic dinners with men, invariably much younger than him. He had broken up with his life partner of nearly thirty years, Stuart Hay, and since then, according to Stuart, had been *like a schoolboy in a sweetshop*.

Among Rod's known lovers during the early part of 2004, there was an air steward from Kuala Lumpur, a Chinese film director, a Spanish philologist and a young Barbadian man. None of these relationships had seemed to mean much to Rod but, later that year, in the spring, he met a Korean, Seok Kyu Choi, with whom he thought he might be falling in love.

Stuart continued to keep in close touch with Rod even though they had separated. They had been 'married', after all, since 1974. They had met in London, where Stuart, who was two years older than Rod, was studying English literature. They still loved each other even now they were apart. In fact, lately, they had been growing closer again. Rod's sister, Ann, thought it more than likely that they would reunite sooner or later, and grow old together.

Stuart had his own account of the first time Rod met Ozzy. It was during a period when, Stuart felt, Rod had wanted to punish him. Rod kept Stuart informed of all the new men he was meeting – partly, Stuart was convinced, out of a sense of revenge. Rod was still angry with Stuart for leaving him. The argument that had led to their separation had come at the end of a dinner at the Troubadour café in Earl's Court the night of March 15, 2002. Stuart was sure of the exact date because it was the day before his birthday. Both he and Rod had ordered organic hamburgers.

When the bill arrived, Stuart remembered that the café didn't accept credit cards. He had always intended to pay, but he didn't have a cheque or any cash on him. So he asked Rod to pay. To Stuart's astonishment, Rod was outraged. *Not only do I have to look after all my clients, and Clare and Charlotte at the agency, but I have to look after you too.*

Stuart became angry. *How dare you fucking speak to me like that.*

It wasn't just Rod's snapping at him: it was an accumulation of emotion that had somehow, in that restaurant, at that moment, reached crisis point. Rod liked to *nurture.* That's what he did. He took people under his wing. But Stuart suddenly realized that he didn't want to be under anybody's wing any more.

They both wore identical Jaeger-LeCoultre Reverso watches that they had bought twelve years before as tokens of love and loyalty to each other. As they left the restaurant, Stuart took his watch off and made to fling it in front of an oncoming bus.

Rod caught his arm and pleaded, *Don't...*

As soon as Rod said that, Stuart knew that he wanted revenge for what he saw as another humiliation and he decided then that the dynamics of the relationship had to change. He could no longer carry on being Rod's little boy.

At the end of March, Stuart moved out of their flat in Earl's Court and went to stay with friends. In the summer they sold the flat. Rod moved into an 'architect-designed' loft in Southwark, and Stuart bought a place in Brixton.

It was after the separation that Rod – who had always been loyal and monogamous – started to have frequent sexual encounters with very young men. He said he wanted a stable, loving relationship, yet he was drawn to men with whom he could never have that, not among the gay S&M community, not among twenty-year-old boys.

I know, said Rod. *But they're beautiful.*

In spite of their separation, Rod still often came over to Stuart's flat, where he spent time on computer dating sites – Gaydar usually, or MSN Dating & Personals – showing off to Stuart the other men he had sex with or was planning to meet.

One evening in March 2004, Rod called Stuart on his mobile phone as he made his way to meet yet another man he had encountered through the Internet. Roddy – Stuart usually called him Roddy – was walking towards Southwark Cathedral along Borough High Street at about six p.m., just as the dusk was gathering.

I can see him. Standing outside the cathedral. He was giving Stuart a commentary on his new assignation. *He's fucking gorgeous. He's just over there. I've got to go now. See you. Bye!*

He hung up, leaving Stuart feeling irritated and – he had to accept – jealous. Which is what, he suspected, Rod had intended.

Rod never spoke to Stuart again about the man he met that night, which was unusual. Rod talked about all his lovers to Stuart or Charlotte, and more often than not to both of them. But this one was different.

Without Stuart or Charlotte's knowledge, Rod had for some time been advertising on an S&M website that he was looking to be someone's 'slave'. If they had known what he was doing, they would both have been surprised. Rod had been mildly curious about S&M when he was with Stuart – nothing more than what Stuart called 'schoolboy stuff' – but Stuart wasn't interested and Rod hadn't pressed it. Not even after they split up did Stuart ever see marks or bruises on Rod's body.

Rod was an unlikely devotee of S&M. He was squeamish. The sight of blood made him queasy. He couldn't even look at a broken fingernail and Stuart was later convinced that Rod's attraction towards masochism was rooted in self-hatred. He was sure that Rod saw his separation from Stuart as a deep rejection. Rod had been abandoned and he was lonely and now he was punishing himself. The self-hatred, thought Stuart, was all mixed up with Rod's upbringing, in particular his relationship with his father, Tom. He had constantly sought approbation from his father, but he felt that he never received it.

Rod was six and his sister, Ann, was nine when their father gave up commuting to his job as a banker in London and moved the family from their West Sussex home to a fruit farm in East Sussex. Rod was moved from a private school in Burgess Hill to Blackboys, the local state primary in Framfield. Both children were bullied when they first arrived, partly for being incomers, partly for being 'posh'. Rod was a generous boy, but also precocious and selfish. *He was an 'I wanter',* Ann told me. *Always 'I want, I want'. He was a spoiled boy. His mummy spoiled him.*

Even so, the children worked hard. In the summers, Rod and Ann would be up until ten at night helping with the farm, packing strawberries, apples, raspberries. Ann remembers it as a happy childhood. Their mother cared for them; she was an old-fashioned housewife. Their father read to them every night. They felt secure and loved.

Rod Hall fishing in Vivien Leigh's garden

Their provincial life was made more interesting by the presence of their neighbour, the film star Vivien Leigh. She had separated from her second husband, Laurence Olivier, in 1960, and afterwards used Tickerage Mill, the Queen Anne house next to the Halls' cottage, as a retreat. Leigh was forty-eight when Rod first met her, but the first time she opened her kitchen door to find Rod and Ann standing there nervously clutching their autograph books and Brownie cameras, he thought she looked about fourteen.

Leigh befriended the children. She always called them 'darlings', but they were careful, in spite of her divorce, to call her 'Lady Olivier'. Rod and Ann would go often to her immaculate house to play with her huge puppet-theatre. The dining-room walls were lined in green silk and hung with oil paintings. She pointed out the Picassos and the van Gogh, and explained the background to each painting. Among them was Augustus John's unfinished portrait of her: Olivier had halted the sitting after John developed too great a passion for his subject.

Ann remembered playing with Vivien's make-up in her dressing room – Rod was amazed that anyone should have a room in which to do nothing other than get dressed – and he went fishing in her pond. He was the only person, Leigh told him, allowed to do so. It made him feel very special. They were also allowed to ride in her grey Rolls-Royce, driven by her liveried chauffeur, with Rod waving out the window like royalty. They met movie stars at the house, among them Jack Hawkins and Peter Finch. When Princess Margaret came to visit, Vivien told them in advance so that they could stand at the gate and wave.

Rod was able to play the piano by ear. He was musical, with a good voice, and sang in the local church choir. He was sensitive and clever, and at eleven easily gained entrance to Lewes Grammar School. He was in his mid-teens when he started to suspect that he was gay. James Reeves, the blind poet and novelist, lived near the school and had requested volunteers to read to him. Rod was among the boys who visited Reeves at home and they formed a close friendship.

When Rod was sixteen, Ann asked him about a local girl called Zoe he had been linked with. Rod started to cry.

But I'm in love with a boy.

He didn't tell his parents that he was homosexual until years later, and only because they were bound to discover anyway, after he founded the Gay and Lesbian Society at the University of Edinburgh.

Rod's father had felt physically sick when he found out his son was gay and, although a loving father, he never came to terms with Rod's homosexuality. According to Stuart, Rod never recovered from the realization that his father could not accept him for what he unalterably was.

Rod started to receive the text messages at the office in April 2004. He couldn't hide them from Charlotte, because Rod didn't normally 'do' text messages. He thought it was something more suited to teenagers. Now he was getting them – sometimes as many as six or seven – every day. Charlotte asked him who they were from. He'd say, *No one you know. You wouldn't approve anyway.*

Charlotte kept pushing. In the end, Rod gave in and said, *It's this guy I'm seeing called Ozzy. He's twenty and he's beautiful.* He said that Ozzy was a Muslim who wasn't yet 'out', and that – only half-jokingly – he believed that Ozzy's family would kill him if they found out about the relationship. Charlotte, who in her own way loved Rod as much as Stuart did, told him to keep away from Ozzy.

Rod kept receiving texts. It seemed that there was a problem between him and Ozzy, because some of the texts were threatening. One said, pointedly, that Ozzy knew where Rod's mother lived in Sussex. Another suggested that Rod's clients might like to know what it was he did in his private life. Then, a few weeks later, Rod came into the office, agitated. He sat down in front of Charlotte's desk. *I think I've pissed that Ozzy off. Someone's got hold of my Gaydar profile and made it look like I'm a paedophile.*

Charlotte asked how Ozzy could possibly have known his password. Rod made a face as if to say, *You're going to shout at me for this.* Then he said, *I was in the shower and Ozzy said he didn't have a profile on Gaydar so could he borrow my login.*

Charlotte told him once again to have nothing more to do with Ozzy. *Maybe you're right,* said Rod.

That was the last Charlotte heard about Ozzy until one Friday a few weeks later in May. She and Rod were going to a lunchtime reading of a play in the West End, and Rod said to Charlotte, *You'll never guess who phoned me and confessed to that Gaydar thing. It was Ozzy. He wants to come and see me tonight.*

Charlotte said, *I hope you're not going to see him.*

Rod replied, *Well, he's twenty and he's beautiful.*

Ozzy called a few more times later that afternoon. Rod was too busy to speak to him, but in the end he took one of the calls. Afterwards, Rod told Charlotte that he had made an arrangement for Ozzy to phone him at 10.30 that night but would not be seeing him, adding, as he left the office, *You know you've talked me out of a shag tonight, don't you?*

And he laughed.

When Rod didn't appear at Charlotte's engagement party the following night, she wasn't concerned, although she was disappointed. Stuart, who had been invited, was also absent. The next day, Charlotte, beginning to worry when she had still heard nothing from Rod, called Stuart, but he diverted her calls. He hadn't been in the mood to go to the party, and now he wasn't in the mood to make excuses.

At about five p.m., Charlotte rang Ann, who was still living in the grounds of her parents' cottage in Framfield. She stayed close to the farm to look after her mother – Margaret Hall – who had suffered a series of severe strokes and was now an invalid. Ann had been worried about Rod since the last time she saw her brother a few weeks before. She knew that he wasn't happy. He had said to her, *Ann, I don't much like myself at the moment.*

He told her about the dates he had been arranging through the Internet. She warned him to take care, fearing the dangers of his meeting up with strangers for sex. He said he didn't like what he was doing but that he was addicted to it.

Before Rod left that day, there had been an odd exchange when he had insisted on discussing his will with her. He wanted to amend it, leaving half of everything he had to Stuart, and the other half to Ann. Before, Stuart had been the sole beneficiary. Ann told him not to be so silly, talking about death at his age. He was, after all, only fifty-three. Now, here was Charlotte, ringing to tell Ann that Rod could not be found.

Ann decided to phone Stuart. Stuart said, *If anyone is going to go round there, it ought to be me*, meaning to Rod's flat in Southwark.

Charlotte told Stuart to make sure that he went with someone and, on Ann's advice, he took a close friend with a calm disposition, Andy Philips.

Ozzy's real name was Usman Durrani. He was born on July 5, 1983, and had been named after Uthman, the third Caliph. He lived in Forest Gate, in east London, with his mother, Khalida, two older brothers, Ali and Khurram, and a sister, Sadia. Two other sisters lived away from home, one in Surrey and the other in the United States. His father, Mahmoud, had died some years previously. Usman was the youngest, after his sister Sadia, by eight years.

Forest Gate is a poor and run-down area, with large and long-settled immigrant communities from Pakistan and Bangladesh. The Durrani family was well known there. They were respected, traditional and devout Muslims. Before his death in 1999, Usman's father had been a wholesaler in the rag trade, dealing in leather and sheepskin. The family lived in a double-fronted house in a pleasant tree-lined street with rose bushes and a small patch of grass at the front, and a concrete drive to park the car. The front door was flanked by decorative coach lamps. The impression was not of the impoverished inner city, but of prosperous suburbia.

Usman, the last, late baby, was adored by the whole family, particularly his mother. They saw him as a gift from Allah. He was overindulged, spoiled, a mummy's boy. As he grew up he seemed less clever or able than any of his brothers or sisters. His father, who had ambitions for all his children, was disappointed in him. At primary school Usman was generous and kind, always giving out presents. He often brought friends home. He was well behaved and hated lying. He even disliked jokes, claiming that they were just another form of lying.

At the age of eleven he failed to get into either of the first-rate schools to which his successful brothers had been admitted. Instead, he went to a state comprehensive in the neighbouring borough of Redbridge, where he found it difficult to make friends. In all the years he was there, he didn't bring a single friend back home.

As lonely boys often are, Usman was bullied. At one point, another boy tried to push him out of an upper-floor window. He never told his family. They found out what had happened only when the school contacted them. Soon afterwards, he started to become distant and closed off. He began to lie and steal – not only at school, from which he was frequently a truant, but at home.

In the summer of 1996, when Usman was thirteen, his father was diagnosed with cancer and soon afterwards his grandmother was seriously injured in a car crash. A series of burglaries at the house resulted in the family receiving death threats, apparently from the intruders. It was around this time that Usman began to steal money from members of both his close and his extended family. Sometimes he stole small change, sometimes hundreds of pounds.

No one could understand what was happening to him. He couldn't explain why he stole. On one occasion he showed his sister Sadia a very long list of all that he'd taken and who or where from. He knew that one day he had to return what was stolen and said that he intended to do so. It was part of the Islamic religion that if you took something from someone you must give it back. The whole family tried to talk to Usman about his behaviour, but he felt he was being persecuted and just became silent. At one point, he was cautioned by the police for stealing from a supermarket. Again, he wouldn't talk to the family about why he did it.

He was particularly fond of stealing sweets, or money for sweets. It appeared this was a way of trying to make himself more popular with the other children at school. He would also bring home sweets for his family. He even got a nickname – 'Mr Tuck', or sometimes 'Abu Hamwa', which Usman told Sadia means 'Father of Sweets' in Arabic. Much later, when advertising on the Internet for sexual partners, he used the name 'Sweetsmaster'.

In his mid-teens, Usman made a suicide attempt by taking an overdose of tablets. He was hospitalized and referred to psychiatric services for a brief period. The stealing and the lying and truanting and self-harm continued. He made several bomb threats against the Canary Wharf Tower from his home phone number. He was quickly caught, but was let off with a caution because of his age and immaturity.

His family were uncomfortable about the idea of bringing in outsiders to help with their problems. But some time during 1997 or 1998, a social worker in Camden named Rajah Khan, who Sadia knew from her work as a schoolteacher, started to meet and talk to Usman informally. It did not help: Usman's behaviour continued to deteriorate. He no longer trusted the family. He had decided – perhaps because of the sexual abuse he later claimed to have suffered by an older, male relative in Pakistan – that the family was against him.

By 1999, Usman's father, Mahmoud, was in hospital in west London, and close to death. The family often stayed with him overnight in the same room. Usman was at the hospital when Mahmoud died on the night of July 28, but he was in the bathroom having a shower as his father took his last breath. Afterwards, he felt guilty that he was there and yet not there. But he reacted differently from the rest of the family, never once talking about his father's death. He never cried. He seemed unable to grieve.

Shortly after his father's death, Usman signed on at Newham College for a course in business studies. Once there, his lies became even more fantastical. On one occasion he told the family that he worked as a bodyguard for Michael Douglas and Nicole Kidman and had taken them to see Buckingham Palace. In fact, he was struggling with his studies and, on several occasions, was told to leave, only to be reinstated.

His exclusions from college had occurred after he had made outlandish claims against staff, saying that he was being victimized. In what appeared to be an attempt to get both attention and sympathy, he forged a letter from St Bartholomew's Hospital explaining that he was suffering from terminal brain cancer. The deception was exposed when the letterhead, on inspection, read not 'St Bartholomew's Hospital' but 'St Bartholomew's Canoe Club' (it had been downloaded from the Internet).

Usman had by this time become an enthusiastic user of the Web. Sadia began to worry that her brother was spending too much time online and that it was becoming an obsession. She searched his cookies and temporary Internet files and found a picture of a young white man in a suggestive pose. She said nothing to Usman, but told her eldest brother, Ali. Ali spoke to Usman about the picture, and was satisfied that it was merely 'research'. It was never made clear what it was research for.

The L-shaped apartment Rod had bought was part of a converted Victorian primary school in Southwark, south-east London, called the Tabard Centre, designed in the early 1990s by the architects Julian de Metz and Amit Green. To enter his part of the building, you had to go through a steel door with an inscription carved above it that read BOYS. The body of the flat was two former classrooms knocked into one room which made 1,500 square feet of floor space under a high vaulted ceiling that incorporated the original Victorian timber trusses.

The flat had cathedral-like windows, around twelve feet high, and at its highest point, about twenty feet up, a small bathroom had been installed in the original bell tower with windows looking out on three sides over the city. The oval bath was panelled with cedar and had a single tap that curved from the floor into the centre of the bath.

Once you reached the tower, via a spiral staircase, you could continue climbing, up, up, another twenty feet through the timbered beams which criss-crossed the tower, right into the crow's nest, a tiny rooftop area from which you could see the entire vista of London.

De Metz had this to say about it in *Lofts*, a style book: *You can survey the city, and feel part of it, and yet always feel secure. It is an escapist fantasy made manifest, a fairy-tale gothic structure.*

The main room comprised the long part of the 'L' shape. A modern kitchen area had been installed which incorporated a work surface of stainless steel standing three feet away from, and parallel to, the main wall. Around the corner, in the short part of the 'L', was a snug or library room, which led into a wet room, lined in pale limestone. Suspended above the snug was a mezzanine-level bed platform, which was reached by a shorter, spiral staircase. Susan Culligan, the young banker who had originally commissioned the loft, saw the platform, on which she slept in a four-poster bed, as part of the fairy-tale fantasy that she wanted to evoke. But Rod slept there on a simple super-king-sized Scandinavian bed, elegantly minimalist, as always. There was nothing else in the room.

In the living area of the flat, he had a 1960s-style sofa upholstered in soft, sage-green leather. There was a large wooden dining table that he had handmade for him by Charles Rutherford, to celebrate when the movie *Billy Elliot* was nominated for three Oscars. Around it were eight chairs, designed by Bellini, in ox-blood leather. There was a 1920s Scandinavian-style oak desk, a Jacobean inlaid drum table and a corner chair of the same period. There were oil paintings, notably by Terry Frost and Maurice Cockerill. There was, too, a slightly twee watercolour that perhaps reminded Rod of the fruit farm at Framfield.

Stuart arrived at the flat with Andy on Sunday evening. The blinds were drawn and the lights were on low. Rod's car, a black Saab convertible, was in the car park. When they had made their way through the two CCTV-monitored security doors and up five or six flights of stairs, to the rough steel front door of Rod's flat, it was just before nine. There was a wired glass panel in the door at head height, through which the identity of visitors could be checked. The deadlock at the bottom of the door was open. That meant Rod was certainly in the apartment. Rod never left the front door unlocked when he went out.

Andy and Stuart let themselves in. It was very warm and stuffy. The lighting in the flat was low. There was a whirring sound – the extractor fan in the downstairs wet room, off to the right, in the short part of the 'L', underneath the bed platform. Stuart was conscious of a loud, unsettling noise. He saw that Poppy, Rod's Siamese cat, was alone in the middle of the cathedral-like room. Her head was thrown back. She was screaming.

Stuart ignored Poppy, and followed the sound of the whirring fan round the corner to the right and into the snug. The door to the wet room, where the sound was coming from, was ajar, and there was a shaft of light beaming from it. It seemed to Stuart that this path of light was premeditated and theatrical, designed to lead him into the room.

He went in. The light was on, which was why the fan was running. Immediately, he saw that there were lacy footprints, in blood, in the shower, and a flannel with some blood on it. There were some spatters of blood on the floor, on the bidet and toilet seat. The blood didn't amount to very much, and Stuart thought Rod might have cut himself shaving.

The cat had calmed down. Leaving the wet room and returning to the snug, Stuart now decided to take a look at the mezzanine bed platform, which was suspended above his head. He made his way up the short spiral staircase very slowly. By now, he was frightened. In the back of his mind was the thought that Rod had committed suicide. He felt sure that Rod had been suffering emotionally for some time. Behind him, Andy was saying, *Be careful, just be careful.* They were both whispering. They didn't know why.

Stuart arrived at the top of the staircase. Nothing was out of place except a pair of black socks on the floor. He walked up to the bed and pulled the bedclothes back. The bed was empty. He retreated slowly back down the spiral staircase, and returned to the snug. There was a sense of absolute stillness, no noise from either inside or outside the flat.

He made his way back into the main room. He peered at the stainless-steel kitchen unit through the gloom, this awful murky light.

It was so terribly hot. The huge windows had darkened with the dusk.

Stuart looked up at the high spiral staircase that led to a white sliding door and into the second bathroom. Rod always kept it open, but it was closed. As he walked past the kitchen island, towards the staircase, Stuart noticed that there was a cafetière half full of coffee. The sink was full of dirty, greasy plates. Stuart thought, *Roddy wouldn't leave it like this.*

He looked up at the closed door at the top of the staircase. He knew he was going to have to walk up it. He had to do it. *It was diabolic*, he thought, like the set of a horror film. Everything had been designed. He was being led. It was like it had been arranged, just for him, and the downstairs bathroom had simply been a teaser.

He began, slowly, to walk up the staircase. Twenty steps in all, round and round in tight circles. Andy stayed close behind. They reached the platform at the top. In front of them was a white bath towel, spread out on the floor. It was covered with brown stains. Stuart thought it was covered with shit. It didn't occur to him that it might be dried blood.

Stuart stepped over the bath towel. The sliding door ran from right to left. He pushed it open, slowly. He walked into the bathroom inside the bell tower. Stuart noticed a pool of black on the floor to his right. He couldn't work out what it might be. Then he noticed a number of tea-light holders, which he remembered buying in Heal's on Tottenham Court Road years ago. They were arranged in an arrow shape, pointing away from the bath towards the east.

Stuart looked in the direction of the bath. Rod's feet were protruding from it. They were black and spattered. He saw that there were white objects scattered on the floor, like pebbles, and his eyes travelled up beyond Rod's feet, up his legs. Rod's body had been ripped from his neck to his navel. His head was up against the wall. He had been completely disembowelled.

Stuart looked into Rod's face. His mouth was open. His eyes were wide open. His face was red and green. There was some kind of fluid all over his face that had turned it the colour of verdigris. It had created a terrible mask, like something out of a voodoo ritual. Stuart was thrown back by the force of what he saw. If Andy hadn't been behind him, he would have fallen back over the spiral staircase to the ground. Stuart started screaming. *We've got to get out, we've got to get out. It will come and get us.*

They ran down the spiral staircase and out of the flat. They hammered on the door of the next apartment on the landing. Stuart was shaking and screaming, *They've murdered him.*

Soon afterwards, the air was filled with helicopters and searchlights and barking dogs and paramedics. Someone offered Stuart an oxygen mask. He refused it. He kept saying, *I killed him, I murdered him. If I hadn't separated from him this would never have happened.*

At some point, his phone rang. It was Ann calling to find out if her brother was all right.

He's dead, he's here, he's in the bath, oh it's terrible, Ann, he's dead.

Andy took the phone from Stuart and said to Ann calmly, *We've found Rod, Ann. He's dead.*

When the police knocked on Ann's door at five a.m., she was expecting them. She had been convinced that her brother had killed himself and was sure she could have done something to prevent it. So when she was told that he had been murdered, she felt a kind of relief. Then came the rage and the grief.

Back in London, Charlotte didn't speak to Stuart until six the following morning. He had spent most of the night at Southwark police station.

Stuart said, *Do you know?*

And Charlotte said, *Yes I know. Rod is dead. Ann told me.*

Stuart said, *Yes, but do you know?*

Charlotte said, *Do I know what?*

Stuart said, *Rod was murdered.*

Charlotte, like Stuart, felt physically knocked back by the impact of what had happened. She was in the middle of the bedroom when the phone call came; then she found herself collapsed in the corner. She still clung on to the phone. She screamed into the mouthpiece, *I know who did this.*

Stuart told her to call the police. She was put through to an investigating officer. She told him, *I know who did this. His name is Ozzy, he's a student at Stratford College, his phone number begins with 0208 534. His mobile number is in Rod's Filofax, which is in his brown Gap bag which will be leaning up against the island in the kitchen. It will be under 'O' for Ozzy.*

One of Charlotte's great strengths as an agent was that she had an excellent memory for details.

Usman had arrived at Rod's flat some time around 11.30 that Friday night. He had promised to have sex with Rod. Rod, who was exchanging text messages with Seok Kyu Choi in Korea, buzzed him in through the two sets of security doors and into his flat. Some time later, Usman tied Rod up in the bathroom, with Rod's consent. A holdall with sex toys was found in the bathroom. Whether it was Rod's or Usman's was uncertain. It contained a leather hood with eyeholes, a whip, handcuffs and ropes. Rod's hands had been manacled behind him and his feet bound with rope. He had been suspended from a crossbeam above the bath. He wore the hood over his head. Once he was secure above the bath, Rod would have been able to see Usman through the eyeholes in his hood. Usman took a camera out and began photographing Rod. Rod would have been able to watch him as he did so. He would also have been able to see him produce the knife.

Usman began stabbing Rod. After the first few wounds, Rod managed to break free of his bonds. He fell on Usman. He wrestled with him in the bath, as best he could. The bath was slippery with blood. He fought, but Usman would not stop. He stabbed Rod between thirty and fifty times. Any one of seven major traumas may have led to his eventual death. He then disembowelled Rod, removing his internal organs and leaving them on the floor. These were the small white pebbles that Stuart had seen. Then Usman took a video of Rod's body with a digital camera. He poured Jeyes fluid on to Rod's face, which turned it green. He then gave the flat a cursory clean and took a shower. He rested, possibly even slept, in Rod's bed.

Usman left the flat early the next morning. He was seen by a neighbour wearing a heavy, long coat – Rod's coat – and a pair of Rod's shoes. It struck the neighbour as unusual that he was wearing such a coat, since it was warm. He was carrying a black bin-liner which contained the camera, a wallet, Rod's Jaeger watch and a diamond tiepin. Usman thought this would help to make it look like a robbery. In the bag, presumably, was also the murder weapon, which was never found, and Usman's shoes, too soaked with blood to wear.

After leaving Rod's apartment, he went to the flat he secretly shared with his wife, Nabela, in Beckton. They had met early in 2003 when she and Usman were both students at Newham College. Nabela Razak was divorced and had two children at primary school. Her ex-husband had committed an honour killing some years before and was still in prison. Without telling any of his family, Usman married Nabela in November 2003 under an Islamic law known as a *nikah*. They did not require an imam. All that was required was for a *wali* – a trusted friend – to be present as a witness. Nabela asked her best friend's husband, Stephen Ramgit Rainer, a dispatch rider living in Leytonstone, east London, to be their *wali*.

After they were married, Usman hardly ever stayed the night with Nabela. He only came to the flat during the day. His wife was left alone on most evenings. Rainer did not think it was the way a husband should behave.

On Saturday, May 22, the night of Charlotte's engagement party, the night after Rod was murdered, Rainer and his wife were getting ready to go to a barbecue in Harold Hill, near Romford, in east London, when Nabela telephoned. They had been expecting to meet Nabela and Usman at the barbecue but Nabela asked Rainer if he would come to the flat in Beckton. She spoke calmly, but she said it was urgent. It took him about forty minutes to drive to Beckton and when Nabela answered the door she was distraught, shaking. They sat at the kitchen table and, weeping, Nabela told Rainer that two months earlier, Usman had been abducted by four white men in Earl's Court. They had stopped as he waited at a bus stop, asked for directions, then bundled him into the back of their van, where each of them had raped him.

Please don't tell anyone about this, Nabela said. *It's so much shame and embarrassment.* She was sobbing and, as Rainer tried to comfort her, Usman came in. He'd heard the sound of his wife crying.

Rainer asked him about the rape. *Is this true?*

He said it was. He described to Rainer what had happened, and then, bafflingly, explained that rather than reporting the men, he had befriended them after meeting them again by chance a few weeks later at the Olympia exhibition centre in west London, where he said he was working as a security guard for a pop concert.

After this, Usman said, he talked to them regularly on the phone. He said he only had a number for one of them – a man called Roderick. When pressed, he said the other men were called John, Paul and George. He wouldn't give any further details.

Nabela confirmed that a posh man by the name of Roderick, who sounded white, had been phoning Usman on his mobile. Rainer was angry. He didn't believe anything Usman said. He asked him more about the men. Who were they? Why would he befriend them? Usman told him it was because he had wanted revenge.

It was then that Usman confessed to Rainer and his wife that he had gone to the Tabard Centre in Southwark the previous night and murdered Rod. Usman said, *I wanted to hurt him, but I didn't want to kill him. I just went mad. I wanted him to feel the pain I felt.*

No way, said Rainer, *I've had enough of this bullshit. You're lying.*

Rainer still didn't believe what Usman had told him. Nor did Nabela. He had lied so many times, he had dramatized his life so often, that anything he said was in doubt. Rainer thought this was just another of his fantasies. He got into his car and set off to drive home. But he had a puncture and returned soon afterwards. While he waited for the RAC, Nabela pleaded with him to help.

Usman still had the black bin-liner. He said he needed help to get rid of the contents. Rainer asked him, *If you did kill this man why do you still have these things in your possession?* Usman said simply that he didn't know what to do with them. Rainer asked him about the man he had killed. Usman said, *A literary agent. Fame. A well-known person. Homosexual. Rich.*

Thinking that the contents of the bag were merely stolen property, Rainer and Nabela drove Usman around the local streets disposing of the evidence. Rainer said, *If these need to be got rid of, I'll get rid of them.* If Usman had stolen them, then he wouldn't want to throw them away, thought Rainer. Nabela agreed that this was the best course. She wanted to protect her husband. She thought he might be a thief; she didn't believe he was a murderer.

The Jaeger watch, the symbol of Stuart's devotion to Rod, was thrown down a drain. The clothes were scattered at the back of a supermarket and were never found. The camera was later recovered, with the pictures in it of Rod suspended over the bath.

After they had finished disposing of the evidence, they bought some food and returned at about eleven p.m. to Beckton, where Usman and Nabela spent the night. The next day, Rainer returned to Beckton. He and Nabela decided they needed to contact Usman's brothers, Ali and Khurram. They arranged to meet the brothers in Docklands, in east London, at a quiet location. Usman stayed in Beckton. This was the first time that Ali and Khurram, or any of the family, were aware that Usman was married. Nabela told her brothers-in-law what had happened. Then Nabela and Rainer returned to Beckton. Later that day, Ali, Khurram, Khalida and Sadia all arrived to see Usman. A short while later, Rainer left the flat and returned to Leytonstone. He was not party to the family's decision to send Usman to Pakistan. The next day Usman and one of his brothers were on a flight via Dubai.

While Usman was on the plane, a police officer turned up at the Durrani family house and confirmed that Usman was suspected of murder. The officer searched Usman's room. He couldn't find his passport anywhere. He told the family that if Usman was trying to flee the country, someone ought to get in touch with him and make sure that he returned immediately. The family, now aware that Usman had actually done what he had claimed, contacted the brothers, who received the message in Dubai. Usman was brought back to London.

The next day, the whole family together – Khalida, Ali, Khurram and Sadia – walked Usman to the police station in Forest Gate, only a few minutes away, on Romford Road. He was arrested, but later released on bail. The police observed him over the next few days. At one point, young men were seen to be kissing his hand in the street. The police speculated that he had achieved a measure of respect among the community as a result of claiming to have carried out an honour killing. While he was out on bail, Usman checked himself into the mental health unit of Newham University Hospital. It was a week or so later before an officer from Lewisham police station arrived to take him into custody. He was formally charged with the murder of Rod Hall.

When Usman met the detective who was going to interview him, he seemed friendly and talkative. The detective used the word *bouncy*. Usman talked quite happily about football, college and his wife. Sometimes he would take a photograph of Nabela out of his wallet and stare at it. However, when he went into the formal interview he was silent. He gave the interrogating officer a catatonic stare, looking right through him. The officer, who had dealt with numerous homicides, found it disturbing.

He could do the stare, he could look right through you. Most people can't do that. It's very strange. Unsettling. He was a very chilling person.

Usman Durrani wouldn't even speak to give his name.

Homosexuality, sadomasochism and religion, according to the prosecution psychiatrist who assessed Usman while he was in custody, are a 'toxic brew'. He had seen the same combination in cases of extreme violence and murder again and again. Religion has the power to inspire shame and guilt. Many homosexuals who are religious or come from religious families are tormented by their sexuality. At Usman's trial, the prosecuting counsel asked his sister Sadia about the predominant attitude towards homosexuality in the Muslim community. She said:

> *I think the attitude comes from the story of Lot* [in the *Qur'an*, Lut]. *And it is a curse and a cursed act. It is something that is seen as unnatural so if anyone is to have tendencies for that it is to suppress it. In our community, it is seen as a very bad thing and in our religion as a major sin. There is not actually a case I know of in our local community of anyone being openly homosexual so I am pretty sure they would be ostracized.*

Usman showed emotion at his trial only when the counsel for the prosecution suggested he was a homosexual – then, he rose to his feet, shouted out and gesticulated angrily.

Male homosexuality is another ingredient in the 'toxic brew' because it is often the case that gay men seek out the transgressive more than heterosexuals or lesbians. S&M, the third ingredient in the brew, can run out of control. Passion becomes anger; what is at one moment arousing may in the next be unbearably painful. Crucially, the tools to do harm are there at hand.

It may simply be that Usman Durrani is insane. But none of the psychiatrists who assessed him after his arrest – acting for the prosecution or the defence – thought that he was mentally ill by any technical definition. The assessment at the psychiatric unit of the John Howard Centre in Homerton, east London, where he was referred for psychiatric tests, was that he fulfilled the criteria for a diagnosis of personality disorder. Personality disorder is not a mental illness.

There is, however, a mental process – not an illness – defined in psychiatric medicine as catathymia. A sufferer may have some underlying conflict that produces powerful feelings that gather momentum until the person thinks the only solution to the psychic turmoil is to kill someone. Usman may have had confused feelings about the relative who, he claimed, abused him as a child. Rod was much older than Usman, like his abusive relative, and powerful, like his domineering father, whom he also resented. Or Usman's frenzied violence may not have been about feelings at all – but about the deadening of them.

The defence psychiatrist was convinced by the arguments of James Gilligan, a leading American forensic psychiatrist. Gilligan has suggested that one of the most dangerous conditions in the risk of violence is shame. Profound shame, according to Gilligan, can lead to emotional numbness, a state in which one can commit acts of great extremes in an attempt to generate feeling – any feeling.

There would have been a huge amount of shame associated with homosexuality in an Islamic family. In addition to that, a secret marriage with an older woman with children would have added to the burden. If Usman did suffer from a personality disorder, catathymia or deadening shame, he was still a seductive and attractive young man. He was, in the words of the prosecuting psychiatrist, *self-centred, narcissistic, effeminate, exasperating, evasive, elusive and unreliable.* The defence psychiatrist called him *coquettish* and said that he saw himself only *as a victim*. Usman showed no understanding of the effect of what he had done, on either his or Rod's family. Impulsive and grandiose, he expressed no guilt or regret. He cried sometimes during consultations, but his tears seemed false or were those of self-pity. It was both psychiatrists' opinions that he would be capable of committing another murder.

Usman was extremely manipulative. He had a soft, girlish, classless voice. He had a habit of lowering his head and looking through his fringe of floppy hair. So powerful was his ability to influence people that members of the prison staff at Feltham Young Offenders' Institute made personal visits to Usman at the psychiatric ward at the John Howard Centre (and one member of the Feltham staff wrote him sympathetic letters). After his arrest, Usman continued to seek attention. During his time at the John Howard unit he would scratch at himself with a pencil, enough to draw blood, and scream and rage out loud. He seemed to have a deep fear of being abandoned.

Catathymia, shame, sexual stimulation, rage, loneliness: could any of these explain Usman's frenzied attack? The prosecution psychiatrist summed up Usman's behaviour in the language of his trade: *A single behavioural act must always have a multiple of determinants. You don't kill someone for 'a reason'. You kill them for multiple reasons. Your unconscious mind being one of them.*

As unfathomable as Usman Durrani's behaviour might have been, Rod Hall's was also mysterious. Why would you invite an immature and unstable, if highly manipulative, young man into your flat late at night and allow him to tie you up and place a hood over your head, so that you were completely helpless, especially when this person had threatened you and your family? Why did Rod, so intelligent and worldly, allow this to happen?

The prosecution psychiatrist made an attempt to explain the appeal of submissive S&M: *If you are dominant in everyday life you can relive childhood experiences when you were the submissive one. That's a kind of release. Surrendering to others so you don't have to be the one in control.*

Promiscuity combined with S&M could hardly be described as simply an erotic game. It's obviously risky. How can you be sure how far the other person wants to go? It can be a fine line between what is arousing and what is enraging. Some people, psychiatrists point out, do have fantasies about being killed or mutilated. Killing is the most extreme form of sadism. It could also be the case that being murdered is the most extreme form of masochism. And that death, too, is a release.

Stuart, Ann and Charlotte do not believe that Rod wanted to be murdered. Perhaps they do not believe this because they knew him too well; knew the kind of man he was. Or perhaps they do not believe it because such a possibility is simply too painful to contemplate.

The trial of Usman Durrani began at the Old Bailey in London in July 2005. Usman pleaded guilty to 'manslaughter due to diminished responsibility' as a result of suffering a significant abnormality of mind. His two brothers, Ali and Khurram, were in court every day. They wore conventional suits rather than their usual traditional Muslim dress, since the trial was taking place a few weeks after the London Underground bombings of July 7, and they didn't feel it would help their brother's case to advertise their culture and religion.

Charlotte and Stuart attended most days of the trial, Ann less frequently. Charlotte had kept the Rod Hall Agency going without Rod and almost all the clients had remained loyal. Having arranged for a priest to 'clear' the flat in a ceremony, Stuart helped Ann to sell it to an unsuperstitious Australian couple who were pleased to buy it at a reduced price. The money raised from the sale was split between Stuart and Ann, under the terms of Rod's amended will.

As at his police interviews, Usman never spoke during the trial. In the dock, he wore a dark grey suit that was too big for him, a white shirt and blue tie. He was slight, intense, angular, with very fine skin, dark circles round his eyes, a high brow and thick, straight black hair. Charlotte had been scared of seeing him. She didn't want to fill in the blanks in her mind of Rod's death. But when she did see Usman, all she felt was *an overwhelming sense of nothing*. Stuart wanted to hate him. He had the most terrible fantasies about physically punishing him, until he saw him. But there in the courtroom Stuart found he couldn't. There were times when he even felt sorry for him. He looked so young and unimpressive. *He was just a little boy.*

For much of the trial, Usman stared at the floor or flicked casually through the evidence folder, looking at pictures of the crime scene and the post-mortem photographs and diagrams. *Like it was the Argos catalogue or something*, said Charlotte. That he could even look at the evidence file was astounding to her. But Usman never showed a flicker of shame or recognition.

When he was not looking at the file or the floor, he read a book called *Fortress of the Muslim: Invocations from the Qur'an and Summah*. There are 134 invocations and supplications. These include: 'Invocations if You Are Stricken by Doubt'; 'Invocations for When the Wind Blows'; 'What to Say to the Unbeliever if He Sneezes and Praises Allah'; 'What to Say When You Feel Frightened'; 'Invocation to be Recited Before Intercourse'; 'What to Say When Slaughtering or Sacrificing an Animal'; 'Repentance and Seeking Forgiveness'.

The trial lasted for the best part of three weeks. Usman read his book, scrutinized the evidence folder, stared at the floor. On one occasion he complained to the judge that a man in the public gallery, a friend of Rod's, was staring at him. Other than that, he seldom looked up. Khurram, Ali, Khalida and Nabela did not take the stand, but Sadia Durrani and Stephen Rainer both testified.

The claims that Rod and three other men raped Usman were discredited. Even the defence accepted that the story was fabricated. Usman had his guilty plea for manslaughter rejected and was accordingly sentenced to life imprisonment for murder. He will become eligible for parole – because of his youth and lack of previous convictions – in 2016. But it was the view of both the defending and prosecuting forensic psychiatrists that he was unlikely to be granted parole for many years beyond that date. It is also the view of the defending psychiatrist that, as Usman begins to accept what he has done, he will be a major suicide risk. *For there can be no atonement for what he has done*, the defence psychiatrist said.

There can be no forgiveness.

Rod's funeral took place on June 26, 2004 at the St Thomas à Becket church in Framfield, shortly after Usman was charged with his murder. It was a warm day. There were mainly family and friends present, about a hundred people in all. Rod's closest clients were there – Lee Hall, Jeremy Brock and Simon Beaufoy among them.

Stuart read John Donne's *Holy Sonnet X*, a reflection upon death:

... And soonest our best men with thee do go,
Rest of their bones, and soul's delivery.
Thou'rt slave to fate, chance, kings, and desperate men...

Charlotte felt despairing. *I just couldn't think of anything but the coffin. It was awful*, she said. *The coffin was fucking enormous. So wide. And Rod was so skinny. I kept thinking about his teeth. He spent a fucking fortune on his teeth. He always said they would outlast him.*

After Rod was buried, the mourners returned to the cottage in Framfield. Charlotte didn't know what to say to Rod's ailing mother. Margaret had suffered several strokes that had affected her speech and understanding and Charlotte assumed that she scarcely knew what was going on. But when she finally found the courage to talk to Margaret, the two women held one another, and Charlotte began to shake with tears. Margaret said, *Don't cry, dear. I've cried all the tears.*

It was clear that Margaret knew exactly what was going on. She had the burden of her son's death to bear until her own death on Christmas Day 2007.

Rod Hall had died as he had lived, theatrically. He had died as if one of his clients had written the story. But if one of those clients had taken the story to him, would he have found it believable?

He usually began his critique of writers' work with praise. In this instance, and for this story, he would have told the author that he enjoyed the *back story*, the historical tapestry of the characters in the drama, and how they were drawn towards each other because of the odd similarities in their otherwise very different lives. Even if it was slightly improbable, this part of the narrative, Rod might have agreed, was dramatically effective and convincing. He would have enjoyed the irony of the obvious parallels between victim and perpetrator, and perhaps even found them plausible. He would have noted that there were reasons for attraction between the two main characters which went beyond that of mere physical impulse.

Both men, Rod might have noted, were lonely. Both had overbearing fathers and were indulged by their mothers. Both came from close, loving, conventional families whose fathers hated the idea of homosexuality. They each wanted their life to be dramatic, to be special. They concealed from those closest to them their deepest secrets. They both wanted revenge of different kinds – Usman on his father, his relative and on Rod himself; Rod on Stuart, the lover who had rejected him.

Rod would have liked the power of the idea of *shame* in the narrative, since both men were deeply ashamed. Usman was ashamed by his lack of any ability that would have pleased his father; of the apparent suffering at the hands of the relative who he claimed abused him. He was ashamed of his femininity, unpopularity and homosexuality. And Rod would have liked the conceit that although Usman was ashamed of all these things, he was entirely unashamed of a brutal and pitiless murder.

As for the other character in the drama, the rich, successful protagonist, he was ashamed of growing old. He was ashamed of his secret desire to be dominated – to be the slave. He was ashamed of his addiction to promiscuity and sadomasochism. Above all, perhaps, he was ashamed of being lonely.

Rod would then have moved on to what he saw as serious problems. Firstly, and not insignificantly, there were political or, if you preferred, practical problems. The story punched buttons that the theatre and film business may have found too sensitive to touch – Islamic conservatism and the sexual extremism of gay men. Rod would have known that many producers would have wanted to keep away from such subjects. The film and theatre businesses, for all their professed desire for work that is challenging and provocative, are in some respects also deeply conservative.

More seriously, there were flaws in the actual story itself, most particularly in the denouement. After all, could any audience seriously be asked to believe that the final act of murder would take place in a bell tower, which, as a symbol, combined both the invocations of an angry, ancient God and the uncontrollable urges of the cock? To cap it all, the bell tower was appropriated to evoke a fairy-tale narrative: that is, it was specifically designed to act as a theatre for the playing out of a myth. A corrupted fairy-tale tower into which a visitor, a storyteller and fantasist, entered as the witching hour approached to enact the perfect antithesis of a happy ending.

Rod would certainly have insisted that this part of the narrative be edited out or toned down. No one believed in phallic symbols any more. *You need to introduce some consistency here*, Rod might have said. *Is it a fairy-tale tower, or a religious tower, or a phallic tower?* The writer might have pressed on. *It doesn't matter. The point is, in the tower, on that night, certain gods revealed themselves to one another and came into conflict. Usman's God was there: paternal, stern, unforgiving, demanding and, in his immature mind, the expiation of sin by blood, the judgement of Lut. But our gods were there too: Eros and Thanatos; pleasure, freedom, gratification.* Rod might have paused, searching for a kind way to deliver his conclusion. Then he would have shaken his head and said, *It just doesn't happen that way, and no one is going to believe it. And besides, no one takes Freud seriously any more.* If the writer had pressed on, Rod would, as gently as he knew how, have delivered the final blow to the author's vanities. *It's dramatic, I agree. But there's no redemption in it, no lessons, no hope. It's just too sad.*

Rod was one of four friends or acquaintances of mine who died suddenly in 2004. This accumulation of shocks had shaken loose some deep-buried moorings in me. I was having trouble coping. I felt numb and lonely. My mind seemed unsteady sometimes. For the first time since suffering a serious breakdown twenty years earlier, I felt the power of the drive towards nothingness moving within. It was as if a thick, opaque shield that had protected me from a too-acute sense of my own mortality had suddenly crystallized and become brittle and thin.

Usman's act had reached out to me, a virtual stranger. What happened was affecting my marriage, my family. Depressed, I had – perhaps self-destructively – quit my main source of income, a London newspaper column. My wife was worried about me. I was so scared. I had become so scared of death.

At Rod's memorial, in September, at St James's Church in Piccadilly, I was still fragile and cold, as cold as the church itself. I stood by my younger brother, Jack, and we sang hymns and listened to the eulogies and dedications. I wondered if I would still love Jack if he had done what Usman Durrani had done. I felt certain that you had no choice in such matters. It clarified for me the suffering Usman had inflicted not only on Rod and all who were close to him, but on his own family who had loved him and had no choice but to continue doing so.

There was a string quartet playing. Jeremy Brock and the playwright and poet Liz Lochhead gave speeches. Brock talked of Rod's clothes, specifically of his fondness for leather trousers. He talked of his love of champagne, his taste, his aestheticism, his passion for food. I felt he didn't say anything very important about Rod.

Nobody there who spoke seemed to know Rod all that well, or that's how it appeared to me on that frozen, darkening day.

At the end, they played 'Funeral for a Friend' by Elton John. Its brash, gothic chords felt out of keeping. Everything, in fact, seemed out of joint. That was perhaps the nature of tragedy, even the definition of it. Above all, I felt that it was loneliness that hung in the air that day more than grief. Perhaps it was mine. Perhaps it was an echo of Rod's. Perhaps it was Usman's. Perhaps even now, as he awaited trial in Belmarsh, he clung to his loneliness, the loneliness that had started as a child when he was abused out of innocence. Because to abandon it would be the start of his understanding of not only what he had done but what he had suffered. Or was the story of his abuse just another lie, another fairy tale, the convenient invention of someone who had cast himself as the eternal victim-hero?

As the service concluded, I was aware that I felt nothing. I felt nothing at all. I just felt empty. I was almost the first one to leave the church. I couldn't fucking wait to get out of there and forget about death and its fearful implacability. As I stepped out on to the street, all I wanted to do was look away from the part of me that was seduced by the tower; that in my most hidden self ached for it.

I think Rod knew that feeling, that longing for nothing, for non-feeling, for death itself. I think Rod, in those final moments in the tower, found out all that there was to know about seduction and of fairy tales and of gods. ■

---

www.granta.com
Read an interview with Tim Lott

FICTION

FAMILY MAN

Annie Proulx

The Mellowhorn Retirement Home was a rambling one-storey log building identifying itself as western – the furniture upholstered in fabrics with geometric 'Indian' designs, lampshades sporting buckskin fringe. On the walls hung Mr Mellowhorn's mounted mule deer heads and a two-man cross-cut saw.

It was the time of year when Berenice Pann became conscious of the earth's dark turning, not a good time, she thought, to be starting a job, especially one as depressing as caring for elderly ranch widows. But she took what she could get. There were not many men in the Mellowhorn Retirement Home, and those few were so set upon by the women that Berenice pitied them. She had believed the sex drive faded in the elderly but these crones vied for the favours of palsied men with beef-jerky arms. The men could take their pick of shapeless housecoats and flowery skeletons.

Three deceased and stuffed Mellowhorn dogs stood in strategic guard positions – near the front door, at the foot of the stairs, and beside the rustic bar made from old fence posts. Small signs, the product of the pyrographer's art, preserved their names: Joker, Bugs and Henry. At least, thought Berenice, patting Henry's head, the Home had a view of the enclosing mountains. It had rained all day and now, in the stiffening gloom, tufts of bunchgrass showed up like bleached hair. Down along an old irrigation ditch willows made a ragged line of sombre maroon, and the stock pond at the bottom of the hill was as flat as zinc. She went to another window to look at the coming weather. In the north-west a wedge of sky, milk-white and chill, herded the rain before it. An old man sat at the community-room window staring out at the grey autumn. Berenice knew his name, knew all their names: Ray Forkenbrock.

'Get you something, Mr Forkenbrock?' She made a point of prefacing the names of residents with the appropriate honorifics, something the rest of the staff did not do, slinging around first names as though they'd all grown up together. Deb Slaver was familiar to a fault, chumming up with 'Sammy', and 'Rita', and 'Delia', punctuated with 'Hon', 'Sweetie' and 'Babes'.

'Yeah,' he said. He spoke with long pauses between sentences, a slow unfurling of words that made Berenice want to jump in with word suggestions.

'Get me the hell out a here,' he said.

'Get me a horse,' he said.

'Get me seventy year back aways,' said Mr Forkenbrock.

'I can't do that, but I can get you a nice cup of tea. And it'll be Social Hour in ten minutes,' she said.

She couldn't quite meet his stare. He was something to look at, despite an ordinary face with infolded lips, a scrawny neck. It was the eyes. They were very large and wide open and of the palest, palest blue, the colour of ice chipped with a pick, faint blue with crystalline rays. In photographs they appeared white like the eyes of Roman statues, saved from that blind stare only by the black dot of pupil. When he looked at you, thought Berenice, you could not understand a word he said for being fixed by those strange white eyes. She did not like him but pretended she did. Women had to pretend to like men and to admire the things they liked. Her own sister had married a man who was interested in rocks and now she had to drag around deserts and steep mountains with him.

At Social Hour the residents could have drinks and crackers smeared with cheese paste from the Super Wal-Mart where Cook shopped. They were all lushes, homing in on the whisky bottle. Chauncey Mellowhorn, who had built the Mellowhorn Retirement Home and set all policy, believed that the last feeble years should be enjoyed, and promoted smoking, drinking, lascivious television programmes and plenty of cheap food. Neither teetotallers nor bible-thumpers signed up for the Mellowhorn Retirement Home.

Ray Forkenbrock said nothing. Berenice thought he looked sad and she wanted to cheer him up in some way.

'What did you used to do, Mr Forkenbrock? Were you a rancher?'

The old man glared up at her. 'No,' he said. 'I wasn't no goddamn rancher. I was a hand. I worked for them sonsabitches. Cowboyed, ran wild horses, rodeoed, worked in the oil patch, sheared sheep, drove trucks, did whatever. Ended up broke.

'Now my granddaughter's husband pays the bills that keep me here in this nest of old women,' he said. He often wished he had died out in the weather, alone and no trouble to anyone.

Berenice continued, making her voice cheery. 'I had a lot a different jobs too since I graduated high school,' she said. 'Waitress, day-care, house-cleaning, 7-Eleven store clerk, like that.' She was engaged to Chad Grills; they were to be married in the spring and she planned to keep working only for a little while to supplement Chad's pay cheque from Red Bank Power. But before the old man could say anything more Deb Slaver came pushing in, carrying a glass. Berenice could smell the dark whisky. Deb's vigorous voice pumped out of her ample chest in jets.

'Here you go, honey boy! A nice little drinkie for Ray!' she said.

'Turn around from that dark old winder and have some fun!' She said, 'Don't you want a watch *Cops* with Powder Face?' (Powder Face was Deb's nickname for a painted harridan with hazelnut knuckles and a set of tawny teeth.) 'Or is it just one a them days when you want a look out the winder and feel blue? Think of some troubles? You retired folks don't know what trouble is, just setting here having a nice glass of whisky and watching teevee,' she said.

She punched the pillows on the settee. 'We're the ones with troubles – bills, cheating husbands, sassy kids, tired feet,' she said. 'Trying to scrape up the money for winter tyres! My husband says the witch with the green teeth is plaguing us,' she said. 'Come on, I'll set with you and Powder Face a while,' and she pulled Mr Forkenbrock by his sweater, threw him on to the settee and sat beside him.

Berenice left the room and went to help in the kitchen where Cook was smacking out turkey patties. A radio on the windowsill murmured.

'Looks like it is clearing up,' Berenice said. She was a little afraid of Cook.

'Oh good, you're here. Get them French fry packages out of the freezer,' she said. 'Thought I was going to have to do everthing myself. Deb was supposed to help but she'd rather tangle up with them old boys. She hopes they'll put her in their will. Some of them's got a little property or a mineral rights cheque coming in,' she said. 'You ever meet her husband, Duck Slaver?' Now she was grating a cabbage into a stainless-steel bowl.

Berenice knew only that Duck Slaver drove a tow truck for Ricochet Towing. The radio suddenly caught Cook's attention and she turned up the volume, hearing that it would be cloudy the next day with gradual clearing, the following day high winds and snow showers.

'We ought to be grateful for the rain in this drought. Know what Bench says?' Bench was the UPS driver, the source of Cook's information on everything from road conditions to family squabbles.

'No.'

'Says we are in the beginning of turning into a desert. It's all going to blow away,' she said.

When Berenice went to announce dinner – turkey patties, French fries (Mr Mellowhorn still called them 'freedom fries') with turkey patty gravy, cranberry relish, creamed corn and home-made rolls – she saw that Deb had worked Mr Forkenbrock into the corner of the settee, and Powder Face was in the chair with the bad leg watching cops squash the faces of black men on to sidewalks. Mr Forkenbrock was staring at the dark window, the coursing raindrops catching the blue television flicker. He gave off an aura of separateness. Deb and Powder Face might have been two more of Mr Mellowhorn's stuffed dogs.

After dinner, on her way back to the kitchen to help Cook clean up, Berenice opened the door for a breath of fresh air. The eastern half of the sky was starry, the west a slab of basalt.

In the early-morning darkness the rain began again. He did not know but would have understood the poet's line 'I wake and feel the fell of dark, not day'. Nothing in nature seemed more malign to Ray Forkenbrock than this invisible crawl of weather, the blunt-nosed cloud advancing under the lid of darkness. As the dim morning emerged, like a photograph in developing solution, the sound of the rain sharpened. That's sleet, he thought, remembering a long October ride in such weather when he was young, his denim jacket soaked through and sparkling with ice, remembered meeting up with that old horse-catcher who lived out in the desert, must have been in his eighties, out there in the rattling precip limping along, heading for the nearest ranch bunkhouse, he said, to get out of the weather.

'That'd be Flying A,' said Ray, squinting against the slanting ice.

'Ain't that Hawkins's place?'

'Naw. Hawkins sold out couple years ago. A fella named Fox owns it now,' he said.

'Hell, I lose touch out here. Had a pretty good shack up until day before yesterday,' the horse-catcher said between clicking teeth and went on to tell that his place had burned down and he'd slept out in the sage for two nights but now his bedroll was soaked and he was out of food. Ray felt bad for him and at the same time wanted to get away. It seemed awkward to be mounted while the man was afoot, but then he always had that same uncomfortable, guilty itch when he rode past a pedestrian. Was it his fault the old man didn't have a horse? If he was any good at horse-catching he should have had a hundred of them. He foraged through his pockets and found three or four stale peanuts mixed with lint.

'It ain't much but it's all I got,' he said, holding them out.

The old boy had never made it to the Flying A. He was discovered days later sitting with his back against a rock. Ray remembered the uncomfortable feeling he'd had exchanging a few words with him, thinking how old he was. Now he was the same age, and he had reached the Flying A – the warmth and dry shelter of the Mellowhorn Retirement Home. But the old horse-catcher's death, braced against a rock, seemed more honourable.

It was six-thirty and there was nothing to get up for, but Ray put on his jeans and shirt, added an old man's sweater as the dining room could be chilly in the morning before the heat got going, left his boots in the closet and shuffled down the hall in red felt slippers, too soft to deliver a kick to stuffed Bugs with the googly eyes at the foot of the stairs. The slippers were a gift from his only granddaughter, Beth. Beth was important to him. He had made up his mind to tell her the ugly family secret. He would not leave his descendants to grapple with shameful uncertainties. He was going to clear the air. Beth was coming on Saturday afternoon with her tape recorder to help him get it said. During the week she would type it into her computer and bring him the crisp printed pages. He might have been nothing more than a ranch hand in his life but he knew a few things.

Beth was dark-haired with very red cheeks that looked freshly slapped. It was the Irish in her he supposed. She bit her fingernails, an unsightly habit in a grown woman. Her husband, Kevin Bead, worked in the loan department of the High Plains Bank. He complained that his job was stupid, tossing money and credit cards to people who could never pay up.

'Used to be to get a card you had to work hard and have good credit. Now the worse your credit the easier it is to get a dozen of them,' he said to his wife's grandfather. Ray, who had never had a credit card, couldn't follow the barrage of expository information that followed about changing bank rules, debt. These information sessions always ended with Kevin sighing and saying in a dark tone that the day was coming.

Ray Forkenbrock guessed Beth would use the computer at the real estate office where she worked to transcribe his words.

'Oh no, Grandpa, we've got a computer and printer at home. Rosalyn wouldn't like for me to do it in the office,' she said. Rosalyn was her boss, a woman Ray had never seen but felt he knew well because Beth talked often about her. She was very, very fat and had financial trouble. Scam artists several times stole her identity. Every few months she spent hours filling out fraud affidavits. And, said Beth, she wore XXXL blue jeans and a belt with a silver buckle as big as a pie tin that she had won at a bingo game.

Ray snorted. 'A buckle used to mean something. A rodeo buckle, best part of the prize. The money was nothing in them days. We didn't care about the money. We cared about the buckle,' he said, 'and now fat gals win them at bingo games?' He twisted his head around and looked at the closet door. Beth knew he must have a belt with a rodeo buckle in there.

'Do you watch the National Finals on television?' she said. 'Or the bullriding championship?'

'Hell, no,' he said. 'The old hens here wouldn't put up with it. They got that teevee lined out from dawn to midnight – crime, that reality shit, fashion and python shows, dog and cat programmes. Watch rodeo? Not a chance,' he said.

He glared at the empty hall beyond the open door. 'You wouldn't never guess the most of them lived on ranches all their life,' he added sourly.

Beth spoke to Mr Mellowhorn and said she thought her grandfather could at least watch the National Finals or the PBR rodeos considering what they were paying for his keep. Mr Mellowhorn agreed.

'But I like to keep out of residents' television choices, you know. Democracy rules at the Mellowhorn Retirement Home and if your grandfather wants to watch rodeo all he has to do is persuade a majority of the inhabitants to sign a petition and—'

'Do you have any objection if my husband and I get him a television set for his room?'

'Well, no, of course not, but I should just mention that the less fortunate residents might see him as privileged, even a little high-hat if he holes up in his room and watches rodeo instead of joining the community choice—'

'Fine,' said Beth, cutting past the social tyranny of the Mellowhorn Retirement Home. 'That's what we'll do, then. Get him a snooty, high-hat television. Family counts with me and Kevin,' she said. 'I don't suppose you have a satellite hook-up, do you?' she asked.

'Well, no. We've discussed it, but – maybe next year—'

She had brought Ray a small television set with a DVD player and three or four discs of recent years' rodeo events. That got him going.

'Christ, I remember when the finals was in Oklahoma City, not goddamn Las Vegas,' he said. 'Of course bullriding has pushed out all the other events now, goodbye saddle bronc and bareback. I was there when Freckles Brown rode Tornado in 1962. Forty-six year old, and the ones they got now bullriding are children! Make a million dollars. It's all show business now,' he said. 'The old boys was a rough crew. Heavy drinkers, most of them. You want to know what pain is, try bullriding with a bad hangover.'

'So I guess you did a lot of rodeo riding when you were young?'

'No, not a lot, but enough to get broke up some. And earned a buckle,' he said. 'You heal fast when you're young but the broke places sort of come back to life when you are old. I busted my left leg in three places. Hurts now when it rains,' he said.

'How come you cowboyed for a living, Grandpa Ray? Your daddy wasn't a rancher or a cowboy, was he?' She turned the volume knob down. The riders came out of a chute, again and again, monotonously, all apparently wearing the same dirty hat.

'Hell no, he wasn't. He was a coal miner. Rove Forkenbrock,' he said. 'My mother's name was Alice Grand Forkenbrock. Dad worked in the Union Pacific coal mines. Something happened to him and he quit. Moved into running errands for different outfits, Texaco, California Petroleum, big outfits.

'Anyway, don't exactly know what the old man did. Drove a dusty old Model T. He'd get fired and then he had to scratch around for another job. Even though he drank – that's what got him fired usually – he always seemed to get another job pretty quick.' He swallowed a little whisky.

'Anymore I wouldn't go near the mines. I liked horses almost as much as I liked arithmetic, liked the cow business, so after I graduated eighth grade and Dad said better forget high school, things were tough and I had to find work,' he said. 'At the time I didn't mind. What my dad said I generally didn't fuss over. I respected him. I respected and honoured my father. I believed him to be a good and fair man.' He thought, unaccountably, of weeds.

'I tried for a job and got took on at Bledsoe's Double B,' he said. 'The bunkhouse life. The Bledsoes more or less raised me to voting age. At that point I sure didn't want nothing to do with my family,' he said, and fell into an old man's reverie. Weeds, weeds and wildness.

Beth was quiet for a few minutes, then chatted about her boys. Syl had acted the part of an eagle in a school play and what a job, making the costume! Just before she left she said off-handedly, 'You know, I want my boys to know about their great-granddad. What do you think if I bring my recorder and get it on tape and then type it up? It would be like a book of your life – something for the future generations of the family to read and know about.'

He laughed in derision.

'Some of it ain't so nice to know. Every family got its dirty laundry and we got ours.' But after a week of thinking about it, of wondering why he'd kept it bottled up for so long, he told Beth to bring on her machine.

They sat in his little room with the door closed. ' "Antisocial," they'll say. Everybody else sits with the door open hollering at each other's folks as if they was all related somehow. A regional family, they call it here. I like my privacy.'

She put a glass of whisky, another of water and the tape recorder, smaller than a pack of cigarettes, on the table near his elbow and said, 'It's on, Grandpa. Tell me how it was growing up in the old days. Just talk any time you are ready.'

He cleared his throat and began slowly, watching the spiky volume metre jump. 'I'm eighty-four years old and most of them involved in the early days has gone on before, so it don't make much difference what I tell.' He took a nervous swallow of the whisky and nodded.

'I was fourteen years old in nineteen and thirty-three and there wasn't a nickel in the world.' The silence of that time before traffic and leaf blowers and the boisterous shouting of television was embedded in his character, and he spoke little, finding it hard to drag out the story. The noiselessness of his youth except for the natural sound of wind, hoof beats, the snap of the old house logs splitting in winter cold, wild herons crying their way downriver. How silent men and women had been in those times, trusting to observational powers. There had been days when a few little moustache clouds moved, and he could imagine them making no more sound than dragging a feather across a wire. The wind got them and the sky was alone.

'When I was a kid we lived hard, let me tell you. Coalie Town, about eight miles from Superior. It's all gone now,' he said. 'Three-room shack, no insulation, kids always sick. My baby sister Goldie died of meningitis in that shack,' he said.

Now he was warming up to his sorry tale. 'No water. A truck used to come every week and fill up a couple barrels we had. Mama paid a quarter a barrel. No indoor plumbing. People make jokes about it now but it was miserable to go out there to that outhouse on a bitter morning with the wind screaming up the hole. Christ,' he said. He was silent for so long Beth backed up the tape and pressed the pause button on the recorder. He lit a cigarette, sighed, abruptly started talking again. Beth lost a sentence or two before she got the recorder restarted.

'People thought they was doing all right if they was alive. You can learn to eat dust instead of bread, my mother said many a time. She had a lot a old sayings. Is that thing on?' he said.

'Yes, Grandpa,' she said. 'It is on. Just talk.'

'Bacon,' he said. 'She'd say if bacon curls in the pan the hog was butchered wrong side of the moon. We didn't see bacon very often and it could of done corkscrews in the pan, would have been okay with us long as we could eat it,' he said.

'There was a whole bunch a shacks out there near the mines. They called it "Coalie Town". Lot of foreigners.

'As I come up,' he said, 'I got a pretty good education in fighting, screwing – pardon my French – and more fighting. Every problem was solved with a fight. I remember all them people. Pattersons, Bob Hokker, the Grainblewer twins, Alex Sugar, Forrie Wintka, Harry and Joe Dolan – we had a lot of fun. Kids always have fun,' he said.

'They sure do,' said Beth.

'Kids don't get all sour thinking about the indoor toilets they don't have, or moaning because there ain't no fresh butter. For us everthing was fine the way it was. I had a happy childhood. When we got bigger there was certain girls. Forrie Wintka. Really good-looking, long black hair and black eyes,' he said, looking to see if he had shocked her.

'She finally married old man Dolan after his wife died. The Dolan boys was something else. They hated each other, fought, really had bad fights, slugged each other with boards with nails in the end, heaved rocks.'

Beth tried to shift him to a description of his own family, but he went on about the Dolans.

'I'm pretty set in my ways,' he said. She nodded.

'One time Joe knocked Harry out, kicked him into the Platte. He could of drowned, probably would of but Dave Arthur was riding along the river, seen this bundle of rags snarled up in a cottonwood sweeper – it had fell in the river and caught up all sorts of river trash. He thought maybe some clothes. Went to see and pulled Harry out,' he said.

'Harry was about three-quarters dead, never was right after that, neither. But right enough to know that his own brother had meant to kill him. Joe couldn't never tell if Harry was going to be around the next corner with a chunk of wood or a gun.' There was a long pause after the word 'gun'.

'Nervous wreck,' he said. He watched the tape revolve for long seconds.

'Dutchy Green was my best friend in grade school. He was killed when he was twenty-five, twenty-six, shooting at some of them old Indian rock carvings. The ricochet got him through the right temple,' he said.

He took a swallow of whisky. 'Yep, our family. There was my mother. She was tempery, too much to do and no money to do it. Me, the oldest. There was a big brother, Sonny, but he drowned in an irrigation ditch before I come along,' he said.

'Weren't there girls in the family?' asked Beth. Not content with two sons, she craved a daughter.

'My sisters, Irene and Daisy. Irene lives in Greybull and Daisy is still alive out in California. And I mentioned, the baby Goldie died when I was around six or seven. The youngest survivor was Roger. Mama's last baby. He went the wrong way. Did time for robbing,' he said. 'No idea what happened to him.' Under the weeds, damned and dark.

Abruptly he veered away from the burglar brother. 'You got to understand that I loved my dad. We all did. Him and Mother was always kissing and hugging and laughing when he was home. He was a wonderful man with kids, always a big smile and a hug, remembered all your interests, lots of times brought home special little presents. I still got every one he give me.' His voice trembled like that of the old horse-catcher in the antique sleet.

'Remembering this stuff makes me tired. I guess I better stop,' he said. 'Anymore two new people come in today and the new ones always makes me damn tired.'

'Women or men?' asked Beth, relieved to turn the recorder off as she could see her only tape was on short time. She remembered now she had recorded the junior choir practice.

'Don't know,' he said. 'Find out at supper.'

'I'll come next week. I think what you are saying is important for this family.' She kissed his dry old-man's forehead, brown age spots.

'Just wait,' he said.

After she left he started talking again as if the tape was still running. 'He died age forty-seven. I thought that was real old. Why didn't he jump?' he said.

Berenice Pann, bearing a still-warm chocolate cupcake, paused outside his door when she heard his voice. She had seen Beth leave a few minutes earlier. Maybe she had forgotten something and come back. Berenice heard something like a strangled sob from Mr Forkenbrock. 'God, it was lousy,' he said. 'So we could work. Hell, I liked school. No chance when you start work at thirteen,' he said. 'Wasn't for the Bledsoes I'd of ended up a bum,' he said. 'Or worse.'

Berenice Pann's boyfriend, Chad Grills, was the great-grandson of the old Bledsoes. They were still on the ranch where Ray Forkenbrock had worked in his early days, both of them close to the century mark. Berenice became an avid eavesdropper, feeling that in a way she was related to Mr Forkenbrock through the Bledsoes. She owed it to herself and Chad to hear as much as she could about the Bledsoes, good or bad. Inside the room there was silence, then the door flung open.

'Uh!' cried Berenice, the cupcake sliding on its saucer. 'I was just bringing you this—'

'That so?' said Mr Forkenbrock. He took the cupcake from the saucer and instead of taking a sample bite crammed the whole thing into his mouth, paper cup and all. The paper massed behind his dentures.

At the Social Hour Mr Mellowhorn arrived to introduce the new 'guests'. Church Bollinger was a younger man, barely sixty-five, but Ray could tell he was a real slacker. He'd obviously come into the home because he couldn't get up the gumption to make his own bed or wash his dishes. The other one, Mrs Terry Taylor, was around his age, early eighties despite the dyed red hair and carmine fingernails. She seemed soft and sagging, somehow like a candle standing in the sun. She kept looking at Ray. Her eyes were khaki-coloured, the lashes sparse and short, her thin old lips greased up with enough lipstick to leave red on her buttered roll. Finally he could take her staring no longer.

'Got a question?' he said.

'Are you Ray Forkenknife?' she said.

'Forkenbrock,' he said, startled.

'Oh, right. Forkenbrock. You don't remember me? Theresa Worley? From Coalie Town? Me and you went to school together except you was a couple grades ahead.'

But he did not remember her.

The next morning, fork poised over the poached egg reclining like a houri on a bed of soggy toast, he glanced up to meet her intense gaze. Her red-slick lips parted to show ochre teeth that were certainly her own, for no dentist would make dentures that looked as though they had been dredged from a sewage pit.

'Don't you remember Mrs Wilson?' she said. 'The teacher that got froze in a blizzard looking for her cat? The Skeltcher kids that got killed when they fell in a old mineshaft?'

He did remember something about a schoolteacher frozen in a June blizzard but thought it had happened somewhere else, down around Cold Mountain. As for the Skeltcher kids, he denied them and shook his head.

On Saturday Beth came again, and again set out the glass of water, the glass of whisky and the tape recorder. He had been thinking what he wanted to say. It was clear enough in his head, but putting it into words was difficult. The whole thing had been so subtle and painful it was impossible to present it without sounding like a fool. And Mrs Terry Taylor, aka Theresa Worley, had sidelined him. He strove to remember the frozen teacher, the Skeltcher kids in the mineshaft, how Mr Baker had shot Mr Dennison over a bushel of potatoes and a dozen other tragedies she had laid out as mnemonic bait. He remembered very different events. He remembered walking to the top of Irish Hill with Dutchy Green to meet Forrie Wintka who was going to show them her private parts in exchange for a nickel each. It was late autumn, the cottonwoods leafless along the grim trickle of Coal Creek, warm weather holding. They could see Forrie Wintka toiling up from the shacks below. Dutchy said it would be easy, not only would she show them, they could do it to her, even her brother did it to her.

Dutchy whispered as though she could hear them. 'Even her stepfather. He got killed by a mountain line last year.'

And now, seventy-one years later, it hit him. Forrie's father had been Worley, Wintka was the stepfather who had carried the mail horseback and in Snakeroot Canyon had been dragged into the rocks by a lion. The first female he had ever ploughed, a coal-town slut, was sharing final days with him at the Mellowhorn Retirement Home.

'Beth,' he said to his granddaughter, 'I can't talk about nothing today. There's some stuff come to mind just now that I got to think my way through. The new woman who come here last week. I knew her and it wasn't under the best circumstances,' he said. That was the trouble with Wyoming; everything you ever did or said kept pace with you right to the end. The regional family again.

Mr Mellowhorn started a series of overnight outings he dubbed 'Weekend Adventures'. The first one had been to the Medicine Wheel up in the Big Horns. Mrs Wallace Kimes had fallen and scraped her knees on the crushed stone in the parking lot. Then came the dude ranch weekend where the Mellowhorn group found itself sharing the premises with seven elk hunters from Colorado, most of them drunk and disorderly and given over to senseless laughter topping 110 decibels. Powder Face laughed senselessly with them. The third trip was more ambitious; a five-day excursion to the Grand Canyon where no one at the Mellowhorn Retirement Home had ever been. Twelve people signed up despite the hefty fee to pay for lodging and transportation.

'You only live once!' cried Powder Face.

The group included newcomers Church Bollinger and Forrie Wintka, aka Theresa Worley, aka Terry Dolan and, finally, Terry Taylor. Forrie and Bollinger sat together in the van, had drinks together in the bar of El Tovar, ate dinner at a table for two and planned a trail-ride expedition for the next morning. But before the mule train left, Forrie asked Bollinger to take some photographs she could send to her granddaughters. She stood on the parapet with the famous view behind her. She posed with one hand holding her floppy new straw hat purchased in the hotel gift shop. She took off the hat and turned, shading her eyes with her hand, and pretended to be peering into the depths like a stage character of yore. She clowned, pretending she was unsteady and losing her balance. There was a stifled 'Oh!' and she disappeared. A park ranger rushed to the parapet and saw her on the slope ten feet below, clutching at a small plant. Her hat lay to one side. Even as he climbed over the parapet and reached for her the plant trembled and loosened. Forrie dug her fingers into the gravel as she began to slide towards the edge. The ranger thrust his foot towards her, shouting for her to grab on. But his saving kick connected with Forrie's hand. She shot down the slope as one on a water slide, leaving ten deep grooves to mark her trail, then, in a last desperate effort, reached for and almost seized her new straw hat.

The subdued group returned to Wyoming the next day. Again and again they told each other that she had not even cried out as she fell, something they believed denoted strong character.

Ray Forkenbrock resumed his memoir the next weekend. Berenice waited a few minutes after Beth arrived before taking up a listening post outside the room. Mr Forkenbrock had a monotonous but loud voice and she could hear every word.

'So, things was better for the family after he got the jobs driving machine parts around to the oil rigs,' he said. 'The money was pretty good and he joined one of them fraternal organizations, the Pathfinders. And they had a ladies' auxiliary which my mother got into; they called it "The Ladies", like it was a restroom or something. They both got real caught up in Pathfinders, the ceremonies, the lodge, the good deeds and oaths of allegiance to whatever.

'Mother was always baking something for them,' he said. 'And there was kid stuff for us, fishing derbies and picnics and sack races. It was like Boy Scouts, or so they said. Boy Scouts with a ranch twist, because there was always some class in hackamore braiding or raising a calf. Sort of a kind of a mix of Scouts and 4-H which we did not belong to.'

Berenice found this all rather boring. When would he say something about the Bledsoes? She saw Deb Slaver at the far end of the hall coming out of Mr Harrell's room with a tray of bandages. Mr Harrell had a sore on his shin that wouldn't heal and the dressing had to be changed twice a day.

'Now don't you pick at it, you bad boy!' yelled Deb, disappearing around the corner.

'Anyway, Mother was probably more into it than Dad. She liked company and hadn't had much luck with neighbours there in Coalie Town. The Ladies got up a program of history tours to various massacre sites and old logging flumes. Mother loved those trips. She had a little taste for what had happened in the long ago. She'd come home all excited and carrying a pretty rock. She had about a dozen rocks from those trips when she died,' he said.

In the hall Berenice thought of her sister toiling up rocky slopes, trying to please her rock-hound husband, carrying his canvas sack of stones.

'The first hint I got that there was something peculiar in our family tree was when she come home from a visit to Farson. I do not know what they were doing there, and she said that the Farson Auxiliary had served them lunch – potato salad and hot dogs,' he said.

'One of the Farson ladies said she knew a Forkenbrock down in Dixon. She thought he had a ranch in the Snake River valley. Well, my ears perked up when I heard "ranch",' he said.

'And Forkenbrock ain't that common of a name. So I asked Mother if they were Dad's relatives,' he said. 'I would of liked it if we had ranch kin. I was already thinking about getting into cowboy ways. She said no, that Dad was an orphan, that it was just a coincidence. So she said.'

At dinner that night, once Forrie Wintka's dramatic demise had been hashed through again, Church Bollinger began to describe his travels through the Canadian Rockies.

'What we'd do is fly, then rent a car instead of driving. Those interstates will kill you. The wife enjoyed staying at nice hotels. So we flew to San Francisco and decided to drive down the coast. We stopped in Hollywood. Figured we'd see what Hollywood was all about. They had these big concrete columns. Time came to leave, I got in and backed up and crunch, couldn't get out. I finally got out but I had a bad scratched door on the rental car. Well, I bought some paint and I painted it and you could never tell. I drove to San Diego. Waited for a letter from the rental outfit but it never came. Another time I rented a car there was a crack in the windshield. I says, "Is this a safety problem?" The guy looks at me and says, "No." I drive off and it never was a problem. We did the same thing when we went to Europe. In Spain we went to the bullfights. We left after two. I wanted to experience that.'

'But are they wounded?' asked Powder Face.

Mr Bollinger, thinking of rental cars, did not reply.

When Berenice told Chad Grills about old Mr Forkenbrock who used to work for his grandparents, he was interested and said he would talk to them about it next time he went out to the ranch. He said he hoped Berenice liked ranch life because he was in line to inherit the place. He told Berenice to find out all she could about Forkenbrock's working days. Some of those cagey old boys managed to get themselves situated to put a claim on a ranch through trumped-up charges of unpaid back wages. Whenever Beth came with her tape recorder Berenice found something to do in the hall outside Ray Forkenbrock's room, listening, expecting him to tell about the nice ranch he secretly owned. She didn't know what Chad would do.

Ray said, 'I think when she heard about the Dixon Forkenbrocks Mother had a little feeling that something wasn't right because she wrote back to the Farson lady thanking her for the nice lunch. I think she wanted to strike up a friendship so she could find out more about the Dixon people, but, far as I know, that didn't happen. It stuck in my mind that we wasn't the only Forkenbrock family.' Beth was glad he didn't pause so often now that he was into the story, letting his life unreel.

'The last day of school was a trip and a big picnic. The whole outfit usually went on the picnic, since learning academies of the day was small and scattered. When I was twelve the seventh grade had only three kids – me, one of my sisters who skipped a grade and Dutchy Green. We was excited when we found out the trip was to the old Butch Cassidy outlaw cabin down near the Colorado border. Mrs Ratus, the teacher, got the map of Wyoming hung up and showed us where it was. I seen the word "Dixon" down near the bottom of the map. Dixon! That's where the mystery Forkenbrocks lived. Dutchy was my best friend and I told him all about it and we tried to figure a way to get the bus to stop in Dixon. Maybe there'd be a sign for the Forkenbrock ranch.

'As it turned out,' he said, 'we stopped in Dixon anyways because there was something wrong with the bus. There was a pretty good service station in Dixon that had been an old blacksmith shop. The forge was still there and the big bellows which us boys took turns working, pretending we had a horse in the stall. I asked the mechanic who was fixing the bus if he knew of any Forkenbrocks in town and he said he heard of them but didn't know them. He said he had just moved down from Essex. Dutchy and me played blacksmith some more but we never got to Butch Cassidy's cabin because they couldn't fix the bus and another one had to come take us back. We ate the picnic on the bus on the way home. After that I kind of forgot about the Dixon Forkenbrocks,' he said. He was beginning to slow down again.

'I didn't think about it until Dad died in an automobile accident on old route 30,' he said.

'He was taking a short cut, driving on the railroad ties, and a train come along,' he said.

'I'd been working for the Bledsoes for a year and hadn't been home.'

At the mention of the Bledsoes, Berenice, out in the hallway, snapped her head up.

'Mr Bledsoe drove me back so I could attend the funeral. They had it in Rawlins and the Pathfinders had took care of everything,' he said.

Beth looked puzzled. 'Pathfinders?'

'That organization they belonged to. Pathfinders. All we had to do with it was show up. Which we done. Preacher, casket, flowers, Pathfinder's flags and mottoes, grave plot, headstone – all fixed up by the Pathfinders.' He coughed and took a sip of whisky, thinking of cemetery weeds and beyond the headstones to the yellow wild pastures.

Berenice couldn't listen any more because the chime for Cook's Treats rang. It was part of her job to bring the sweets to the residents, the high point in their day trumped only by the alcoholic Social Hour. Cook was sliding triangles of hot apple pie on to plates.

'You hear about Deb's husband? Had a heart attack while he was hitching the tow bar to some tourist. He's in the hospital. It's pretty serious, touch and go. So we won't be seeing Deb for a little while. Maybe ever. I bet she's got a million insurance on him. If he dies and Deb gets a pile a money I'm going to take out a policy on my old man.'

When Berenice carried out the tray of pie Mr Forkenbrock's door stood open and Beth was gone.

Sundays Berenice and Chad Grills drove out on the back roads in Chad's almost-new truck. Going for a ride was their kind of date. The dust was bad, churned up by the fast-moving energy company trucks. Chad got lost because of all the new, unmarked roads the companies had put in. Time after time they turned on to a good road only to end up at a dead-end compression station or well pad. Getting lost where you had been born, brought up and never left was embarrassing and Chad cursed the gas outfits. Finally he took a sight line on Doty Peak and steered towards it, picking the bad roads as the true way. Always his mind seized on a mountain. In a flinty section they had a flat tyre. They came out at last near the ghost town of Dad. Chad said it hadn't been a good ride and she had to agree, though it hadn't been the worst.

Deb Slaver did not come in all the next week and the extra work fell on Berenice. She hated changing Mr Harrell's bandage and skipped the chore several times. She was glad when on Wednesday, Doc Nelson's visit day, he said Mr Harrell had to go into the hospital. On Saturday, Beth's day to visit Mr Forkenbrock, Berenice got through her chores in a hurry so she could lean on a dust mop outside the door and listen. Impossible to know what he'd say next with all the side stories about his mother's garden, long-ago horses, old friends. He hardly ever mentioned the Bledsoes who had been so good to him.

'Grandpa,' said Beth, 'you look tired. Not sleeping enough? What time do you go to bed?' She handed him the printout of his discourse.

'My age you don't need sleep so much as a rest. Permanent rest. I feel fine,' he said. 'This looks pretty good – reads easy as a book.' He was pleased. 'Where did we leave off?' he said, turning the pages.

'Your dad's funeral,' said Beth.

'Oh boy,' he said. 'That was the day I think Mother begin to put two and two together. I sort of got it, at least I got it that something ugly had happened, but I didn't really understand until years later. I loved my dad so I didn't want to understand. I still got a little Buck knife he give me and I wouldn't part with it for anything in this world,' he said.

There was a pause while he got up to look for the knife, found it, showed it to Beth and carefully put it away in his top drawer.

'So there we all were, filing out of the church on our way to the cars that take us to the graveyard, me holding Mother's arm, when some lady calls out, "Mrs Forkenbrock! Oh Mrs Forkenbrock!" Mother turns around and we see this big fat lady in black with a wilted lilac pinned on her coat heading for us,' he said.

'But she sails right past, goes over to a thin, homely woman with a boy around my age and offers her condolences. And then she says, looking at the kid, "Oh Ray, you'll have to be the man of the house now and help your mother every way you can." ' He paused to pour into the whisky glass.

'I want you to think about that, Beth,' he said. 'You are so strong on family ties. I want you to imagine that you are at your father's funeral with your mother and sisters and somebody calls your mother, then walks right over to another person. And that other person has a kid with her and that kid has your name. I was – all I could think was that they had to be the Dixon Forkenbrocks and that they was related to us after all. Mother didn't say a word, but I could feel her arm jerk,' he said. He illustrated this by jerking his own elbow.

'At the cemetery I went over to the kid with my name and asked him if they lived in Dixon and if they had a ranch and was they related to my father who we was burying. He gives me a look and says they don't have a ranch, they don't live in Dixon but in LaBarge, and that it is his father we are burying. I was so mixed up at this point that I just said, "You're crazy!" and went back to Mother's side. She never mentioned the incident and finally we went home and got along like usual although with damn little money. Mother got work cooking at the Sump ranch. It was only when she died in 1975 that I put the pieces together,' he said. 'All the pieces.'

On Sunday Berenice and Chad went for their weekly ride. Berenice brought her new digital camera. For some reason Chad insisted on going back to the tangle of energy roads and it was almost the same as before – a spider web of wrong-turn gravel roads without signs. Far ahead of them they could see trucks at the side of the road. There was a deep ditch with black pipe in it big enough for a dog to stroll through. They came around a corner and men were feeding a section of pipe into a massive machine that welded the sections together. Berenice thought the machine was interesting and put her camera up. Behind the machine a truck idled, a grubby kid in dark glasses behind the wheel. Thirty feet away another man was filling in the ditch with a backhoe. Chad put his window down, grinned and, in an easy voice, asked the kid how the machine worked.

The kid looked at Berenice's camera. 'What the fuck do you care?' he said. 'What are you doin out here anyway?'

'County road,' said Chad, flaring up, 'and I live in this county. I was born here. I got more rights to be on this road than you do.'

The kid gave a nasty laugh. 'Hey, I don't care if you was born on top of a flagpole, you got *no* rights interferin with this work and takin pictures.'

'Interfering?' But before he could say any more the man inside the pipe machine got out and the two who had been handling the pipe walked over. The backhoe driver jumped down. They all looked salty and in good shape. 'Hell,' said Chad, 'we're just out for a Sunday ride. Didn't expect to see anybody working on Sunday. Thought it was just us ranch types got to do that. Have a good day,' and he trod on the accelerator, peeling out in a burst of dust. Gravel pinged the undercarriage.

Berenice started to say, 'What was *that* all about?' but Chad snapped, 'Shut up,' and drove too fast until they got to the blacktop and then he floored it, looking in the rear-view all the way. They didn't speak until they were back at Berenice's. Chad got out and walked around the truck, looking it over.

'Chad, how come you let them throw off on you like that?'

'Berenice,' he said carefully, 'I guess that you didn't see one a them guys had a .44 on him and he was taking it out of the holster. It is not a good idea to have a fight on the edge of a ditch with five roustabouts in a remote area. Loser goes in the ditch and the backhoe guy puts in five more minutes of work. Take a look at this,' he said and he pulled her around to the back of the truck. There was a hole in the tailgate.

'That's Buddy's .44 done that,' he said. 'Good thing the road was rough. I could be dead and you could still be out there entertaining them.' Berenice shuddered. 'Probably,' said Chad, 'they thought we were some kind of environmentalists. That camera of yours. Leave it home next time.'

Right then Berenice began to cool towards Chad. He seemed less manly. And she would take her camera wherever she wanted.

On Monday Berenice was in the kitchen looking for the ice-cream freezer which hadn't been used for two years. Mr Mellowhorn had just come back from Jackson with a recipe for apple pie ice cream and he was anxious for everyone to share his delight. As she fumbled in the dark cupboard Deb Slaver banged in, bumping the cupboard door.

'Ow!' said Berenice.

'Serves you right,' snarled Deb, sweeping out again. There was a sound in the hall as of someone kicking a stuffed dog.

'She's pretty mad,' said Cook. 'Duck didn't die so she don't get the million-dollar insurance, but even worse, he's going to need dedicated care for the rest of his life – hand and foot waiting on, nice smooth pillows. She's got to take care of him forever. I don't know if she'll keep working and try to get an aide to come in or what. Or maybe Mr Mellowhorn will let him stay here. Then we'll *all* get to wait on him hand and foot.'

Saturday came and out of habit, because she had broken up with Chad and no longer really cared about the Bledsoes or their ranch, Berenice hung around in the hall outside Mr Forkenbrock's room. Beth had brought him a dish of chocolate pudding. He said it was good but not as good as whisky and she poured out his usual glass.

'So,' said Beth. 'At the funeral you met the other Forkenbrocks but they didn't live in Dixon any more?'

'No. No, no,' he said. 'You ain't heard a thing. The ones at the funeral were *not* the Dixon Forkenbrocks. They was the LaBarge Forkenbrocks. There was another set in Dixon. When Mother died me and my sisters had a go through her stuff and sort it all out,' he said.

'I'm sorry,' said Beth. 'I guess I misunderstood.'

'She had collected all Dad's obituaries she could find. She never said a word to us. Kept them in a big envelope marked "Our Family". I never knew if she meant that sarcastic or not. The usual stuff about how he was born in Nebraska, worked for Union Pacific, then for Ohio Oil and this company and that, how he was a loyal Pathfinder. One said he was survived by Lottie Forkenbrock and six children in Chadron, Nebraska. The boy was named Ray. Another said his grieving family lived in Dixon, Wyoming, and included his wife Sarah-Louise and two sons, Ray and Roger. Then there was one from the *Casper Star* said he was a well-known Pathfinder survived by wife Alice, sons Ray and Roger, daughters Irene and Daisy. That was us. The last one said his wife was Nancy up in LaBarge and the kids were Daisy, Ray and Irene. That was four sets. What he done, see, was give all the kids the same names so he wouldn't get mixed up and say "Fred" when it was Ray.'

He was breathless, his voice high and tremulous. 'How my mother felt about this surprise he give her I never knew because she didn't say a word,' he said.

He swallowed his whisky in a gulp and coughed violently, ending with a retching sound. He mopped tears from his eyes. 'My sisters bawled their eyes out when they read those death notices and they cursed him, but when they went back home they never said anything,' he said. 'Everybody, the ones in LaBarge and Dixon and Chadron and God knows where else, kept real quiet. He got away with it. Until now. I think I'll have another whisky. All this talking kind of dries my throat,' he said, and he got the bottle himself.

'Well,' said Beth, trying to make amends for misunderstanding, 'at least we've got this extended family now. It's exciting finding out about all the cousins.'

'Beth, they are not cousins. Think about it,' he said. He had thought she was smart. She wasn't.

'Honestly, I think it's cool. We could all get together for Thanksgiving. Or Fourth of July.'

Ray Forkenbrock's shoulders sagged. Time was swinging down like a tyre on the end of a rope, slowing, letting the old cat die.

'Grandfather,' said Beth gently, 'you have to learn to love your relatives.'

He said nothing, and then, 'I loved my father. That's the only one I loved,' he said, knowing it was hopeless, that she was not smart and she didn't understand any of what he'd said, that the book he thought he was dictating would be regarded as an old man's senile rubbish. Unbidden, as a wind-shear hurls a plane down, the memory of the old betrayal broke the prison of his rage and he damned them all, pushed the tape recorder away and told Beth she had better go.

'It's ridiculous,' Beth said to Kevin. 'He got all worked up about his father who died back in the 1930s. You'd think there would have been closure by now.'

'You'd think,' said Kevin, his face seeming to twitch in the alternating dim and dazzle of the television set. ■

PHOTO ESSAY

THE ARCTIC

Photographs by Gautier Deblonde

Words by Lavinia Greenlaw

There is a place in Lapland called Arctic Circle. You can step across a painted line and receive a certificate, although the actual circle, around 66 degrees latitude north, is unfixed. It wavers over the north like a lasso and slips according to the tilt of the earth on its axis.

Midwinter

The feeling of slippage is immediate. The nights are at least twenty hours long and the world is snow. While my mind gives up trying to keep time, my body clings to any familiar sign of it. The sky pales for three or four hours, although a constant black haze remains over the pole. A small sun inches into view and rolls along the horizon, and the sky takes on a faint wash of yellow and blue. I feel as if I've caught a glimpse of an actual day happening somewhere else. As the sun tips away again, I can't keep my eyes open.

The Arctic Highway runs north from Rovaniemi along a river, only now there is no river, just fields of snow. There is no road either, and the few cars that come this way follow its compacted grey trace past signs that cannot be read because they, too, have been wiped out. This is fairy-tale snow, hanging in glittering swags from trees which double over under its weight. It emphasizes telegraph wires and heaps up cosily against windows. Snow scatters light and flattens perspective. It is absence and substance at the same time, a perfect form of equilibrium. There is nothing to read in it, just a fundamental continuity that makes every place familiar. I am near the edge of the compass. From the pole, whichever way you head is south.

What does minus fifty mean? That the ink in a pen freezes, that water thrown from a cup turns to ice before it hits the ground, that your lungs might bleed. Even now when buildings are heated and sealed and streets can be as brightly lit as a film set there is an inheritance of cold and darkness.

In a hospital in Lapland I meet a Finnish psychiatrist who is an expert in Arctic Personality Disorder. He says that darkness is less of a problem than the cold; it makes the body hoard blood around the heart, depriving the brain. He explains that the Arctic personality is characterized by *sisu* – adaptability and perseverance. Such people have a tendency to be greedy, stingy and ruthless. They hoard information, are suspicious of strangers and are 'sexually specialized'. His other interest is suicide, and he remarks that women have started to kill themselves in the same way as men. They used to take an overdose or drown themselves, 'so as not to leave a mess', but now they are as likely to use a gun.

This darkness doesn't trouble me. I came to the Arctic having lost my imagination and soon feel restored, not because there is nothing to see but because this is such a fundamental way of seeing. Even when it is cloudy, you can catch sight in the sky of wild streaks, sheets and pillars of gaseous colour. The aurora borealis or Northern Lights are a form of elemental disturbance (electron showers stirring up hydrogen and nitrogen) and the rawness of their colours, like the rawness of that small sunset, suggests a time when light was first occurring. The Finns call the Northern Lights *revontulet* or foxfire, after a mythical fox who swept snow into the air with its tail, igniting it. If you talk to the Northern Lights, they will come down and grab you. If you don't wear a hat, they will clutch at your hair.

Not being able to see did not trouble me as I am so short-sighted. My understanding of light begins with fractured auras and haloes, leaky shifting colours and granulated shapes which might or might not become clear. There is a moment, though, when this world becomes very clear indeed, a winter twilight called, in Finnish, *sininen hetki* or the 'blue moment'. It is as if blue light rises out of the snow and, because everything is covered in snow, everything turns blue, so the world is full of its own space and silence and not empty at all.

Midsummer

A night in the port of Bodø in northern Norway, where every building, from the fishery to the church, is compact, functional and low. The town looks as if it has been constructed from a kit and could be packed up and driven off in a single day.

Even softened by cloud, the light is insidious. I am waiting for something to happen, for the sky to break, but nothing will happen and all night people circle the harbour square or ride back and forth in cars and on motorbikes, just passing the time. I lie down for three hours and, once or twice, dip into sleep.

The next day the ferry sails for five hours towards a dark line that breaks down into islands. Their cliffs are so sheer that they veer away from themselves and each island sits in black shadow, giving the impression that it is hovering on the sea. Everything is unanchored. There are too many islands, too much water and too much light.

Vaerøy is one of the Lofoten Islands. Here, the sun does not rise for a month in winter; nor does it set for two months in midsummer. The beach is little more than a ledge of blanched sand; the sea is so thickened by cold and light that it might be glass. For now it is calm, but whatever washes up has been pounded and scoured: heaps of stones worn into huge, beautiful eggs shot through with quartz, a sheep's vertebrae, eye socket and jaw as smooth as paper, translucent shells of crabs, sea urchins and limpets, fraying husks of seaweed.

This is bird land. Their eggs are hidden beneath my feet among the egg-shaped stones. There are no trees so they make do with ground cover: rock, gorse and grass. Oystercatchers run past screaming, warning or distracting. Redshanks blurt from fence posts, their nests scattered among whatever grass they can find. Masses of gulls and terns explode out of the cliffs. Crows mob the oystercatchers, after their fledglings. Cormorants wheel and dive. Auks come into land to breed. They nest on high ledges and lay eggs which have evolved into a tear shape so that they won't roll.

Midsummer is the feast of John the Baptist. Tonight the trolls come out to make mischief and the witches go to meet the devil on the mountain top. By late afternoon, the sun begins to make its way from stage left. People appear along the coast building fires. They share the traditional midsummer feast of dark beer, salami and semolina, but this is no raucous affair. The light is so bright that the flames are invisible. There are no leaping shadows. People gather round long enough to make sure that their unwanted furniture and tyres have properly caught light, and then they go home, long before midnight.

I wait on the beach as the sun makes its way to the centre of the view. At midnight exactly it starts to sink down on to the sea, so smoothly that it looks like a ball about to bounce. And then it does bounce, off the horizon. It is immediately rising again. I feel thrown into reverse. For all my years in the city, in London, my nights manipulated by tungsten, neon and sodium, halogen and sixty-watt bulbs, traffic lights, street lights and security lights, my body insists that this is wrong.

It is wrong to be able to see so far and so clearly that the earth curves, wrong to have a fifty-foot shadow, wrong to be sleepless and wrong to be so happy. Light meets every thought and glance. I have no imagination here. ■

Gautier Deblonde has made five trips to the Norwegian archipelago of Svarlbard in the High Arctic since 2003. Spitsbergen, the main island in the group, lies between latitude 76.5° and 80° north. For 115 days each year, the sun does not rise above the horizon.

Barentsburg is a Russian mining town. It was established by the Norwegians in 1912 and bought by the Soviet Union in 1932. Now it is in decline, with a workforce of around 600 men and women from Russia and Ukraine.

УЗБЕК

Ny Alesund, originally a mining town, is the world's most northerly community, where around 150 scientists work on the Natural Environment Research Council's international research station.

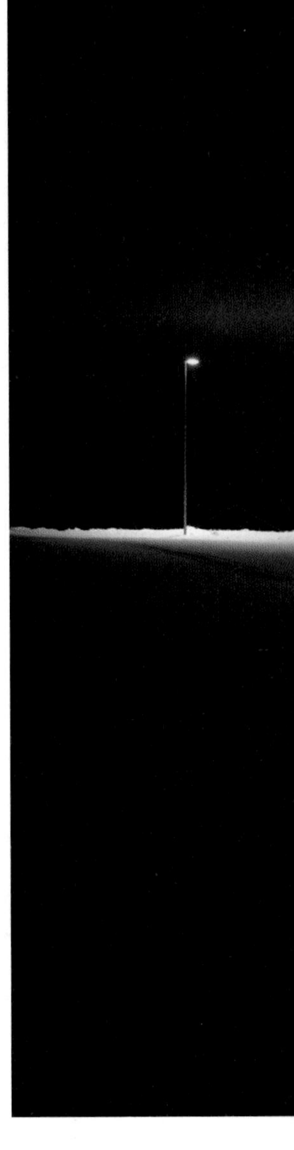

Pyramiden, founded as a mining settlement by Sweden in 1910, was sold to the USSR in 1927. It was abandoned in 1998 and is now a ghost town, though there are plans to redevelop it for tourists.

THE COURTYARD THEATRE
STRATFORD-UPON-AVON FROM 3 APRIL

THE MERCHANT OF VENICE

WILLIAM SHAKESPEARE

Angus Wright who plays Shylock by Jillian Edelstein after Guercino

RSC TICKET HOTLINE 0844 800 1110
(NO BOOKING FEE, CALLS FROM BT LANDLINE COST 5P PER MINUTE)

BOOK ONLINE www.rsc.org.uk
(NO BOOKING FEE)

ALSO THIS SEASON: THE TAMING OF THE SHREW
A MIDSUMMER NIGHT'S DREAM HAMLET LOVE'S LABOUR'S LOST

accenture

Yes, I would like to take out an annual subscription to *Granta* and receive a complimentary *Granta* special-edition **MOLESKINE**® notebook:

PERSONAL SUBSCRIPTION

Your address:

TITLE: INITIAL: SURNAME:

ADDRESS:

POSTCODE:

TELEPHONE: EMAIL:

GIFT SUBSCRIPTION

Gift address:

TITLE: INITIAL: SURNAME:

ADDRESS:

POSTCODE:

TELEPHONE: EMAIL:

Billing address:

TITLE: INITIAL: SURNAME:

ADDRESS:

POSTCODE:

TELEPHONE: EMAIL:

NUMBER OF SUBSCRIPTIONS	DELIVERY REGION	PRICE	SAVINGS	DIRECT DEBIT PRICES	SAVINGS
☐	UK	£29.95	32%	**£24.95**	**43%**
☐	Europe	£35.95	18%	**£32.95**	**29%**
☐	Rest of World	£39.95	10%	**£35.95**	**18%**

I would like my subscription to start from:

☐ the current issue ☐ the next issue

All prices include delivery

GRANTA IS PUBLISHED QUARTERLY

PAYMENT DETAILS

☐ I enclose a cheque payable to '*Granta*' for £ ______ for ___ subscriptions to *Granta*

☐ Please debit my ☐ MASTERCARD ☐ VISA ☐ AMEX for £ ______ for ___ subscriptions

NUMBER ☐☐☐☐ ☐☐☐☐ ☐☐☐☐ ☐☐☐☐ SECURITY CODE ☐☐☐

EXPIRY DATE ☐☐ / ☐☐ SIGNED DATE

Instruction to your Bank or building society to pay Direct Debit

DIRECT Debit

TO THE MANAGER:

(BANK OR BUILDING SOCIETY NAME)

ADDRESS:

POSTCODE:

ACCOUNT IN NAME(S) OF:

SIGNED: DATE:

BANK/BUILDING SOCIETY ACCOUNT NUMBER

SORT CODE

ORIGINATOR'S IDENTIFICATION

9 1 3 1 3 3

Instructions to your Bank or building society Please pay Granta Publications Direct Debits from the account detailed on this instruction subject to the safeguards assured by the Direct Debit Guarantee. I understand that this instruction may remain with Granta and, if so, details will be passed electronically to my Bank/ building society.

Banks and building societies may not accept Direct Debit instructions from some types of accout

☐ Please tick this box if you would like to receive special offers from *Granta*

☐ Please tick this box if you would like to receive offers from organizations selected by *Granta*

Please return this form to: **Granta Subscriptions, PO Box 2068, Bushey, Herts, WD23 3ZF, UK**
Freephone 0500 004 033 or go to **www.granta.com**

Please quote the following promotion code when ordering online: GBIUK101

REPORTER AT LARGE

THE AVIATORS

A son's search for his missing father in an African war zone

Xan Rice

Some men live to fly, and Captain John Wilkinson was one of them. His wife Marie tells a story from early in their relationship when Johnny, as his friends knew him, was a young South African Air Force pilot learning to fly the Hercules cargo plane. 'I love you,' he told Marie, knowing that what he said next would hurt her, 'but you have to remember that flying will always be my first love.' Thirty years later they were still together, and had two daughters and a son, Hilton. Johnny was still flying the Hercules, but in Angola, in a war zone a long way from home.

On December 26, 1998, a Saturday, Johnny woke at first light. The sky over Luanda was pale and clear – ideal flying weather. He worked for Transafrik, an air charter company that flew heavy equipment to diamond mines and food and blankets to many of the casualties of Angola's long civil war. Over the last month the fighting had been especially intense in and around Huambo, a highland city in the centre of the country. Later that morning Johnny would be flying there on a mission for the United Nations.

He showered quickly and put on his fawn one-piece flying overall. His cabin in the Transafrik camp was austere, but he had simple needs. On the shelf were his books, thrillers by Robert Ludlum and the RAF pilot-turned-novelist Gavin Lyall. On a table was the sewing machine that he used to make his own jeans from sheets of denim material. Beside the front door was a row of seedlings that he had carefully planted in Coke cans and food tins.

He was hungry and hurried to the mess. The decorations were still up from the Christmas party of the day before. It had been a rare day off for the pilots, who spent more time in the air in a typical three-month stretch than many commercial pilots did in a year. Johnny's crew was already up and about. Carloa Melgar, a Bolivian, was the flight engineer. Benjamin Montefalcon, one of the numerous Filipinos who worked for Transafrik, was responsible for securing the load. An Angolan pilot, Carlos da Silva, was the first officer. They were happy to be flying with Johnny. He was an old-school pilot who flew with a calculator in his pocket and a cigarette in his mouth, and took notes on the back of his packets of Rembrandt van Rijn 30s. His experience had earned him the respect of his colleagues; his logbook showed 23,000 hours' flying time in the Hercules, more than all but a few other cargo pilots in the world.

His affection for the 'Herc', a four-engine, bulbous-nosed, turboprop aircraft well suited to the short, bumpy airstrips of Angola, was often the source of amusement. After a day's flying, dirty and sweaty from helping the loadmaster secure and unload the cargo, Johnny would remain on the airstrip to talk to the ground engineers about minor adjustments that could be made to the plane.

'Johnny, you can't make love to an aircraft,' the other pilots would call out to him as they hurried back to camp to drink beer under the mango tree.

The company bus was ready to depart. When Johnny first came to live and work in Angola nearly eight years before, the journey to the 4 de Fevereiro airport took twenty-five minutes. But since then a third of Angola's ten million people had been officially displaced, with many of them coming to Luanda to escape the fighting in the bush and the provinces. The Mercedes minivan moved slowly on the potholed roads that morning, and it took nearly an hour to arrive at the airport. Once there Johnny chatted to the UN ground staff about the route that he would be flying: south-east to Huambo, to pick up passengers, and then north-east to Saurimo, a garrison town. In the late afternoon he would return to Luanda. The first leg of flight UN806 was expected to be the most dangerous. Huambo was under attack from anti-government UNITA guerrillas, who had claimed the city as their capital. The only way in and out was by air.

Johnny had flown in other African war zones: Sudan, Rwanda, Mozambique and Somalia. He knew how to minimize risks. In Angola, the main danger to planes was from Stinger surface-to-air missiles that were used by UNITA to bring down government aircraft. To stay out of range of the missiles for as long as possible, pilots waited until they were directly above the safety of the airport before descending in a tight spiral.

With da Silva and Melgar performing the pre-flight checks, Johnny went to the cargo hold to ensure Montefalcon was satisfied that the load was secure. Then he settled into his seat on the left-hand side of the flight deck, placing his bags at his feet. Most pilots and crew members carried a single flight bag, usually holding the aircraft manual, various spare forms, condiments to improve the taste of pre-cooked meals and, perhaps, a porn mag or two for in-flight entertainment. Johnny carried a second flight bag containing his Jeppesen aeronautical charts, which showed the optimal approach and departure routes for most of the world's airports.

He adjusted the seat height and rudder pedals so that he had the correct eye position, and put on his headset. After checking with the crew one last time, he eased back on the control column. The Herc climbed smoothly into the air. An hour later it landed at Huambo airport. The UN supplies were unloaded, and ten people attached to the peacekeeping mission came aboard: three Angolans, two Russian mechanics, an Australian lawyer, a Zambian policewoman, an Egyptian, a Cameroonian and a Namibian. Shortly before noon, the Herc twisted high into the sky above the airport, before levelling off and setting its course north-east. Johnny made radio contact with air traffic control in Luanda to say that he was headed to Saurimo.

Kurt Frauenstein was the first at Transafrik to discover that Johnny's Hercules had disappeared shortly after take-off. The thirty-five-year-old South African pilot had joined the company with Johnny in 1991 and, like some of the other younger crew, regarded him as a father figure. On the morning of December 26, he had left the camp before dawn and flown to Huambo on a Boeing 727 to deliver a consignment of fuel. He was on the way back to base when an air traffic controller in Luanda radioed to ask if he could try making contact with flight UN806. 'At first I thought little of it,' Frauenstein, who now lives with his family in New Zealand, told me. 'Johnny was probably just out of range, as sometimes happened. But when I could not get hold of him either I started to worry.'

When Frauenstein landed in Luanda, he picked up Ross Coleman, an American flight engineer, and flew back in the direction of Huambo. They circled the area where the plane was thought to have disappeared for as long as their fuel load would allow, but could see no signs of wreckage. Later that night, however, their worst fears were confirmed when a spokesman for the UN announced that Johnny's plane had gone down near Huambo.

By the following morning, Transafrik had made no effort to notify the families of the missing crew. Ross Coleman was indignant. An impulsive former navy man who liked to smoke cigars on the flight deck, he had been close to Johnny and he took it on himself to call the Wilkinson home in Kempton Park, seven miles north of Johannesburg. Marie was away spending Christmas with her two daughters in Durban, and it was Hilton, her twenty-five-year-old son

– and an old schoolfriend of mine – to whom Coleman spoke. Too distraught to phone his mother himself after Coleman's call, Hilton asked a family friend to make contact with her in Durban.

'When I took the call,' Marie told me, 'I said: "Don't tell me. It's Hilton." I thought he'd gone out on the town and had a car accident.'

It did not occur to her that something could have happened to Johnny. He had always seemed somehow indestructible, treating his frequent bouts of malaria as if they were mere colds and always, no matter how bad the mechanical problem, ensuring that his plane and crew returned to safety. Now he was missing.

The disappearance of flight UN806 caused tension between the Transafrik flying crew, who wanted to suspend all operations and go in search of the plane, and management, which, according to Frauenstein, thought the pilots should continue to work. There was uncertainty, too, over exactly what had happened: in the first days, there were reports that suggested the crash had not been fatal. On December 28, Associated Press reported that the downed plane was emitting SOS signals. The next day, Reuters quoted Issa Diallo, head of the UN observer mission in Angola, who said that the aircraft may have landed intact and that there was hope of survivors. Meanwhile, the Angolan government was insisting that UNITA had taken the crew and passengers hostage. All of these conflicting reports gave the Wilkinsons hope that Johnny might still be alive.

At home in Johannesburg, as his mother was preparing to return from Durban, Hilton was desperate for news of the search-and-rescue operation. Had the aircraft been found yet? What of the survivors? He drove to an airport near Pretoria, where Transafrik had an office, to meet Frauenstein, who had flown to South Africa for the day. 'Hilton was very upset but also very determined to do something,' Frauenstein said. 'He seemed like...like a man preparing himself for a mission.'

Frauenstein explained to Hilton that nobody knew quite what was happening and that there was no official search taking place on the ground. Neither UNITA nor the government forces had agreed to a request for a ceasefire to allow the missing plane to be located, and the continued fighting between government troops and rebels meant that it was considered too dangerous to fly low over the area. But Frauenstein did offer Hilton some advice. 'I said: "Hilton, you are not going to find out what happened to your dad by sitting here and listening to the news. If you want the truth you are going to have to come to Angola to find it yourself." '

It was at about this time that I read in the Johannesburg *Star* that a South African pilot named John Wilkinson was missing in Angola. Could it be *that* John Wilkinson? I dialled Hilton's number. He answered after a few rings and I could immediately tell from his voice that it was his father who was missing – the father whom I remembered as a tall, thin man and whom I had seen smoking a pipe as he sat in his car waiting to collect his son at the end of term. I said that I was sorry, and that I hoped Johnny would be okay. I have never been able to forget the desolation in Hilton's voice as he said goodbye. His sister Anne-Audette, then twenty-two, has since told me that she had never before seen her brother cry but that at times during the days after the crash he could not stop crying. She loved her father, too, but Hilton's bond with Johnny seemed to have unfathomable depths. Johnny was more than a father to Hilton: he was a hero, and had been ever since as a young boy Hilton had accompanied him in the Herc on his cargo flights in and around South Africa.

On the morning of December 29, Coleman called Hilton to tell him that a Transafrik flight would be leaving Johannesburg for Luanda the next day. This confirmed to Hilton what he already knew: that he was going to Angola.

He was driven to the airport by his mother.

'I was crying,' Marie says now. 'I kept telling Hilton how much I loved him.'

Hilton seemed excited rather than anxious or fearful. He knew

A Transafrik Hercules

Angola and its airports nearly as well as his father knew them. At the departure gate, he said a few last words to Marie: 'Mum, I'm bringing dad home.'

Hilton Wilkinson was thirteen when, in 1987, he arrived at the High School for Boys in Potchefstroom, a conservative Afrikaans town ninety miles west of Johannesburg, where I was also a pupil. Boys lived in three hostels, the smallest of which was Buxton House, in the far corner of the school. At night we fell asleep to the sounds of trains passing nearby. Boys from the other hostels called us 'the railway kids'.

There were twenty first-year pupils in Buxton and we all lived in the same cramped dormitory on the ground floor. Our beds were a foot apart; you couldn't whisper without somebody at the far end of the room hearing what you were saying. We were woken every morning at five a.m. to run wind sprints across the rugby field or swim lengths of butterfly in the cold pool. Then we showered, dressed, swept the dormitory and fagged for our allocated senior, making his bed, shining his shoes, putting out his clothes, fetching tea and carrying his suitcase to school. We lived in terror, knowing that a beating was never far away. You could be beaten for having a sloppily made bed, a dirty collar, for failing to greet a prefect, for forgetting the name of the First XV rugby fullback or for talking after lights out. Hilton fagged for a prefect whose study opened on to our dormitory. He had a fondness for the Bible and the rod. Hilton was very thin and when he was being beaten we sometimes joked that his legs might snap. That was how he got his first nickname: *Wednesday*. When's dey gonna break.

Hilton spoke hesitantly, which led some to assume that he was slow-witted. The truth was the opposite; he had a sharp and mischievous mind. If there was a prank in the hostel or the classroom he was sure to be involved. Perhaps it was because he was so slight and seemed so innocent, but he somehow managed to get away with things the rest of us wouldn't. Our lives were small and sheltered, governed by alarm bells, the routine of mealtimes and the changing sporting seasons – athletics, swimming, cricket and rugby. We had little sense of how South Africa was about to change, of how we were approaching the end of the apartheid years, and that the black men – Sam and Danny and Abe – who served our food, watery Welsh rarebit and cottage pie in the dining hall, would soon be free to enrol their own children at a school such as ours. If we wanted to survive, let alone thrive, in what was being called the 'new South Africa', we were told that we must study hard to obtain a good university degree in what was considered to be a useful subject such as law, engineering, accountancy or medicine.

Hilton had no interest in any of these subjects or in studying to go to university. From an early age, he knew exactly what he wanted to do. He wanted, like his father Johnny, to be a pilot. He wanted to fly. Even at school he began to cultivate a fly boy image, a construct of romantic imagination. He bought a pair of Ray-Ban Aviators and taught himself to smoke while hunched inside a locker. He wasn't the only pupil experimenting with Chesterfields in the lavatories late at night, but his was no simple act of teenage rebellion. To him, pilots smoked, as his father smoked. At night, he would read by torchlight, tales of flight and wartime adventure: *The Great Escape*, *The Wooden Horse* and *The Colditz Story*. His favourite book was Paul Brickhill's biography of Douglas Bader, *Reach for the Sky*. Hilton's mother, Marie, herself the daughter of a career pilot who flew B-24 Liberator bombers for the Allies during the Second World War, understood what motivated and inspired her son. After all, she was married to an obsessive pilot. 'After a few days at home without flying John would become irritated,' she told me. 'He couldn't help himself, it's just who he was.'

Between an estuary on the Indian Ocean and a steep hill looking out towards the Outeniqua Mountains is the small town of Knysna in the Western Cape, familiar to many British tourists who have stopped off there on their way from Cape Town to Port Elizabeth on the Garden Route. Many of the most expensive hillside houses are owned by so-called out-of-towners, those who have become wealthy through working in banking or IT in Johannesburg or Cape Town. Warwick Sparg, who built himself a grand house on the hill with a garage large enough to accommodate his Porsche, his five BMW motorcycles, a Harley-Davidson and a pool table made his money as a bush pilot. He is fifty-six, fit and tanned, and wears his hair raffishly long. On one recent afternoon, after picking me up from the local airport, he talked about how he got his start. He began as a pilot for a scheduled airline but the work bored him; he was seeking spontaneity and adventure and so began to promote himself as a pilot for hire. One of his first clients was Wouter Basson, the cardiologist who would come to be known as 'Doctor Death' after he was revealed to have led the apartheid government's secret chemical warfare project. Another client was Billy Rautenbach, a white Zimbabwean close to the Mugabe government, who, notoriously, was made chairman of the Democratic Republic of Congo's state mining company, Gécamines, at a time when Mugabe's troops were helping prop up Laurent Kabila's regime. But Sparg's most memorable client was a bearded Angolan rebel leader called Jonas Savimbi.

Known to his followers as O Mais Velho ('The Oldest One'), Savimbi had led the União Nacional para a Independência Total de Angola, or UNITA, since its formation in 1966, when it was one of three liberation movements fighting to end Portuguese colonial rule. By mid-1974, independence for Angola was inevitable. Portugal's fascist dictatorship, first under António de Salazar and then Marcello Caetano, had desperately held on to the country's African colonies even as France, Belgium and Britain had let theirs go. But in April 1974, Caetano's regime had been overthrown in a near-bloodless military coup. Instead of uniting, however, the rebel armies in Angola had begun to fight one another in an attempt to assume sole power once the Portuguese had gone.

'It was a peculiar arrangement: a black nationalist warlord leading an anti-colonial struggle backed by a white racist regime.'

The Cold War made external intervention in the struggle inevitable. The Marxist Movimento Popular de Libertação de Angola, or MPLA, which had the support of the intellectual and mixed-race elite in Luanda, received military and financial backing from the Soviet Union and Cuba. The United States took the side of UNITA. Also assisting Savimbi was the South African government, which was as paranoid as the Americans were about the Communist threat in Africa, especially in southern Africa, where liberation movements in Mozambique, Zimbabwe and what is now Namibia but was then called South West Africa and was an enclave of the apartheid state, were being supported by the Soviet Union. It was a peculiar arrangement: a black nationalist and ruthless warlord leading an anti-colonial struggle while being backed by a white racist regime. 'When you're a drowning man in a crocodile-infested river, you don't argue about who is rescuing you until you're safely on the bank,' Savimbi said later.

As independence came closer in Angola, and the Portuguese elite began to flee the country, South Africa sent troops north along the road towards the Angolan capital in an attempt to prevent the MPLA from seizing power. Cuba, in turn, successfully sent thousands of troops south from Luanda to deter the South African column from advancing further.

On November 11, 1975 the MPLA assumed power, declaring the country independent. In response, UNITA and the FNLA, the third liberation group, came together to set up a rival coalition government, based in Huambo. For much of the next twelve years, Angola was ravaged by civil war, with young, white South African conscripts regularly deployed deep in MPLA-controlled territory, sometimes fighting alongside UNITA and sometimes fighting alone. (The apartheid government denied that its troops were fighting on Angolan soil; a compliant media at home ensured that few South Africans knew exactly what was going on.)

Savimbi used South African airports as the means by which he could travel out of Africa. Whenever he needed to visit foreign capitals such as Washington on fund-raising missions, a South African military plane would fly him from the Angolan bush to Pretoria, where Sparg would be waiting for him in a JetStar II business jet to take him to wherever he wanted to go. 'Savimbi was always the perfect gentleman,' Sparg told me, without irony. 'He greeted the crew as he came aboard and thanked us before leaving the airplane. He always had a white doctor with him, and as the plane began to descend the doctor would hand each crew member an envelope with one thousand dollars inside.'

Working for Savimbi was Sparg's introduction to the war in Angola and soon, using a Malawian passport, since South Africans were officially not allowed in Angola at the time, he began to operate from inside the country, flying UN officials on various missions. When he saw the potential of being a pilot for hire in a country in which it was too dangerous to travel by road, he set up his own charter service. The work was dangerous – Sparg's first aircraft had bulletproof material on the floor and he wore a flak jacket when flying into trouble spots – but it was also lucrative.

By the early Nineties, Balmoral, in which he had a fifty per cent stake, was a thriving business servicing the World Food Programme and other humanitarian organizations with its fleet of small aircraft. Whenever he was back in South Africa, on holiday or maintaining his aircraft, Sparg was approached by pilots looking for work in Angola. Some were attracted by the money: a newly qualified pilot would receive a tax-free income of $5,000 a month. (One of Sparg's pilots flew with a one-dollar bill taped to the instrument panel. 'That's my boss,' he'd tell people. 'George Washington.') Other ambitious pilots wanted to accumulate their flying hours so that they could apply for jobs at large commercial airlines in other countries. Most of them, including the pilot who arrived in Angola with his surfboard, had no idea how difficult and precarious flying was in a country devastated by twenty years of war.

When a slender, smooth-cheeked young man approached Sparg outside the Turbo Prop Service Centre at Lanseria airport on the north-western outskirts of Johannesburg in 1995, there was little to suggest he would be any different from most other youthful pilots looking for work. Hilton was twenty-one. He had completed a year's military service, but had abandoned his ambition of joining the air force after being told he needed a degree. He had earned his private and commercial pilot's licences and had had his tuition fees paid for by his father. He had 210 hours in his logbook. He was ready to fly. 'He was very respectful. He said: "Are you Mr Sparg?" and I said that I was. He said he wanted to fly in Angola. I looked at him and thought: *You are very young and very skinny*. I said to him: "What do you know about Angola?" He said: "My dad flies for Transafrik." I hired him on the spot.'

Before he had completed his first year of flying in Angola, Hilton was captain on both the Cessna 208 Caravan, a single-engine plane that took nine passengers, and the Beechcraft King Air 200, a twin-turboprop aircraft. His instructor at Balmoral, Graham Woodhouse, told me in an email from Kabul, where he was delivering a plane, that Hilton's 'flying ability was well above average'.

The work was intense and exhausting. Hilton flew for up to seven hours a day, five or six days a week. It was nothing like flying school. Many of the airstrips were littered with the wrecks of crashed or abandoned planes. The gravel runways of Angola had been eroded by heavy freight planes and were perilous for smaller aircraft. Hilton learned how to spiral in and out of dangerous areas, how never to trust the Russian pilots when they reported their altitude and positions, and how to remain calm even when the windscreen of his King Air shattered in mid-flight, as it did on one occasion soon after he arrived in Luanda.

But his most important lesson was how to avoid being hit by ground fire or surface-to-air missiles. When flying short distances between airports, the trick was to fly fast and low, just above the tree line, giving the rebels no time to line up a shot. For longer trips it was necessary to spiral up above the airport to get out of missile range. Though Angola was experiencing a lull in fighting when Hilton first arrived in the country, UNITA still had a large stockpile of missiles, as his father knew well. In the early Nineties, Johnny had often flown alongside Don Rogers, an American flight engineer who had worked aboard Hercules aircraft since the late Sixties, when he supported US ground troops stationed in Saigon for the Vietnam War. Immediately before joining Transafrik, Rogers had worked for a small American air charter company called St Lucia Airways, whose main customer was the Central Intelligence Agency. 'We were contracted by the CIA to fly Stinger surface-to-air missiles from Kelly Air Force Base in Texas to an abandoned Belgian airfield in Zaire [now the Democratic Republic of Congo],' says Rogers, who is retired and these days lives in Florida. From there he flew with the missiles across the border to Savimbi's military stronghold in Jamba, in south-eastern Angola. 'It did occur to me when I joined Transafrik that I could be taken down by one of the Stingers that I had delivered.'

Sparg was proud of the young man; he saw Hilton not just as a good pilot, but as a kindred spirit in the bush-flying world. 'Many pilots can only "drive" a plane,' he said. 'Hilton could really "feel" the aircraft. I could identify with him. We would drink hard, smoke hard and play hard. But you could not frighten us with work.'

Hilton lived with six other male Balmoral pilots and crew in a house in downtown Luanda, which had armed security guards at the door. The only female in the house was the local cook. While some of the crew members argued over who should have the largest rooms, Hilton was content with the smallest, little more than a storage cupboard beneath the stairway, where he slept sprawled out and naked on a mattress on the floor with the air conditioning on high. The cold air against his skin helped him wake up in the morning, he said, even though he was always the last one to rise, drinking only a Coke, his 'Black Magic', for breakfast, before hurrying to the airport. On a Saturday night, the flying crews and humanitarian workers in Luanda usually gathered for a house party or headed out to a pub known as the Pink Palace or to one of the nightclubs on the beach road, where whores loitered.

Sometimes, at Luanda airport, Hilton watched Johnny take off in the Herc, and he would ease back on an imaginary control column, as if mimicking his father's actions. The other pilots noticed how Hilton had unconsciously adopted Johnny's body language: the slightly sagged right shoulder, the cigarette hanging on his lower lip. Given their hectic flying schedules, father and son seldom saw each other, except on Sunday evenings, when Hilton would drive a

Korean-made Rocksta jeep from his downtown digs to the Transafrik camp. It was against company policy to drive alone at night, but a safety rule was not going to stop him from seeing his father. Out at the camp, alone together, Hilton and Johnny talked about flying, just as they had always done at home, to the irritation of Marie and the girls. 'We would worry about Hilton, thinking that he'd had an accident or something,' said Riaan Theron, a South African pilot who flew with Hilton at Balmoral. 'But at two or three in the morning we always heard him come rumbling back in the jeep from visiting his father.'

The Transafrik camp, which was originally built as the Filipino Consulate in Angola, was situated on a dirt road twelve miles south of Luanda, in an area called Corimba near the coastal highway. Most of the 150 staff seldom ventured beyond the nearby village that they named 'Smokey Mountain' because of the haze caused by all the cooking fires there in the morning and evening. Some of the Transafrik workers had local girlfriends in the village. On Sundays, a few of the Filipino personnel organized cockfights there and many of the pilots and crew would go along to bet on them, returning to camp with pockets stuffed full of near-worthless Angolan kwanzas. During weekday evenings, if they weren't flying – Transafrik was a twenty-four-hour operation – the pilots listened to Voice of America or the BBC World Service in their cabins, or sat on plastic chairs under the mango tree, drinking Castle Lager flown in from South Africa or the local Diamond Beer. Back in South Africa, Marie tolerated her husband's long absences from home even as they strained their marriage. She was concerned that Johnny had begun to drink too much, that on his visits home he was oddly 'distant' from her and that, when he wasn't busy repairing something, he would simply sit in silence in the lounge, reading.

Hilton defended his father when Marie complained of Johnny's strange silences. 'He'd say: "Mum, there's stuff that has happened to Dad while flying that he just can't talk about,"' Marie told me one afternoon at her house near Johannesburg's main international airport. Marie knew that Hilton was at least partly right; Johnny did not want to alarm her by revealing just how dangerous his job could be. While he discussed his more bizarre assignments, such as when he flew pot plants from South Africa to Zaire for Mobutu Sese Seko or when he was arrested in Libya while transporting spare parts for drivers in the Paris–Dakar rally, he never told her how his plane was shot up while flying over Mogadishu. She learnt of the narrow escape only years later when one of Johnny's colleagues showed her a photograph of the bullet-sprayed plane.

After each two-month stint in Angola, Hilton had four weeks at home in Johannesburg. His friends knew when he was back in town because their phones would ring late at night, with Hilton announcing that he was coming to pick them up for a few drinks. He was generous, paying for friends in restaurants; those who refused to accept his generosity would find hundreds of rands left on their car seats the next day. He was an extravagant tipper and loans invariably became gifts.

Hilton had no interest in or knowledge of contemporary popular culture. He was hopelessly, happily, oblivious to it. What interested him was the culture – the songs, the films, the cars – of his father's late adolescence and early adulthood. While most of us were listening to alternative or indie music, he played Elvis songs on the stereo of his white MGB sports car. When he took a holiday to London, the highlight of the trip, he said, was watching the Buddy Holly musical in the West End.

It was a good life, but scarcely a stable one. After Hilton had spent nearly three years in Angola, Johnny had encouraged him to search for a more settled job in South Africa – and a safer one. Accidents were frequent in Angola, and two of Balmoral's most senior pilots were killed when a wing of their King Air had broken off in a violent thunderstorm. For several days Balmoral stopped all commercial work, using every one of its planes to search for the wreckage. 'When a colleague goes down that's what you do,' Sparg said. 'You forget the business side.'

As part of the search effort, Hilton was especially affected by the experience. To Marie, and to his friends at home, it seemed as though somebody who always considered himself to be, as he put it, 'bulletproof' had become vulnerable, had begun to consider the dangers of a life in the sky. 'He started talking more and more about his "box party", his expression for a funeral,' Hilton's closest friend, Richard Brady, says now. 'He would say to Marie: "Mum, I want there to be a bagpiper, and he must play 'Amazing Grace' ". She hated that.'

In the spring of 1998, Hilton finally left his job. He had enough flying hours and enough money to take his senior commercial pilot's licence in Connecticut in the United States. Back in Johannesburg, he circulated his CV to numerous charter airlines, requesting a job as a cargo pilot. If all went well, he hoped soon to be flying a Herc, like his father, but in South Africa. As he waited for replies, he planned for a bit of fun over Christmas, especially as his mother would be away in Durban and he would be alone at the family house. Johnny had been home on leave in November, celebrating his fifty-first birthday with Marie on December 2 and flying back to Angola a week later.

On Christmas Eve, Hilton took Johnny's old Land-Rover and picked up Richard Brady. Together they drove the short distance from his home to Caesar's Palace casino, had dinner there and gambled until dawn. On their return to Hilton's house, Richard went to bed. Hilton, meanwhile, was dressing for church: like Johnny, he was not especially religious, but the two of them still went to the local Methodist church on Easter Sunday and on Christmas Day, if they were home. At church Hilton, who was still drunk, fell asleep in the pews. The woman seated next to him woke him up when the service was over.

Hilton flew into Luanda on December 29. He was met at the airport by John Nagel, a Balmoral aircraft engineer. In spite of the differences in their ages – Nagel was forty-one and married with two children, while Hilton was sixteen years younger and single – they had become close friends during Hilton's time in Angola. As soon as Hilton cleared customs, he and Nagel set out on the road, driving all over Luanda as they searched for anyone with information about flight UN806. After making enquiries at the Transafrik office, they went to Johnny's camp. Their best hope for information was the United Nations, which had a special department that controlled air operations in Angola. Nobody seemed to know much at all – or at least, if they did they weren't saying.

Hilton returned to the airport, asking the pilots on inbound planes if they knew anything. Then they met Frauenstein, who had just returned from Huambo. He explained how he had persuaded Transafrik to let him take a Hercules to Huambo to see if he could convince the Angolan army to escort him to the crash site. The fighting in the area made it impossible. As he and his translator slept in a UN camp overnight, they could hear the shells falling nearby.

'Hilton was level-headed, but emotional,' said Nagel, who is back working in Angola, this time for the state oil company Sonangol. 'He kept saying that if his dad survived the crash, he would get out as he was not the type of guy to piss off his captors. But he was realistic. He also knew that the longer we spent without news the less chance there was of finding Johnny alive.'

Hilton was not the only one who had flown into Luanda to help with the search. In Nairobi, where he was on a temporary assignment, Ramon Dumlao had heard about the crash. A fifty-five-year-old Filipino, Dumlao had been with the company for fourteen years and was Transafrik's chief pilot. He and Johnny, his deputy, liked each other. Dumlao was just a few months away from retirement, and the easy option would have been to stick to his holiday plans when news of the crash reached him. Instead, he phoned his wife to say he would not be able to spend New Year with her and their four children in Manila, and returned to Luanda.

There were no New Year's celebrations in the Transafrik camp. Five days had passed since the crash. The mood was one of desolation. Whatever their individual differences, the flying crews regarded themselves as one big family – and now four family members were missing.

Hilton had asked Balmoral if he could borrow a small plane for a search-and-rescue mission. The answer was yes, but he would have to wait a few more days. Hilton was becoming exasperated: he had been in Angola for three nights already, and had not made it out of Luanda. Then an opportunity arose. Dumlao was asked to fly to Huambo and back on a routine mission for the United Nations. Flight UN806A was due to depart on Saturday January 2, 1999, exactly a week after Johnny had flown into Huambo.

Ross Coleman was listed as the flight engineer. He spoke to Dumlao and they agreed to smuggle Hilton on board. They told Hilton that, on the way back to Luanda, they would fly low over the area where Johnny's plane had gone down. The aircraft was to be a Hercules, which had a large viewing area from the flight deck. Hilton called his mother in Johannesburg to tell her the news. Though she did not realize how dangerous the mission would be, Marie was happy, even if she didn't share her son's optimism about finding Johnny alive. 'I did not have much hope,' she says now. 'It had been a week already. We'd heard nothing. There'd been no leads.'

After Jonas Savimbi was shot dead on a riverbank by government troops in 2002, peace had come quickly to Angola. Five years on, the stability, and the booming oil prices, have created huge wealth in the capital Luanda. But most of it is controlled by a small elite within or close to the MPLA-led government, who can afford to live extravagantly in what has become one of Africa's most expensive cities. Meanwhile, hundreds of thousands of people subsist in squalid shanty towns. Walking along the Marginal, the city's seafront drive, one afternoon last winter, I counted six new Hummer 4x4s. One of them was parked next to the pavement; a man with stumps for legs lowered himself on to the tarmac and urinated against its wheel.

For Transafrik, peace meant a decline in business. As the inland roads were cleared of landmines, lorries began to do the work that the Hercs and Boeing 727s did during the war, but at a considerably reduced cost. In September 2006, the company shifted its headquarters to Entebbe, in Uganda, closer to the lawless eastern Democratic Republic of Congo, where a huge humanitarian operation remains ongoing to this day as rebel groups continue to ravage the local population. The Luanda office had not closed completely by the time I arrived there during the winter of 2007.

Pimentel Araújo, the general manager of Transafrik, continued to live in the city and I had come to meet him. We drove to his office located in an old, white shipping container, decorated with maps and model planes. Araújo has neat, thinning grey hair and rimless glasses. His parents were Portuguese but he was born and raised in Angola, and was one of only a few thousand whites who stayed on after independence.

In the year before the MPLA took power, more than 300,000 Portuguese, over ninety-five per cent of the white population, fled the country. Those who left did so by air, but not before packing their belongings in giant crates that were piled up at Luanda's port creating, as Ryszard Kapuscinski wrote in *Another Day of Life*, his account of the last days of Portuguese rule, a new wooden city within a city. 'Now it was spread out at the very edge of the sea, illuminated at night by harbour lanterns and the glare of lights on anchored ships. By day, people wound through its chaotic streets, painting their names and addresses on little plates, just as anyone does anywhere in the world when he builds himself a house… It was carried off by a great flotilla with which, after several hours, it disappeared below the horizon. This happened suddenly, as if a pirate ship had sailed into the port, seized a priceless treasure, and escaped to sea with it.'

Araújo remains nostalgic for the days before the Portuguese left. 'Before, back then, Luanda was such a beautiful city. Now,' he says, with anger, 'it is shit. Before independence, all the public servants were Portuguese. When they left, there was nobody trained in how to run the country. I found a job in a bank. You learned by making mistakes – there was no one to teach you.'

He soon left the bank to work for TAAG, the national airline, and then, later, took a job with Transafrik, when it was set up in 1984. I asked him about Johnny. Araújo looked to his bookshelf for the company's guide to flying in Angola, which described the various airports, runways and flying conditions. The guide was given to all new members of crew. 'Johnny wrote it for us, and we still used it long after he was gone. I am not one who says somebody had great qualities if they didn't. But he was a good man. He was focused on flying and never complained. In the end he was very unlucky. He was in a bad place at a bad time.

'When news of the crash became known, our pilots wanted to search for their colleagues. I had to stop the other pilots going to look for the plane straight away. We had heavy aircraft so it was too dangerous to be flying low. But it was hard to explain to the crews. They lived together and flew together. They were here for the money but they developed strong feelings for one another.'

Huambo today has little of the claustrophobia, squalor and chaos of Luanda. A truck collects rubbish. Workers in reflective bibs repair the roads. Women sweep the streets. There are hawkers on foot everywhere. An old man with a school satchel offers you a fistful of pens. A woman balances a basket of bread rolls on her head; another pushes a wheelbarrow full of toiletries. Girls sell the fattest strawberries you have ever seen. A boy rests on a bench, his merchandise, dozens of pairs of orange-handled scissors, hanging from a string around his neck. It is not difficult to see why the Portuguese called the city Nova

Lisboa. The streets are wide and the houses and buildings, even though many of them are run down with bullet-scarred facades, are recognizably European in architectural style. Opposite a square, where old men sit talking on park benches, is a large, pink, colonial-style building, the headquarters of the MPLA. There are two signs outside.

> PAZ
> PARA SEMPRE
> UM SO POVO
> UMA SO NACAO.
> (Peace for all, one people, one nation.)
>
> MPLA
> E UMA
> BARREIRA
> INTRANSPONIVEL
> (MPLA is an impenetrable barrier.)

A few blocks down is the UNITA office, on the second floor of a corner office block. There are no slogans, only a fluttering party flag on which is depicted a black cockerel against a red sunrise. There is no doubt as to who won the war.

In 1991, UNITA and the MPLA agreed to contest an election, during which both parties campaigned hard. At rallies in support of Savimbi, officials shouted, '*Nosso galo?*' (our cockerel), to which the crowd roared, '*Voa*' (it flies). But the cockerel never flew, and, instead, scurried back into the bush. Savimbi rejected the poll results, which saw him losing narrowly to President José Eduardo dos Santos, and returned to doing what he did best – fighting a ruthless war. In January 1993, UNITA attempted to seize Huambo, laying siege to the city for fifty-five days, pummelling it with mortars and gunfire. As many as 10,000 people died during the siege, many of them from the very same Ovimbundu ethnic group that provided UNITA with its core support, before Huambo fell. Less then two years later, it was back under government control. South Africans had been dragged back into the war, although this time it was a private army, Executive Outcomes, fighting there rather than the national force.

On January 2, 1999, a Saturday, Hilton woke at first light. The sky over Luanda was pale and clear – ideal flying weather. He showered quickly and put on his pilot's uniform. Under his white short-sleeved shirt was a money belt containing $5,000. If he saw the crash site and the plane appeared intact he would ask Ramon Dumlao to return to Huambo and drop him off at the airport. If he could make contact with UNITA, he was sure he could buy his father's freedom. He had breakfast with Nagel, and they argued. Nagel knew how desperate Hilton was to find his father, but he wanted him to pause, to be patient, to wait a few more days. An agitated Hilton would not hear of it and so, reluctantly, Nagel drove him to the 4 de Fevereiro airport. Dumlao and Ross Coleman were there, together with the Filipino loadmaster Bernabe Vicarme and an Angolan first officer. The five of them boarded the Hercules, though the manifest showed only the names of the official crew. Hilton was an illegal passenger.

After landing at Huambo, they picked up four UN passengers, three Angolan men and a Namibian, and loaded two Toyota Land Cruisers into the cargo hold. Shortly before three p.m., flight UN806A took off for Luanda, but instead of climbing quickly to 20,000 feet, the plane flew low towards Tchikala-Tcholohanga, as Hilton would have wanted.

At home in Johannesburg that night, Marie Wilkinson waited for her son to call. But he did not. Perhaps he had arrived home late, she thought, or had nothing to report. Perhaps he was still in Huambo. *He'll speak to me in the morning.*

After a disturbed night, Marie called Nagel at home in Luanda the next morning. She asked if her son was there with him.

'I said: "What's going on? Don't tell me something has happened to Hilton?" When he said yes, I just went crazy.'

As I had dinner in a small roadside restaurant near my hotel in Huambo one evening in late August last year, I thought back to January 4, 1999, when I read with disbelief a story in the *Star* about a second United Nations plane that had gone down in Angola in the same part of the country as the first. Again, the name Wilkinson was mentioned. This time, it was Hilton Wilkinson. He had been on that second plane and, like his father, he was missing.

In the years that followed I would always feel uneasy when I heard or read anything about Angola. For me the country had become synonymous with Hilton and Johnny – a haunted place, a place of war and loss. When I told people what had happened there to a father and son they just shook their heads. Could that be true? It was, I assured them, but I knew only the basic facts, the beginning and the end: two planes falling from the sky within a week of each other. From time to time I would search the Internet for more information, but I could never find anything new. I promised myself that one day I would travel to Angola to discover what had really happened to my schoolfriend and the father he called 'Pops'.

In Huambo I was met that morning at my hotel by a policeman to whom I had been introduced by a stocky, jovial Afrikaner named Waal de Waal, who had served in Angola as part of the South African special forces. A friend of the policeman would act as my driver and guide, and shortly after six o'clock he pulled up in a white Toyota Land-cruiser. We drove east out of the city and the road turned to dirt, with occasional islands of tar in the middle. As the pale sky brightened to blue we passed an old factory shorn of its roof and women washing clothes in a river. After forty-five minutes we arrived at the village of Tchikala-Tcholohanga. We turned left, and drove in the direction of a Catholic church that was being rebuilt by workers perched on wooden scaffolding. A UNITA flag was flying. We were looking for a local headman called Matias Nhanga. He controlled the area when Johnny's plane came down and we needed his permission to travel freely to the crash site. Nhanga's hut was empty, but he soon returned from a nearby field. He wore a dirty cowboy hat and a faded black nylon jacket on which was written HARLEY OWNERS GROUP, LIVE THE LEGEND, 1983. He brought some chairs from his hut, gesturing for us to sit.

De Waal had warned me when we met in Pretoria that Nhanga would expect some sort of gift. I took a framed photograph of Nhanga that de Waal had taken. Nhanga was delighted. We could visit the crash site, he said. Before we left, I asked him if he was in the area when the first plane crashed. He nodded. 'All the people of the village were hiding in the bush because of the war,' he said, speaking through a translator. 'We saw the plane, and there was a big noise. We saw fire. It crashed and there was too much smoke. The ordinary people could not go there, only the soldiers.'

The soldiers were from UNITA, he said.

'They looted the plane and cut a tree to cover it. There was a big hole in the ground. The soldiers were very happy to have shot the plane. They thought it belonged to the government.'

On the far side of the village a team of men wearing overalls and long see-through visors were clearing landmines from an open field. We drove on and soon turned right on to a track, heading towards a shallow green valley. At a rocky outcrop, we turned left, drove on for another hundred metres and then stopped. My driver, Amocachi, led the way on foot. The soil was soft. The wind was blowing strongly now, enough to cause a shiver. There was no human habitation in sight. I heard a rustle, like tinfoil crumpling. I looked down. It was a piece of tough metallic fabric.

'This is the place,' said Amocachi.

In front of us was a crater, several metres wide, which had been recently filled in. Sticking out were pieces of charred metal: rods, springs, cogs, a tangle of wires. I picked up a small piece of metal. There was writing on it.

SINGER
VAP AIR DIVISION
VAPRO CORPORATION
CHICAGO, IL.

Nearby was a seat belt buckle and a piece of white plastic that said FIRST AID KIT. These were the remains of flight UN806, Johnny's flight, but they could just as easily have been another relic of war.

Amocachi and I left the crash site and rejoined the main dirt road, passing the rusty shell of an abandoned tank and driving through groves of eucalyptus trees. In the clearings, the grass had been burned crisp and black. The smell of fire lingered. As we emerged from a dip, an old farmhouse came into view. Amocachi parked on the side of the road. We had driven twenty-four kilometres. I got out of the car and saw the charred carcass of a 4x4 vehicle a few metres away. It was one of the vehicles that the second downed plane had been transporting. In the field nearby was a large, shallow ditch. Reeds were spouting out of it, amid which were large chunks of burnt and twisted metal: the debris from flight UN806A. So this was where Hilton's quest for his father had ended. There was no grave marker or plaque to indicate what had happened here. I spoke one word, the name of my lost friend.

Near the farmhouse the workers were having lunch. One of them came over to talk and we sat down together on a fallen log among the trees. His name was Domingues Satula and I asked him what he knew about the crashed aircraft. Like Nhanga, he spoke of how he was hiding in the woods about a mile from here on the afternoon of January 2. Was this possible or was Satula merely trying to be helpful? Even if he had been here in January 1999, I was not sure whether to believe that he had merely been an innocent spectator or whether he had been on active duty for UNITA. During the war this was staunch UNITA-controlled territory, and most men of his age would have been conscripted into the rebel army.

Satula told us that the government had been using fighter planes and helicopters to attack UNITA positions in the area and there was intense fighting all around. 'There was much fear when we saw an aircraft approaching,' he said, speaking in Umbundu, the Ovimbundu language.

At the time, UNITA was using the farm as a defensive position; among the trees I discovered old trench lines. On top of the hill were the foundations used to secure the anti-aircraft gun that lined up the Hercules in its sights as it flew low over the field, searching for the wreckage of Johnny's plane. I thought of Hilton and how he must have been feeling that afternoon as he peered down from the viewing area of the Hercules, so anxious and yet perhaps still so hopeful. Or had he already begun to accept that his father was gone, that he would not be bringing him home after all?

Satula said that he saw the Hercules catch fire in the air after it was hit. As it descended it burst apart, spilling its cargo, before impacting with the ground. 'It was a time of war,' he said softly.

I asked if he knew that one of the dead was the son of the man piloting the plane that crashed near Tchikala-Tcholohanga. 'Yes, we heard that later,' he said. 'We are sorry for that.'

Under guard from the Angolan army, a team of UN air-accident investigators spent two hours at the first crash site on January 9, 1999. Sixteen days later, UNITA allowed the team to spend an hour at the location of the second crash site. They found close similarities in the way that each wrecked plane had been plundered and then covered with branches and leaves. The voice recorders and black boxes had been neatly removed from both planes.

The official UN inquiries into the crashes have never been made public, but I have spoken to some of those who are familiar with their contents. A piece of audiotape belonging to flight UN806 was recovered. It revealed two loud bangs. The first, the UN inquiry concluded, was a surface-to-air missile hitting the plane at about 18,000 feet. The second was the plane impacting the ground. The depth of hole indicated that Johnny's plane had spiralled nose first into the ground at tremendous speed. Everyone would have been killed immediately. There was no effort made to identify which group had fired the missile, or to apportion blame, but the balance of probabilities suggested that it was UNITA.

Evidence gathered from the second site showed that Hilton's plane had been hit by artillery fire, almost certainly UNITA's. Dumlao had attempted to make an emergency landing: the flaps were down on the aircraft's wings, and the landing wheels were out. A fire had started when the plane was hit and this caused it to break up in the air. The tail section, riddled with bullet holes, was found on a hilltop adjoining the field. The entire passenger section was destroyed. The likelihood of anyone surviving the crash was remote. The inquiry found that a breakdown in relations between the UN and UNITA meant that Savimbi's generals had not given their clearance for the flights. UNITA has never accepted responsibility for shooting down either plane.

On February 9, 1999 Marie Wilkinson flew to Luanda with her daughters to attend a memorial for the victims of flights UN806 and UN806A. They stayed a night with John Nagel's family and a night at Johnny's old cabin at the Transafrik camp. The ceremony was held at the UN headquarters in the capital. Relatives of the victims flew in from all over the world. The elderly mother of one of the Russian mechanics gripped Marie's hand tightly throughout the service, muttering angrily.

For Marie the service provided little comfort; if anything, being around the families of the other crew and passengers made grief even worse. 'As the captain's wife, you feel some sort of responsibility because he was in charge of the aeroplane,' she told me.

On her return to South Africa, Marie organized a second memorial service for her husband and son. A bagpiper played 'Amazing Grace', as Hilton had requested for his 'box party'. His friends drank too much and fondly recalled his eccentricities and pranks. Later, Marie cleared out Hilton's room, and gave away many of his possessions, including his cherished Brno rifle, given to him by Johnny when he left school. She sold the family home, moved into a small apartment in a gated compound in a nearby suburb and found a job in the export department of a chemical company. And she tried to dim the world by drinking a bottle of wine each night. 'Losing a husband is one thing, but losing a son is totally something else,' Marie said. 'I had tremendous anger. And I knew that John and Hilton were still rotting in that godforsaken place.'

During her loneliest moments she would listen to Hilton's voice, locked inside a tape on the telephone answering machine. Callers to the Wilkinson home can even today hear his gravelly greeting: 'Hello there. This is the Wilkinson residence. Please go ahead after the tone and have a good day.'

One afternoon in November 2006, Marie Wilkinson took a call at work. She was asked if she was related to Captain John Wilkinson and Hilton Wilkinson. 'My immediate thought was: "They're alive!" It seems crazy but I had always imagined that I would see the two of them casually walking into the house one day.'

The call was from a woman at South Africa's Department of Foreign Affairs. She told Marie that the UN had, finally, begun formal attempts to identify the victims of the two air crashes and that what was required were DNA samples from the victims' relatives.

The UN teams arriving at the crash sites in January 1999 had collected human remains and sent them to the South African Police Service's forensic science laboratory in Pretoria. There, DNA profiles from twelve people had been collected from bone fragments but nothing more had been done to aid the process of identification. In 2004, with the war in Angola at an end, a Norwegian medical doctor named Christen Halle was asked to investigate the case by the United Nations. He decided that both crash sites should be exhumed and the human remains found there added to those already being held in

Pretoria. In October 2006, after more than a year of planning, a specialist recovery team flew into Huambo, one of its members being the old Afrikaner military man Waal de Waal.

At the crash sites, numerous human bones were discovered, the largest being a femur nine inches long. They were placed in a body bag, which was covered with a United Nations flag and flown to South Africa.

Finding and then contacting the families of the victims was problematic. In the Philippines, appeals went out on national television. In Bolivia, national radio was used. By February 2007, twelve sets of relatives of the twenty-three victims had been located. Most of the families not traced were Angolans. The Angolan government had little interest in the project; to this day it has refused to give consent to a UN memorial stone being laid at each crash site.

Marie gave a blood sample for her son, Hilton; her daughter Judith for John. When the results came back there were six positive matches. The Zambian policewoman, the Namibian army officer, the Bolivian flight engineer Carloa Melgar, Ramon Dumlao and his fellow Filipino Bernabe Vicarme. And Hilton.

From Marie Wilkinson's house in Johannesburg it is a short drive to the Pretoria highway. Heading north, the international airport slips by on the right, and then you pass through miles of yellow veld, small factories and new housing developments in the distance. Eventually, you reach the Pretoria East cemetery. Inside, the trees are bare and the dry winter grass crunches underfoot. Men in overalls fill in a grave, shovelling soil; mourners in black leave the cemetery and walk slowly towards their cars.

The marble and granite tombstones are set out in neat rows. Most are engraved with biblical verses in Afrikaans. Headstone K473, erected in April 2007, is not. Instead, there is a flight number, UN806, and a date, December 26, 1999. Underneath are fourteen names; the sixth down is John A Wilkinson. A second row of names is listed opposite the first, beneath another flight number: UN806A, and a second date, January 2, 1999. The fourth name from the top is Hilton Wilkinson. It is his remains that are buried a few feet beneath. At the bottom of the tombstone is a single line: THEY DIED FOR PEACE IN ANGOLA.

That may have been true of Johnny Wilkinson, perhaps, but of Hilton?

I recalled my recent flight out of Huambo, where I'd seen a crew member wearing a black peaked cap that said TRANSAFRIK: HERCULES. We chatted and he told me his name was Jaime Oliveira. He had been a loadmaster with Transafrik until quite recently. On Christmas Eve 1998, he had flown with Johnny – two days before the crash. He invited me to his flat in downtown Luanda, and told me of how he had seen Hilton at the airport the day before his final flight. Oliveira recognized him because he had flown as a passenger on one of Hilton's Balmoral flights a year or so before. They talked briefly about the missing plane. Hilton was 'calm and very determined', not at all despondent.

'The son was a young man,' Oliveira said as we sat in his cramped living room, facing a wooden bar-counter on which stood a bottle of whisky and a replica of a Transafrik cargo plane. 'He had a career. But he came back for his father.'

He looked at me with sad eyes.

'The son came, and the son died.' ■

---

www.granta.com
Jason Cowley talks to Xan Rice

FICTION

MORE AFRAID OF YOU

Joshua Ferris

ILLUSTRATION BY TOM GAULD

On Bainbridge Island, across the Puget Sound from Seattle, there are two modes of living: downtown and inland. The downtown way of life centres near the ferry that brings tourists and residents over from the mainland. Here you'll find a lively strip of art galleries, bookstores, boutiques and restaurants, and in the summer you can sit outside at the pub and look on the sailboats anchored in the marina while eating the fresh fish of the Pacific Northwest. Wing Point Country Club is nearby, as is a complex of high-end condos and culs-de-sac of quaint clapboard houses. Lucinda Wagner lived in one such house with her husband Paul. They had commissioned a man-made pond in the backyard where wild frogs pounded out throaty calls during the mating season so loudly it sometimes woke her from a dead sleep. But this was to be expected on an island that offered in high contrast a second way of life.

Lucinda's mother, Tess, lived inland among the island's ancient forests. Tess's house, set back from Miller Road in a woody clearing, operated on a septic tank and drew water from a well. A spiky crown of cedars and Douglas firs kept the house well shaded for all but an hour or two in the summertime. Nearby the Grand Forest, with its damp air and overhung vegetation, marked the island as still belonging to nature, no matter the waterfront art galleries and coffee shops. Tess owned a mother-daughter house, but occupied only the smaller, three-room studio while renting the upstairs to tenants. Her most recent tenants had moved out, however, and at the time of her dissolution, she was having difficulty filling the upstairs vacancy and the main rental remained empty.

'I can't find Ambrose,' Tess told her daughter over the phone. Lucinda was due at Harborview in an hour. She had just finished her shower and stood draped in towels at the kitchen counter as her morning coffee spat and hissed. She removed the carafe prematurely and retreated to her bedroom with only half a cup. She listened to her mother give her the details of the missing cat. It had been twenty-four hours and Ambrose never missed a meal.

'Are you sure he isn't inside the house?' asked Lucinda, sitting down on the bed with her coffee and recalling how Ambrose's last disappearance was only a temporary hiatus on a stack of Robert's old clothes, folded on the top shelf of the closet.

'I've looked,' said Tess. 'The place isn't very big, you know.'

'Remember where we found him last time?'

'I looked there, Lucy. He's not there.'

Lucinda sighed, but not so her mother could hear. 'Tell you what,' she said. 'I have to make the 8.30 ferry, but I don't have anything but rounds, so after rounds I'll come back and you and I can look for Ambrose.'

'You can't come now?'

'It's important that I see my patients, Mom.'

'You'll come over right after?'

'Promise.'

That was the summer the hummingbirds went missing. For all

the years Tess had owned the house, a hummingbird feeder hung outside the northern window. She sat at the kitchen table every morning and marvelled at those bright elegant birds. That summer, though, she had seen only one or two hovering over the feed dish.

'Only one or two, Lucy, three at the most,' the older woman had informed her daughter as soon as she noticed. 'Do you think it might be weather patterns?'

'It could be.'

'Where do hummingbirds migrate from? Do they migrate? They must migrate.'

'I think so.'

'You know what I think it is? All the developments downtown. You can't do all that to this beautiful island without consequences. And I'm afraid it's the hummingbirds that have to suffer.'

'I doubt that's it, Mom.'

'Well, I know something's going on, Lucy, when I only see one or two hummingbirds.'

As the summer progressed, talk of the hummingbirds gave way to talk of the squirrels. The squirrels were also missing. They were not scurrying across Tess's yard or bounding up and down the trees. They were not springing from branch to branch or chasing each other with the electric-current rhythms of summers past.

'I can't help but think it's all these developments,' she told Lucinda over the phone. 'They've driven the squirrels away.'

'The developments would drive them further inland, Mom. If anything, you should be seeing more of them from the developments.'

'Well, it's not natural. Please explain to me then where the squirrels have gone.'

Lucinda was in a chaise longue by the artificial pond. She set her magazine down and gazed out at the plastic reeds planted in the water, the lily pads and the miniature water mill gently churning.

'Tell me how you're noticing that the squirrels have all gone missing. How did you become aware of this trend?'

'I'm looking out at the lawn,' she said, 'and I'm telling you, I haven't seen more than two squirrels the entire summer.'

'Well, I agree that's weird.'

'And not one chipmunk.'

'No chipmunks either?'

'This place was crawling with chipmunks last summer. This year I haven't seen so much as a hole in the ground.'

Lucinda ended the call with her mother just as her husband stepped outside and handed her a refreshed drink. She took a sip, crunching a little ice before speaking. 'Mom's going faster than I thought.'

After her rounds Lucinda returned to the island from the mainland and drove north on Miller Road past the Grand Forest. The tall trees let in little light, so despite a sunny day the air coming through the windows was cool, almost wintry. She slowed at the sight of the familiar mailbox and climbed the gravel road that wound around to her mother's secluded house.

In years past Tess and Robert, Lucinda's stepfather, had been the only residents in their Miller Road clearing, but then the land was parcelled off and developers tore down decades-old trees to build new homes, and now there were six or seven houses clustered together. Tess had disliked the loss of privacy and Robert lamented the felled trees – but Robert was dead now and heavy foliage still buffered one house from the next. Tess's house remained more or less in the wild, home to squirrels and hummingbirds and rabbits and chipmunks.

Lucinda pulled up to the house to find Tess in the yard sitting on a stepladder. She was wearing a housecoat made of a cheap plush velvet that easily picked up white thread and other stray clingy bits. It was out of season but Tess wore it anyway, keeping the housecoat clasped at her neck with a choking hand. She clenched hard enough to bring out thin white tendons and heavy blue veins. She wore thick sweatpants under the housecoat, the hems of which were tucked into wool socks. The sight of her mother on the stepladder burdened by winter wear would have been odd if Lucinda were seeing it for the first time. As it was, she stepped out of the car and said simply, 'Where is it?'

Tess pointed inside the house.

Lucinda stepped into the small hallway laid out with a narrow Persian runner. It led to a strip of tilework off to the left that was the kitchen floor. There she located the Tupperware bowl. She lifted the bowl and a small spider immediately darted for her feet. Startled, she backed up to gain the advantage and then brought the toe of her shoe down on the manic black movement. Her dislike of spiders did not border on the pathological, as it did with her mother, and killing them always made her feel a little guilty.

'Did you get it?' asked Tess through the window.

'I got it.'

'Let me see.'

Tess was no longer able to do the daily chores – dusting and vacuuming, overturning the furniture, lifting rugs and beating them with a broom – necessary to keep her house spider-free. She saw more of them now than ever. She tormented herself with visions of a spider creeping along her shoulder and falling down her nightgown, sneaking up on her vulnerable flesh under the toilet bowl as she sat frail and slow-moving, or making contact with her feet as she lay under the covers at night. Lucinda helped her mother with her housework when she could, but it was impossible to beat the rugs and sweep under the furniture every day. She came over when her mother called; she readied her shoe; she squashed the little bugger. Then she gathered it in a paper towel and threw it away.

When a spider did not stick around for Lucinda to show up, she came down on an imaginary one, so that Tess would not feel the anxiety of an escaped spider. For a long time Tess failed to catch on. One night, however, she asked to see the remains and when Lucinda had nothing to show her, Tess began to require visual proof.

'Oh, that's disgusting,' said Tess, after re-entering the studio and peering into the paper towel. 'Are they more scary alive, or more disgusting dead?'

Lucinda tossed the paper towel in the bin under the sink. 'So when was the last time you saw Ambrose, Mom?'

'If I knew where, I'd go look for him there.'

'No, not where, Mom. When.'

'Oh,' said Tess, who began to think.

Her thinking was interrupted by a noise coming from the bedroom.

'Is that the sound?' said Lucinda, turning.

'That's it!' cried Tess. 'That's it! Finally! See, I'm not making it up.'

'No one ever claimed you were making it up,' said Lucinda. She moved inside the bedroom. 'Where is it coming from, exactly?'

'I think it's coming from the closet,' said Tess.

The closet was an open doorway leading to a small cluttered space. There was no door to seal it off from the bedroom. Lucinda entered and Tess followed and with the two of them inside among the boxes and the hanging clothes, there was no space left to move. They stood still and listened.

The clawing was muted but raucous. The two women in the closet were buffered from whatever was on the other side of the wall, but the scratching was proof of something alive and determined. The relentless consistency of it – dumb, instinctual and monotonous – disturbed them both.

'Told you,' said Tess.

'I really never doubted you, Mom.'

'What do you think it is?'

'I think you're right. It's probably a raccoon. And the reason you haven't been hearing it during the day is because raccoons are nocturnal.'

'The reason you haven't been hearing it during the day is because you never come around.'

'What do you mean? I stop by every day.'

'For five minutes,' said Tess. 'World's Greatest Daughter. Daughter of the Year, ladies and gentlemen.'

Lucinda frowned and took her mother by the hand. She led Tess out of the closet, sat her down at the kitchen table and made her a sandwich. Tess would often skip lunch on days Lucinda was in surgery.

Despite her mother's suspicions, Lucinda had believed her when Tess began saying two or three weeks earlier that a raccoon had burrowed under the deck on the second level and was scratching at her bedroom wall as if to get in. Now that she'd heard it for herself, she thought it explained Ambrose's disappearance. There was little hope when a cat ran afoul of one of the island's raccoons.

'We'll find Ambrose, Mom,' she said, setting the sandwich down in front of her mother. She bent and kissed the top of her mother's disappearing grey hair.

After Robert's heart attack Tess cried herself to sleep until there were no more tears to cry. Then she lay in bed with eyes wide open, the impenetrable darkness all around her, and spoke to God out loud of all the business between them. She had trouble sleeping until the medicine took effect, and in the time between lights out and real sleep, she had an active, lonely, ruminating, sorrowful mind. She found herself rephrasing sentences spoken thirty years ago so that memory of them no longer caused her shame or embarrassment; she apologized to those who were dead or lost for slights forgotten long ago; she said the names of her two dead husbands aloud. On the day she first heard the thing on the other side of her wall, she had taken to singing herself to sleep with half-remembered lyrics from songs of her youth.

She sprung to life at the first sounds of the animal, the dirt-blind rooting and clawing going on behind her. She felt the need to leap up and run away. She also felt an equally persuasive, self-protecting impulse to remain as still as possible. She froze with uncertainty. But of course it didn't matter what she did: the animal was on the other side of the wall.

Her fear gave way a few nights later to curiosity. What was the creature and what was its business so far down in the earth? What was in the comfort of a wall?

In another night or two she came to believe that the animal's actions were intuitive, maternal: it was nesting in preparation of giving birth. After establishing that fact, she could not be shaken from it, and along with it came an unexpected kinship with the animal. Before a week of nights had passed, she had come to look forward to the sound as something almost companionable before sleep.

Lucinda spent the rest of the afternoon at the Miller Road house and then cooked her mother dinner. She left just after nightfall. An hour later Tess took her medication. Still dressed in her housecoat, she got into bed and waited for the pills to take effect. Soon the sound on the other side of the wall started up. She listened for a while and was on the brink of drifting off when the sound broke through.

She was awake in an instant. Everything that initially frightened her about the sound returned, as if she were hearing it for the first time. The room had life in it, unknown and unpredictable life. As she lay with open eyes useless in the dark, she pictured a paw, black and clawed, boring through the drywall, stirring the still air with a crude curiosity. A few minutes of silence passed, and the scratching started up again, sharper now, as if cotton had been removed from her ears. Raw silence again, and then another round of clawing, a sound almost of shaving away. Plaster from the drywall fell to the floor. She felt it palpably: it was standing inside the closet.

'Robert!' she whispered. 'Lucy?'

She heard a series of soft steps. Her fear engorged like a sickened heart. The room turned very, very small. Even if she could have moved there was nowhere for her to go. Then the creature did exactly what she feared the most: it walked inside the bedroom. Then it did the unfathomable: it began to climb the bed.

The first step placed a light pressure on the mattress, causing a gentle shift in weight down by her feet. There came another step up near her knee, a good distance from the first step. A third settled on the other side of her trembling legs and yet a fourth step landed near her left hand. With the fifth, the mattress hung considerably heavier. A sixth step arrived, landing directly on her thin, frail forearm and, failing to gain a purchase, slid off. It took everything she had not to cry out. A round shiny mass moved over her legs. Seventh and eighth almost weightless steps settled far from one another until, one by one, the pressure started to reverse itself. Step by step it climbed off the bed on to the wall. Tess did not look. Her eyes were wide open, but she saw nothing. Her body quivered. She had furrowed her brow with fear and her lips called out mutely the names of the living and the dead. She remained like that until daylight.

Lucinda's pager went off three times in ten minutes, and by the time she could break away it had logged seven calls from the Miller Road house. She spoke to Tess from a common area where other doctors were eating lunch and working on laptops.

'What's wrong?' she asked.

'It broke through the wall,' said Tess. There was a quality in her voice, an affectless tone that Lucinda recognized as belonging to the recently traumatized.

'What broke through the wall?'

'Not a raccoon.'

Lucinda asked her mother what it was if not a raccoon.

'Help me!' her mother cried.

'What? Mom?'

'Help me!' said Tess. Then the phone went dead.

Lucinda hurried out of Harborview. She ran down to the dock and had to wait an agonizing twenty minutes for the next ferry. She tried calling Tess but the machine kept picking up. She would have called Paul but he was away on business. She almost began to cry with frustration. Once on the island, she drove down Miller Road past the Grand Forest at twice the speed limit. At last she pulled up to the house. She was relieved to find her mother sitting on the stepladder in the middle of the lawn.

'I've been calling and calling,' said Lucinda. 'Why haven't you picked up your phone?'

'I'm not going inside until that hole is boarded up.'

'What hole?'

'Last night I was crawled over by a giant spider,' said Tess.

Lucinda shut the car door and began to walk towards her mother. Tess kept the housecoat clinched at the neck and in her other hand held an aerosol can of insect spray. A wave of pity and tenderness swept over Lucinda as she realized that this was what her mother had come to. 'A spider?' she said.

'A giant spider. Go look at that hole if you don't believe me.'

Lucinda entered the studio, which she found dishevelled. There was a blouse on the floor which she had never seen on her mother, and the Japanese scroll hung off-kilter on the wall. She stepped inside the bathroom and opened Tess's medicine cabinet. There were a dozen medications, including Latravosil. Despite the advice of Tess's internist, Lucinda did not agree that her mother should be on Latravosil, which sometimes did funny things to the brain. She pocketed the pill container and shut the mirror door, which resumed its reflection of the shower curtain. She left the bathroom.

In the closet she got down on her hands and knees and shone the kitchen flashlight at the hole. There it was, larger than she would have imagined, more precisely circular, and damp, too, as if gnawed around the edges. Would the raccoon have chewed at the wall?

She found a piece of plywood in the garage and with a handful of nails covered the hole. Then she led her wary mother through the door, down the hallway and into the bedroom closet where she could see for herself that there was nothing more to fear. Afterwards she removed the bottle of Latravosil from her pocket and said, 'Mom, I want you to stop taking these.'

'You don't believe me about the spider.'

'It's not that I don't believe you,' said Lucinda. 'It's that this is a strong medicine with a lot of side effects and I was never convinced you should be on it in the first place.'

'A spider,' said Tess, 'came into my room last night, crawled on to my bed, and stepped over me with its eight legs.'

Lucinda did not want to contradict her. 'How big was the spider?'

'Bigger than a raccoon. Half the size of the bed. I don't know.'

'How could a spider that big crawl through that hole?'

'They can make themselves very small,' said Tess. 'I saw a special on it. But that's not what you should be asking. How does a spider even get that big? That's what you should be asking.'

Lucinda led her mother out of the closet and back into the kitchen. The older woman was still clutching the can of bug spray when she sat down at the table. She looked around her, darted her eyes over the nearby surfaces and across the floor around her feet. Lucinda made her lunch and then remained with her throughout the afternoon. The two women had dinner together for the second night in a row. Tess drank her nightly glass of wine as Lucinda persuaded her to cut down on the Latravosil, to take half a pill that night instead of the prescribed dosage. As dusk deepened, Lucinda noticed her mother staring more frequently out of the window, not at anything in particular but at the darkness itself. The natural fortification of the tall trees let in none of the moon. She might have been gazing into a startling and inconceivable void.

Lucinda tried to convince her mother, not for the first time that day, to come stay at her house, but Tess refused. She did not want to abandon her memories. She did not want to give up what little was left of Robert's presence.

'I know what happens,' she said. 'One step out of the house is one step into the grave.'

'But it's just for one night, Mom.'

'It always starts with just one night.'

Then she turned suddenly to look at Lucinda with tears in her eyes. 'Stay with me,' she said. Her delicately boned hands gripped her daughter's. 'Stay just until I know the noise isn't coming back.'

Lucinda sat in the corner of her mother's bedroom in a hardback chair under a cushion support and read the day's newspaper while her mother struggled for sleep. Her occasional glances at Tess revealed eyes wide open, a vacant stare at the ceiling, or at the wall when she turned. She wrestled with her pillows, she flinched for no reason, she said random words out loud. Whenever she spoke, Lucinda looked up, but she quickly realized that the words had not been intended for her.

After an hour of lying in bed, Tess said, 'I haven't heard it.'

'You must have scared it away,' said Lucinda.

They sank back into silence. Another hour and Tess was asleep. Lucinda stayed an additional hour to make sure her mother didn't stir, and then she removed the can of bug spray from her bed and quietly retreated from the room. She had a labour-intensive operation to perform in the morning on a man who had come from Arizona with a tumour in his brain and she too needed to sleep.

Tess did not stir until late in the night, an hour or so before dawn, after the medicine had seen its half-life come and go. Initially woozy with sleep, she quickly recalled the previous night, and her mind tingled with alarm. The sound that had roused her was not a mindless rooting behind the wall but a crinkling, a familiar plastic rustle. She could not immediately place the sound, though she knew it came from somewhere inside the house.

It kept up for ten seconds, twenty, and then all went silent. She searched her bed for the can of bug spray. She didn't find it. She put her hand down to the floor and patted the carpet. She moved her hand forward six inches. She felt to the left and then to the right. She moved forward and then back, under the bed. She reached as far back as she could go without tumbling off the bed, and then she stopped. Tears formed in her eyes.

She knew that sound. That sound was the rustle of the shower curtain. Something had been moving the shower curtain.

They boarded up the hole, but it had never left.

She withdrew her hand. A moment later, she felt the bed bend under the first step. It landed not down by her feet as it had the night before, but up by her shoulder. She clinched her eyes shut and began to cry as soundlessly as possible when it stepped near her knees and again on the other side of her, hoisting up its odd lithe weight much faster than it had the previous night. This was nature coming to exact its revenge – but then why did the spider not head downtown to bother all those people in condominiums? She could not tell just where all the legs had been planted but she could feel the pulsing heat of its bulby abdomen.

Then it touched her. It was as if the branch of a tree, soggy at the tip, ran across her forehead. The leg brushed her ear and settled on the pillow, catching some of her hair underneath. She could not help herself, she cried out. The cry was loud and useless because she could not move, she could only cry, and when she heard herself, she remembered the one fact that scared her most about spiders – that they had fangs, fangs like snakes or bats – and now that she had cried the spider would dig its fangs into her. But instead of attacking her, it leapt in the air. It leapt and landed on the wall and scurried across the ceiling, and the last she saw of it was its shadow retreating, leg after leg, over the top of the doorjamb and into the other room.

The next morning Lucinda woke at dawn, showered and drove out to the Miller Road house to check on her mother. She expected Tess to be sleeping in the murky dawn of another Pacific Northwest morning, but as she rounded the last turn on the gravel road, she saw her mother high on the stepladder with feet on the final rung, sweatpants and housecoat on, neck sheathed in a scarf, and a winter hat with hunter's flaps on her head. She had placed the stepladder inside a kiddie pool and filled the pool with water. Next to the pool sat a two-gallon gas can. Her right index finger was poised on the trigger of the bug spray. Lucinda stepped out of the car. She noticed the changes to the house: the front door was open, every window was open, every screen had been removed. It was six in the morning.

'What's going on? What happened?'

'It never left.'

'What never left?' Lucinda looked down at the slightly discoloured water in the kiddie pool. 'Mom, did you pour gasoline into the pool?'

'Find it, Lucy!'

'The spider?'

'It's in the shower!'

Lucinda reached up and touched her mother's face. 'Okay,' she said. 'But then you have to come stay with me, okay? You cannot be sitting in a pool of gasoline water at six in the morning because a spider's run you out of the house.'

'You believe me then?'

'Yes, I believe you. Will you come stay with me?'

'Check the shower!' said Tess.

Lucinda left her mother and entered the house. She stepped on the runner in the hallway and stopped. The house was in greater disarray than it had been the day before. More clothes were scattered on the floor, one of her mother's antique candlesticks had fallen to the rug, and just beyond that, all the *Prevention* magazines and *National Geographics* had spilled off the coffee table. When Lucinda realized she had stopped moving, she shook off her disquiet and continued into the studio. She approached the doorway leading into the bathroom slowly. She stood in front of the shower curtain, her back reflected in the medicine cabinet. She didn't fling the curtain open. She inched quietly up to the edge and peeked in. The shower was empty.

She moved through the house more easily after that, turning on lights, getting on her hands and knees and feeling under the furniture. She looked under the bed and in the closet, in every corner of every room, even inside cabinets and drawers. She opened the utility closet and shuffled through piles of clothing. She came out ten minutes later and assured her mother that the house was free of spiders.

'What about the one on the kitchen counter?' asked Tess. 'It's just a little one. I saw it this morning on my way out. I put a glass over it. I'm not going in there until you kill it.'

Lucinda had very little time if she was to make the next ferry. She considered the somewhat extreme alternative of postponing the operation. But she hated to inconvenience her patient like that. He would have restricted his diet the day before and, more importantly, prepared himself mentally for the ordeal. So she hurried back inside to kill the spider under the glass. When she stood before the clear tumbler, however, peering into it, she saw nothing. She lifted the glass. Nothing scurried out. She decided to come down hard on the counter anyway and the sound drew her mother to the window.

'Did you get it?' she asked.

'I got it.'

'Let me see.'

Tess entered the house without any coaxing, which Lucinda took as a good sign: her mother would not spend the day out on the stepladder in the kiddie pool. She could rest inside the house until Lucinda finished at the hospital, and then Lucinda would come directly home and pick her up. For there was no question that she needed to be picked up: when Lucinda showed her the paper towel where the remains of the imaginary spider should have been, her mother peered down into it and drew away. 'Oh,' she gasped.

'Disgusting.'

Later that morning Tess returned the screens that earlier she had ripped from their frames. It was not easy work. The latches confused her, and at least two of the screens no longer appeared to fit in the windows. She stood on the stepladder peering up at the eaves which harboured God-knows-what and almost lost her balance. She dizzied easily. Sometimes she managed to coax the screen back into its grooves and then she heard a satisfying *click* and knew the thing to be in place, but other times it occurred to her that in all her long life she had never encountered a more awkward physical object than a window screen. To be safe, when she returned inside, she shut and locked all the windows.

By noon the sun had breached the tips of the cedars surrounding the house and, though she was sweltering, she refused to remove her heavy clothing. She opened one window in order to move around the still, hot air of the studio. She sat near the window to keep a vigilant eye on it but as the afternoon dragged on she grew tired and dozed. She awoke with hunger pains to discover that the cool air of evening had settled. She stood to close the window and saw with a start that that particular screen, which had caused her the most trouble earlier in the day, had slipped out of its grooves. She looked through the bare opening into the darkening air and the sight of the screen on the lawn caused her to shudder. She turned to scan the walls and ceiling and floor, found nothing and turned back. But it didn't matter now. There was no way she could remain in the studio.

She turned on a nearby lamp so that she could see her way to the phone. She stood at the console table as the phone rang three times. She tried her best to ignore the shadows in her peripheral vision. At last the operator picked up. A confusing exchange led the operator to say that there was no one named Lucinda currently registered at that hospital.

'No, she's not the patient,' said Tess. 'She's the doctor.'

'Oh, she's the doctor. I see.'

'She's the one doing the surgery.'

'I see that now,' said the operator. 'Let me just put you on hold.'

Two long minutes passed before the operator returned. She informed Tess that Lucinda was still in surgery. Tess left a message with the operator. She wanted her daughter to know that she would be waiting for her in the upstairs studio on her return to the island. With that, she hung up.

Inside the console table's little drawer she kept the keys to the upstairs rental. She opened the drawer and removed the keys. Then she walked around the partition that separated the living room from the kitchen. She grabbed a half a can of fruit cocktail and a container of cottage cheese from the refrigerator. She was just about to leave the kitchen when she remembered the need for a spoon and fork. She turned and opened the drawer and thought that she should also take a plate up with her. She could sit in the middle of the upstairs kitchen and have dinner and wait for Lucinda. Before she had the drawer shut, she saw in her peripheral vision a leg crawl out into the doorway.

She dropped the fruit cocktail and cottage cheese and cried out. She cried the name of her dead sister, her two dead husbands, her absent daughter, the name of her house cat, who had always known what to do with a spider but who was now hanging, she was sure, in some massive web, rotting with the chipmunks and the squirrels and the hummingbirds. She called the names of her mother and father, the name of God, the name of a boy who once retied a bow in her hair – the names of everyone who had abandoned her at the moment she needed them most, the moment the spider stepped forward with its silent weightless touch and turned to look at her crouching in the kitchen.

Before the new owners took possession, Lucinda drove out to the house and walked around it a final time. Her mother's stuff had been moved out, sold off, given away, and now the house itself had been bought. Lucinda was there for purely sentimental reasons: the cedars, the pine needles, the cool air she could not experience with the same immediacy downtown, and which reminded her of her mother. She wanted to take the house in one more time before it became only a memory. The last load of her mother's possessions sat in her trunk and she would soon drive off and never return.

It remains a lovely house to this day. If you find yourself on the island, I recommend driving inland down Miller Road past the Grand Forest and having a look at it. The exact address is 11954 Miller Road, Bainbridge Island, Washington. It is the house located at the end of the gravel road and is now owned by relatives of mine. My uncle Woody and aunt Cindy spend most of the year in Indonesia teaching in a school for international children. They rent out the upper part of the house and keep the lower half vacant, and beautifully furnished, for their return in summer. My uncle's '58 Chrysler Windsor sits in the garage, and his Mercedes station wagon kicks up a nasty billow of diesel smoke on starting. In the backyard, where this past summer I played catch with my cousin's fiancé, whose name is also Josh, the roots of the cedars run so deep they threaten the septic tank's drain field, a repair that will cost my aunt and uncle a small fortune in a few years. But those cedars are really something, choked with twisted ivy and sculpted by nature with a marvellously macabre and breathtaking imagination. They also serve to hide the weather-beaten shed that was there nineteen years ago, when my aunt and uncle bought the house from Lucinda. I have heard the story of her and what happened to her mother from my uncle Woody, who is good friends with Lucinda's husband Paul.

Lucinda spent a final moment in back on the wide step of the pine deck, admiring those same cedars. She recalled climbing them as a girl with her father before he died of a heart attack. They are trees made to be climbed on. She had swung on the lower branches and straddled the thicker ones as if they were a horse. Now she stood up, walked over to her favourite tree and touched it. The image of finding her mother crouched in the kitchen and the bad memories of her final days in the hospital had been replaced by earlier times, better times, which prevailed now as she said goodbye to the trees. Then she turned to walk back to the car.

On her way something caught her eye and drew her towards the side of the deck. The smell became more potent as she neared the dead animal. Its hind legs and curled tail lay rotting in the open air between the edge of the house and the white latticework that walled the deck in. She retrieved a strong stick from near the shed and dragged the animal fully out into the light of day, though she already knew what it was: the biggest raccoon she had ever seen, its claws like a bear's, its face contorted by death into a stony, rotting snarl. Lucinda sat on her haunches with the stick in hand, regretful that she had not better protected her mother from her hallucinations, wishful that she had been more attentive, and sorry for Ambrose, who must have met a terrible end.

What Lucinda didn't know, but what my poor uncle would soon learn for himself, was that the spider lived on in the shed behind the house. ■

POPPERFOTO/GETTY IMAGES

Hydrogen bomb test at high altitude over Christmas Island, May 15, 1957

BOMB GONE

Fifty years ago, Britain tested its first H-bomb on Christmas Island. But at what cost?

Owen Sheers

We had been driving along the Bay of Wrecks on the eastern coast of Christmas Island for over an hour and a half when we saw the flock of terns. A few were scattered over the pale tarmac in front of us, but thousands more were wheeling and hovering in the air, suspended above the saltbushes of the island's interior. 'Sooty Terns,' Perry Langston said from the passenger seat beside me. I stopped the car and turned off the engine, leaving the air conditioning washing over us. 'Must be one of their nesting grounds.' For a few minutes we sat there watching them contract and expand in the air. At their tightest point they looked more like a swarm than a flock, turning the sky a flurry of living black.

I got out of the car and the sudden heat of the day hit me again. In the distance, to my left, I could hear the roaring of the reef. On my right a coconut plantation frayed the inland horizon. I began walking towards the terns. They were unperturbed by my presence and I was soon standing directly beneath them. Their high-pitched cries pulsed like electricity in the air. I looked through the edges of the flock towards our destination at the island's south-eastern point. Down there, at the end of the road, was a tapering slip of land, still marked on some maps as 'Ground Zero', off which, fifty years ago, Britain exploded its first hydrogen bomb.

The bomb had been the fourth in a series of nine nuclear and thermonuclear tests, codenamed 'Grapple', conducted in the central Pacific between May 1957 and September 1958. Britain had already developed its own atomic bomb, tested at Maralinga in the Australian desert two years earlier. But the test limit in Australia was fifty kilotons. In their bid to keep pace with the Americans and the Soviets, the British wanted to develop a hydrogen bomb many times more powerful than anything tested in Australia. The first three Grapple tests were conducted off Malden Island. These were airbursts over the ocean, all in the kiloton range. The next six tests were conducted off or over Christmas Island, and of these, three were in the megaton range. This was why Britain had been willing to send 14,000 men and countless tons of equipment to a coral atoll in the middle of the Pacific: to prove to the world and to itself that it could maintain its position and influence among the powers of a new world order.

In the reading I'd done before coming to the island, I'd often found references to its birds. Christmas Island is famous for both the number of species and the size of its colonies. Eyewitness accounts of the Grapple tests often mentioned them. Captain Cook, on first discovering the island on Christmas Eve 1777, was immediately struck by the 'infinite numbers of a new species of tern'. So far though, in the three days I'd been on the island, I'd seen only cormorants and the solitary frigate birds of the northern beaches, their wings like finely turned blades as they slid off the currents with the motion of tethered kites.

I looked up into the birds again. At times one would fly so close I could see its tongue, the layering of its feathers, the light in its eye. Looking back down along the road, I saw Perry had also got out of the car. He was walking towards me, his white beard and yellow

Brazil football shirt bright in the sun. As usual he was talking, but I couldn't hear him. I couldn't hear anything except the cries of the birds. It felt as if I were caught in a woven cage of sound and it was then, standing at the eye of that feathered storm, that I began to understand.

The British, Fijian and New Zealand servicemen stationed on Christmas Island during the tests had witnessed each of the six explosions from the decks of ships at sea or from the island's northern beaches and coconut groves. Sitting in rows on the sand, they'd been ordered to look away from the blast at the moment of detonation. No one had been able to order the birds to do the same.

In 1957 Paul Ahpoy was a twenty-one-year-old sailor in the Fiji Royal Naval Volunteer Reserve. Over the next year he was one of the few servicemen to witness all six of the Christmas Island tests. It was Paul who first told me about the birds, when I met him at the office of the Fiji Nuclear Test Veterans Association in Suva, Fiji's capital.

'For several days after each test,' he explained, 'we would hear the birds flying into buildings and trees. They had been blinded, you see. By the flash.'

That flash, described by another veteran as a light that 'didn't just illuminate the universe, it *is* the universe', was so pervasive that even house birds were vulnerable. Mrs Sui Kiritome, who was living on Christmas Island at the time of the tests, had followed all the precautions recommended before a detonation. She and her husband had taken down any hanging pictures, left their doors and windows open and tried to ensure their animals were kept out of the light. On returning home from the Royal Navy frigate from which they'd witnessed the test, however, they'd found the doors blown off their hinges, the windows broken, a concrete wall split open and their pet frigate bird running around the house, blind.

Birds' eyes are often on the sides of their heads, giving them almost 360-degree vision. Even if flying away from the blast, they would still have been blinded by the flash of detonation. Nobody knows the numbers affected. Some servicemen, such as Barry Cotton, tried to make amends however they could.

'After the light flash, not a sound, nothing. Then suddenly the air was filled with screaming birds. We commandeered our lorry and driver and some heavy sticks and spades and went off into the interior of the island to do a bad day's work. We killed all the blind and maimed birds we could find and buried them. There were hundreds and they were beautiful, but dead. I think we got drunk afterwards.'

The chain of events that led to the blinding of the birds can be traced back to August 6, 1945 when, in a bid to bring the war with Japan to an end, the US Air Force detonated the atomic bomb 'Little Boy' above Hiroshima. From that moment, the world entered the nuclear age and Britain was never going to want to be left behind. But after the passing of the McMahon Act by the US government in 1946, that's exactly what looked likely to happen. The Act made it a crime punishable by death to transmit any atomic information to any country, ending the wartime US–UK cooperation on nuclear development. Given the cold shoulder by its former ally, it was inevitable that in time Britain would try to explode its own hydrogen bomb somewhere in the world.

America had achieved its goal of a fully functioning hydrogen weapon during the 'Castle' series of tests on Bikini Atoll in the central Pacific in March 1954. During these tests, entire coral land masses within the Marshall Islands were obliterated and vast craters blown in the ocean floor. A miscalculation in the material used for the Castle 'Bravo' test meant the bomb registered fifteen megatons instead of the projected five. US servicemen, Marshall Islanders and the *Lucky Dragon*, a Japanese fishing vessel outside the danger zone, were all contaminated by radioactive fallout. When the *Lucky Dragon* returned to port in Japan, there was outrage. The only country to have been a victim of a nuclear weapon had been struck again.

Lewis Strauss, chairman of the US Atomic Energy Commission,

returned from the Bikini tests on March 31. On the same day he read out a statement in Washington. It was intended to calm the public, to assure them that those affected by the fallout would fully recover. It took just one question to unpick any reassurance he might have sown. Just how powerful, a journalist asked, could an H-bomb be?

'In effect,' Strauss answered, 'it can be made as large as you wish; as large as the military requirement demands. That is to say, an H-bomb can be made as...large enough to take out a city.'

'How big a city?' the journalist asked. 'Any city? New York?'

'The metropolitan area,' Strauss replied. 'Yes.'

The next day the *New York Times* ran the headline H-BOMB CAN WIPE OUT ANY CITY. A fierce public debate followed, drawing condemnation of nuclear testing from across the globe. Pope Pius XII used his 1954 Christmas message to call for international efforts to banish nuclear war. The United States, in so effectively testing its 'superbomb', had aroused international opposition that in only a few years would lead to a moratorium on testing in 1958 and to the Partial Test Ban Treaty of 1963.

In 1954, however, just four months after Strauss's press conference, Churchill's government signed Britain up to the development and testing of its own hydrogen bomb. Publicly, Britain appeared willing to join in discussions about a test ban, but behind the scenes, Sir William Penney, the head of the Atomic Weapons Research Establishment in Aldermaston, was being urged to develop a weapon, according to a general instruction from the Ministry of Supply, 'of very high power that is capable of production in reasonable quantity, that can be reasonably easily handled and maintained and that can be accurately delivered'. The only problem was, in 1954, Penney and his team didn't know how to make a hydrogen bomb or how long it would take to find out. What they did know was that time was tight. If Britain was to maintain its influence in the world, if America was to be persuaded to share its nuclear knowledge, then a megaton bomb must be developed and, crucially, tested quickly. Less than two years later, in February 1956, Air Commodore Wilfred Oulton was called to Air Command in London and given his brief for a new operation. 'I want you to go out and drop a bomb somewhere in the Pacific,' his commander, Air Vice-Marshal Lees, told him. 'And take a picture of it with a Brownie camera.'

Within a year, Oulton was expected to establish a fully operational base involving all three armed services at a remote location where Penney and his team could test their experimental weapon. Two possible archipelagos were on the table: the Kerguelen Islands in the southern Indian Ocean and Christmas Island in the central Pacific.

When you travel to Christmas Island it is easy to understand why it was Britain's first choice for the tests. Lying at the northern end of the Line Islands, one of three archipelagos that make up the Republic of Kiribati (pronounced 'Kirimbass'), it is isolated both from the world and from its own country. Kiribati is a nation of ocean, its borders marking out an area from east to west almost as wide as Australia. And yet there is very little of Kiribati: just 300 square miles of land in one and a half million square miles of ocean.

Before I left Britain I typed the I-Kiribati name for Christmas Island, 'Kiritimati', into Google Earth. I watched the Google globe spin on its axis and the screen zoom in on ocean, ocean, ocean, until eventually, literally out of the blue, Christmas Island appeared. It was beautiful: a skeleton of land around a latticework of internal lagoons, vividly green at its centre, fringed by beach echoed curve for curve by a white penumbra of reef. Zooming back out I looked at it again, lonely in all that sea, and understood why the Polynesians originally called it 'Abakiro', 'The Far Away Island'.

I'd been prepared for Christmas Island's isolation. I knew before I got there what a chance of land it was: one serviceman, arriving in 1957, was convinced that if the pilot of their Stratocruiser had deviated from his path by just a fraction of an inch, they'd have missed the island altogether. What I wasn't prepared for was how fragile it would look. Through the plane's window as I flew in from Fiji, just before dawn, it was no more than a shadow on the sea, so flat it seemed one shrug of the ocean would drown it forever. It seemed unlikely that such a place could have sustained a military operation the size of Grapple, let alone survived the thermonuclear explosions the operation had created.

An hour after my arrival I was standing on the shore of the island, my back to the blue-painted single-storey buildings of the Captain Cook Hotel. The waves before me were layered six or seven deep over the shallow reef. The larger ones broke further out in an unending dull roar. The smaller waves extinguished themselves at my feet, firing along the sand like lit fuses of gunpowder. The easterly trade winds pushing at these waves were the second reason, beyond the island's isolation, why Christmas became the site for the nuclear tests. After the contamination scare of Castle Bravo, the British government didn't want to take any chances. Christmas Island's regular easterly winds meant that even if something did go wrong, any fallout would be carried away west, dispersed across thousands of miles of ocean.

Today the hotel caters for the small groups of dedicated fly-fishermen who travel to Christmas to catch bonefish in the lagoons and giant travelley and tuna in the ocean offshore. The buildings and site behind me had once been the Task Force Officers' B mess. The rest of Main Camp would have stretched down the shoreline to my right: regimented rows of greenish-grey military tents coated with white coral dust. A Naafi, a hospital, a supply shop, lorries, cranes, bulldozers, laboratories, an outdoor cinema and even, at one point, a tent selling freshly caught fish and chips, a handwritten sign hammered into the ground at its entrance: FISSION CHIPS.

Around the curve of the beach, I'd already found the remains of one of Main Camp's churches. The salt-laced wind, time and local vandalism had left it roofless. Light switches hung from their sockets, a burnt-out gas canister lay in the chancel and a dead crab floated in the rusty water collected in the well of a shower. A blank rectangle of concrete below a sign, 'Daily Notices', marked the space where a board of events had once been embedded in the wall. In the opposite corner a pair of white clamshells had been set to resemble a pair of angel's wings above the original foundation stone:

THIS STONE WAS LAID ON 12TH SEPTEMBER 1958
BY REV E G ALSOP RAF, ON THE COMPLETION OF THIS CHURCH

It was in churches such as this that those killed during Operation Grapple were remembered. Stone plaques were set into the coral walls bearing the names of the young men who'd drowned swimming or fishing over the reef, or who'd been victims of accidents during the construction of the base, roads and airstrip. Considering the scale of the operation, these plaques were relatively few in number. Many veterans of the tests, though, would argue that the casualty lists are still growing. For these men, the end of the official operation on Christmas Island was only the beginning of their private battles with illness and grief, which for some would extend into future generations.

The tests conducted on Christmas were declared 'clean' by the Ministry of Defence. They were atmospheric airbursts in which no debris from the land or sea was contaminated. Any fallout was blown away from those stationed on Christmas Island or on boats at sea. This was, and is, the official line. Many veterans of the tests, however, do not agree. Since 1983, when the British Nuclear Test Veterans Association was formed, it and similar organizations in New Zealand and Fiji have claimed that their members suffered illnesses and even died as a result of exposure to ionizing radiation during the tests. Most of the surviving ex-servicemen are now in their mid-seventies, but, encouraged by mounting anecdotal evidence, they are still pursuing their cause. They are asking for recognition from the British government that the men who made it possible for Britain to develop a megaton thermonuclear device faster than either the United States or the Soviet Union had done were placed at undue risk and, as a result, exposed to dangerous levels of radiation.

So far, however, their campaigns have been largely unsuccessful. In 1998 two test cases against the Ministry of Defence, claiming war pensions on the grounds that participation in Grapple led to severe illnesses, were both rejected, by five to four, at the European Court of Human Rights. A subsequent appeal in 2000 was also rejected. Several independent epidemiological studies have, meanwhile, failed to convince the British government that the cancers, illnesses and premature deaths of Grapple veterans were because of radiation exposure. One study even concluded that a group of veterans actually had a lower incidence of leukaemia than the national average.

Turning from the sea back towards the hotel I noticed a concrete plinth at the edge of the beach. A brass plaque on one side commemorated the dawn of the new millennium in 2000. Until 1995 the equator and the International Date Line had intersected over Kiribati like the cross hairs of a sniper's sights. But following the 'Kiribati Adjustment' in 1994–95, which saw the Date Line moved to the east of Kiribati, Christmas Island now claimed to be the first inhabited land mass to receive each new day. It struck me, as I stood there watching the land crabs side-scuttle into their sand holes, that for the next week, if I got up early enough, I could be the first person to inhabit the day. For a few seconds I could live in the rest of the world's future, a day in which nothing had happened, in which no one had been born, and no one died.

Touching the plinth, as if it were some kind of lucky charm, I carried on walking back towards my unpacked cases in bungalow number thirty-five. As I did I realized it was perhaps fitting that back in 1957, when this hotel had been the Main Camp, Christmas Island hadn't received the first light of each new day, but the last. Each dawn in the course of the operation was not a few seconds of untouched day but rather the tail end of a date marked by man, signed off six times during Grapple with his most powerful invention yet.

My interest in Christmas Island and the Grapple tests grew from an accident of birth: my own. From 1972 to 1976 my parents worked in Fiji with the Overseas Development Agency. In 1974 I was born in Suva, before moving with my family back to Wales at the age of two. As I grew older I became fascinated by this country of my birth on the other side of the world. That fascination eventually led to a number of return visits. It was during one of these in 2003 that I'd met Paul Ahpoy and Filipe Rogoyawa, two Fijians in their late sixties, in the basement headquarters of the Fiji Nuclear Test Veterans Association on Amy Street, in Suva.

The 'headquarters' had no computers or filing cabinets, only a long wooden table and an assortment of old school chairs. Once my eyes had adjusted from the bright day outside, I saw that the dominant feature of the space was a stack of beige folders piled at one end of the table and along a single shelf on the back wall. These folders, Paul and Filipe explained to me, contained the returned questionnaires that the association had sent out to other Grapple veterans across the Fijian archipelago. Some of them also held the transcripts of interviews conducted with veterans about their experiences on Christmas Island. The stories, memories and medical histories the questionnaires and interviews had generated formed the main body of the association's work. This evidence, along with similar surveys of British veterans by UK associations, would be passed to a team of lawyers in London who were, at that time, preparing a compensation claim against the Ministry of Defence for illnesses suffered because of radiation exposure during Operation Grapple.

As many as 300 Fijian soldiers and sailors served at Christmas Island during 1957 and 1958. All of them were young and all were volunteers. Depending on their duties, their experiences on Christmas varied widely. The Fijian soldiers, unlike their British and New Zealand counterparts, were not allowed beer. The Fijian sailors were given a freer rein, and for many, as Paul confirmed, 'it was the time of our lives'. For forty years none of the Fijians received a pension for their service as it was only in 1999 that Christmas Island was reclassified as an 'active military operation'.

It was in that basement I first heard about the procedure followed for each of the Grapple tests. It was a story I would hear and read repeatedly, with some variation, over the next three years.

'The routine was always the same,' Paul said. 'At four in the morning they told us to go and line up on the beach. They'd play music on the big loudspeakers, all types of military bands. We could hear the jets warming up on the airfield ten or twelve miles away.'

Some of the men were given white cotton overalls and goggles. Others just wore their regular uniforms. They were told to sit down, facing away from the direction of the blast. Lorries nearby were prepared for a possible evacuation, coloured squares attached to the trunks of coconut trees marking out the different escape routes to be followed. At this point Paul got down on the floor of the basement to demonstrate the position they were told to adopt: knees to chest, elbows outside legs and palms pressed hard against their closed eyes.

'They'd count down over the loudspeakers. "Five, four, three, two, one... Bomb gone!" Then all silence, but after that we all start squirming.' Paul wriggled before me on the floor. 'Because someone is holding a big blowtorch behind you, and we could see the flash through our hands, see the bones, y'know?'

After the flash came the immense sound of the explosion and then the shock waves. Paul described how sometimes the stones around them were thrown into the air, then kept there by a succession of after shocks. 'Boom, boom, boom, about six of them.'

When they were allowed to turn around and open their eyes, Paul saw what he and other veterans have described as 'a second sun', so bright it turned the tropical night into day. The men on the beach, and those on the decks of ships out at sea, all watched that second sun rise. As it did, it changed shape, from a perfect sphere into 'a giant ice-cream cone with white cream dripping over its side', then into the now-familiar mushroom cloud, its stem glittering with ice crystals, towering into the sky and on into the stratosphere. Everyone who witnessed such an explosion mentions the immediate silence. According to Nick Harden, a veteran of the tests, 'all sound stopped, chirping, crabs, as if all nature held its breath'. There are some reports of this silence being broken by men crying.

When the Fijian servicemen returned home from Christmas Island, some reported immediate complaints that many have attributed to exposure to radiation: loss of hair, vomiting, dizziness, memory loss. Over the following years some of the men discovered they were sterile while others reported multiple miscarriages among their wives. As more time passed an increasing number suffered from premature cataracts, skin diseases or various forms of cancer, particularly leukaemia. It was only after 1983, however, when the British veterans' association was set up, that the Fijian veterans began to organize themselves around the growing question of the role their service at Christmas Island may have played in their illnesses. As with their British counterparts, this question became more urgent when they suspected it was not just they who had been affected. There was, it seemed, a disturbingly high rate of infant mortality and birth defects among the veterans'children. Paul's daughter died of an undiagnosed illness when she was three. 'She was playing with her toys and she just lay down and went to sleep,' he told me, before adding: 'The lucky ones are those who don't have children.'

In the books I'd read about the tests, I'd found hardly any mention of the I-Kiribati ('Gilbertese' in 1957) islanders living on Christmas at the time. Every now and then a veteran's account would mention the 'Garth'-like physique of the men, or that the local village was strictly out of bounds. Paul Ahpoy told me how the villagers had been evacuated before each test to safety ships offshore, where they'd been shown films in the hold until the test was over. In *Kirisimasi*, a book produced by the FNTVA, there had been just one interview with an I-Kiribati woman. Other than this, I could find no accounts of the I-Kiribati experience of the British tests, or evidence of any follow-up medical studies of the islanders.

The current population of Christmas Island is predominantly Micronesian and numbers around 5,000, higher than at any other time in its history. Compared to Christmas, the other inhabited islands of Kiribati are tiny – elliptical dashes of land, often overcrowded and increasingly under threat from 'king tides' and rising sea levels. While I was on Christmas the Kiribati president spoke at the United Nations of his concerns that in fifty years' time parts of his country may no longer exist. Christmas Island, as the world's largest coral atoll, constitutes seventy per cent of the total land mass of Kiribati. It has, therefore, presented itself to the I-Kiribati authorities as a natural destination for relocation.

Before leaving England, I'd been given the email address of Alice Taukaro, a young I-Kiribati woman who lived on Christmas. She had promised to help me find islanders who still remembered the nuclear tests. As we drove into London, the island's main village, we passed signs of this recent population growth: the newly-built Line and Phoenix island administration offices, several different denominations of church (Mormon, Seventh Day Adventist, Pentecostal, Catholic, Protestant) and two high schools. Other than a few windmill-powered water pumps the land between these buildings and the villages was largely featureless, the low-lying saltbushes and scrubland punctuated by an occasional coconut tree or, further off, the regimented lines of a plantation. After the wind and motion of the coast I was struck by how still the interior of the island was, as if stunned under the heat of the day.

Along the tar-sealed road, red land crabs, many with one oversized prizefighter's claw, scuttled away from the wheels of the car. At the time of the tests these crabs were everywhere. Like the birds, they often couldn't escape the sudden blast and flash of the detonation. One veteran had described how after a test explosion he'd found a crab's empty shell, its claws raised to fight, still facing the direction of the blast. Today the crabs are still everywhere. I'd woken that morning to find one clinging to the mosquito netting over my window. Later that week I went for a run into the interior. For an hour the only sound other than my breath and footfall was the clicking of hundreds of crabs as they parted across the tarmac a few metres in front of me, before closing again behind.

In London, Alice pointed out the main props of the island's infrastructure: the hospital, the bank, the council meeting house, the communications and Internet centre from where she'd emailed me. At the edges of the town I could see the apparatus of the port: loading cranes, storage sheds and fuel depots. This port had been established and expanded by first the British and then the US military, and was now where much of Christmas Island's money was made and spent. Most of what was consumed on the island, from fruit and vegetables to cars and TVs, had to be imported. Much of the island's economy, meanwhile, was driven by the export of copra, or dried coconut kernels, and fish, which left these quays and wharfs for the outside world.

Although this made the constitution of the national economy relatively clear, I found it harder to ascertain exactly how the majority of Christmas's population earned their income beyond subsistence farming or fishing. There was a small service economy of teachers, administrators and a handful of policemen. The Captain Cook Hotel also provided a certain number of jobs, as did a couple of scuba-diving operations. There was work to be had at the port itself, and in the network of services that supported its operation. A weekly export of live tropical fish on the Air Pacific flight to Hawaii indicated that some money could be made by the collection of these specimens. The best-paid occupation, however, was that of a fishing guide to the American and Japanese tourists who flew in each week to fish in the lagoons and from boats offshore. The tips a guide earned alone amounted to a weekly wage far beyond the reach of most islanders.

The physical debris of the Grapple tests – piles of rusting Land-Rovers and bulldozers, steel instrument casings and all the other detritus of the operation – had only recently been removed by a long overdue British clean-up team. A few bunkers remained, as did the concrete bollards at the side of the roads listing which regiments had built that particular stretch, but on the whole the marks of Grapple were slipping away from the island.

One morning, Alice took me to see Tonga Fou, a local historian, on what turned out to be his eightieth birthday. When I arrived he was lying on a bed in the backyard of his house covered by a mosquito net listening to Radio Kiribati, a transistor radio propped by his ear. Flipping back the net he swung his legs to the floor and walked towards me like an elder statesman about to take the stage.

Tonga came to Christmas Island when he was twenty-nine. Like many young Gilbertese men, he'd been recruited from Tarawa to assist with Operation Grapple. When the tests ended, some of the men chose to stay on the island, previously inhabited only by Gilbertese working in the copra plantations. Tonga's experience of the operation had been more intimate than most. During quieter periods he took RJ Cook, the scientific director of Grapple, fishing round the island. Through this connection he ended up working alongside the rest of the Atomic Weapons Research Establishment team. 'Sometimes they would have containers,' Tonga told me, 'which they would tell me not to touch, because it is poison.'

Tonga recalled the time with fondness. His calm, solid face was quick to smile and he often broke into a high, girlish giggle.

'It was a lot of fun – we worked with the soldiers, fishing together, playing together. In these days we don't think about the bomb because we enjoying ourselves.'

It was through these relationships that Tonga and the other Gilbertese learned about the nature of the bombs to be tested.

'During the Second World War,' Tonga said, 'we saw the Japanese bombing on Tarawa. We thought at first it would be like one of those bombs. But then the soldiers, they ask us, "Do you know the H-bomb?" Well, they explained to us for the first time, about the H-bomb. The A-bomb which is being dropped at Hiroshima, about one thousand bombs like that inside the smallest H-bomb.'

I asked Tonga if he was scared when he heard this.

'Oh yes!' he said, frowning and nodding his head. 'What about us if something goes wrong?'

When I showed him some of the books about Grapple I'd brought to the island, his smile returned. He flicked through the pictures, picking out senior members of the Task Force as if discovering old friends in a high-school yearbook. In return he showed me his own collection of Grapple material: some of the operation's pennants and badges sent to him by veterans, a memoir written by Kenneth Hubbard, the group captain of the RAF Valiant squadron that dropped Britain's first H-bomb, and a booklet produced by Air Commodore Oulton for the servicemen arriving from the United Kingdom to participate in Grapple. The booklet opened with the neat, circular reasoning behind the tests:

> In the absence of international agreement on methods of regulating and limiting nuclear test explosions – and Her Majesty's Government will not cease pursuing every opportunity of securing such agreement – the tests which are to take place shortly in the Pacific are, in the opinion of the Government, essential to the defence of the country and the prevention of global war.

Over the following seven chapters, complete with line-drawn illustrations, the booklet outlined the scientific journey towards thermonuclear capability since the end of the Second World War and the roles of the various services in the forthcoming operation. In a chapter discussing the nature of the tests themselves, the limited dangers of high atmospheric airbursts is made clear:

> If the explosion has been high in the air then the explosion will not touch the ground or the sea and the only R.A. [radioactive] material in the rising cloud are the tiny bits of the bomb. These are so small that they are carried to great heights and fall so slowly that they take weeks or even months to reach the earth. By that time their activity will have decayed and in any case they will be very diffuse and will not be dangerous.
>
> From the point of view of fallout a burst high in the air differs greatly from an explosion on the ground or at sea level. In such a case, where the fireball touches the earth or the sea, tons of dirt or water will be drawn up into the cloud. This will become coated with R.A. material from the bomb and there will be greater fallout. As the cloud rises the smallest particles will be taken up with it, but the larger ones will begin to 'fallout' from the stem and the base of the cloud. A burst at ground or sea level will not be included in Operation 'Grapple'.

Tonga wasn't alone in recalling the good times had by those involved in Operation Grapple. On my way to Christmas Island I'd stopped off in Fiji where I once again met up with Paul Ahpoy. This time he brought with him another veteran, Tekoti Rotan. Tekoti was originally from Banaba, an island so catastrophically mined for phosphate by Britain that at the age of eleven, along with every other Banaban, he had been repatriated to the island of Rabi, in Fiji. Twelve years later he had been posted as a stevedore to Operation Grapple. 'None of the European officers who were stationed here wanted to go,' Tekoti told me. 'So they must have known something, eh?'

In the four years since I'd seen Paul, he had travelled widely in the name of the test veterans' cause. 'The best thing to do is for veterans all over the world to get together,' he told me, 'instead of inviting the politicians, because they come and go.' The legal case prepared in 2003 hadn't come to anything, and the material collected by Paul and others was in the process of being passed to another team of solicitors who had taken over the case.

Back in Fiji, more of the association's members had died of cancer. 'I'm afraid there are not many of the talkative ones left,' said Paul. The most significant change, however, was Paul's renewed optimism, founded upon a report on the New Zealand Grapple veterans that was about to be published by Dr Al Rowland of Massey University. Tekoti showed me some newspaper cuttings which suggested the report contained new material that would be beneficial to their case. 'They are still saying those tests were quite safe,' Paul said. 'But probably, with the professor's findings, that will change.'

Both Paul and Tekoti claimed Operation Grapple had caused them and their families suffering (Tekoti's first and second wives had both had multiple miscarriages and his grandson was born with a 'twisted foot'). And yet, like Tonga, their reminiscences of Christmas Island were often remarkably warm. 'We were all young, you know,' Tekoti explained, 'so it was some excitement. It was like a dream. Because we were so out there in the middle of the ocean, I think we forgot about everything.'

'Although we were isolated, as young people, we enjoyed it, eh?' Paul confirmed. 'We would fish, catch land crabs and pick birds' eggs. We went to the Naafi or to the two bars at either end of the beach, and we could drink as much beer as we wanted.'

This attitude was one shared by many of the UK veterans. Some young men on national service even viewed Christmas Island as a 'cushy number'. Living conditions were hard, tempers could fray (when the cinema projectionist played the song 'How'd ya like to spend Christmas on Christmas Island?' one night, the audience wrecked their only source of entertainment), but many speak of their time on the island as one of the best of their lives.

Even when I asked Tonga about the tests themselves, his first response was positive. The mushroom cloud was, he says, 'Nice, very nice to look at.' The films they were shown in the hold of the safety ships, meanwhile, were 'Oh, very nice films, *Jungle Jim*, yes.' Over time, however, his view of those days has darkened. Just as the soldiers first drew his attention to the dangers of the H-bomb, so returning veterans to Christmas Island, in conveying their concerns over contamination, have cast a shadow over Tonga's experiences of Grapple, and a question mark over its legacy on the island.

When I mentioned the veterans' claims, Tonga's tone changed to one of quiet offence, informed, in part, by a retrospective awareness of the colonial order.

'They think of us as someone who does not know anything. But you don't treat him the right way. The question I say is why? Why the British tried their tests on Christmas Island, why they come this long distance? For one reason. One reason. To take a picture of the H-bomb. But why are they not thinking that human beings are staying on the island?'

The possibility of radiation exposure during Grapple had made Tonga reconsider some of the deaths he'd witnessed on the island in the past fifty years.

'We don't know, we don't know,' he admitted, 'but my feeling is that there is radiation. When I think of the people who were there at the bomb, how they died, it was mostly women, suffering with bleeding.' Although healthy himself, Tonga had his own story of loss since the explosions of Grapple. After suffering from intermittent blisters on her face and neck from 1960 onwards, his wife had died in 1990.

When I stood to leave, Tonga shook my hand. I felt guilty. He'd welcomed me with a smile, but now he was looking at the floor, frowning. He held my hand for a moment as we stood there, then looked up again.

'It was not just the people who were there, you know,' he said. 'No. When my wife gave birth to our daughter, the doctor was very surprised. The baby was bleeding from everywhere, her nose, her mouth, her ears, her eyes.' Tonga shook his head slowly. 'But we do not know, because they have sent no one to the island, no expert, no doctor. So yes, I wonder, I just wonder.'

In the forty years that he'd lived in Kiribati, Perry Langston had experienced most of the possible incarnations of a wandering European in the South Seas. Having originally arrived in the area to work for the British colonial service, Perry had since been a fisherman, a fishing guide, a diving instructor, a teacher, a plantation manager and a navigator. Although he was now married and had settled on Christmas, the desire to explore was still with him, however familiar the territory. 'A road trip, eh?' he said when I told him I'd be driving down to the test site on the south-eastern point of the island. 'Sounds good. Mind if I tag along?'

On that long drive south the next day, Perry demonstrated an impressive knowledge of the physics behind the tests, reciting an accurate summary of much of the material I'd been reading that week. How an atom bomb uses nuclear fission, the splitting of the atoms of a very heavy element such as plutonium. How a hydrogen bomb works in the opposite way, using the fusion of atoms of the lightest element, hydrogen. How, in fact, the bombs exploded in the area we were driving towards had been both – an atomic unit used to trigger the hydrogen unit. How that initial implosion had to be 'perfect! That's why the critical mass of plutonium is a perfect sphere, you see.' Perry made the shape of a circle with both his hands. 'Absolutely perfect.'

Although an undying enthusiast for Christmas Island (he marvelled at the unchanging scenery as if seeing it for the first time), Perry was not blind to its problems, not all of them local. Rising sea levels had seen king tides sweeping into the interior of some of the islands with increasing regularity. Both the issuing of more fishing licences and an increase in illegal fishing had led not just to a dangerous lowering of the fish stocks, but also to more international boats docking at Kiribati's ports. This, Perry said, had led in turn to an increase in prostitution, particularly of children. Cases of HIV on the islands were also on the increase. 'Yes,' he continued, looking out at the monotonous scenery of ocean, reef, shore and sky. 'This is a beautiful place. Beautiful. But we have our problems. That's for sure.'

After our stop for the colony of sooty terns on the Bay of Wrecks, it took another half-hour's driving for us to reach the end of the road. When we did, it was abrupt; the tarmac strip simply petered out into the scrub bush. Another half-mile further on and the island itself tapered into the ocean that stretched for thousands of miles away to the south. I turned off the car's engine. The layered waves kept up their rolling static on the reef. The sky was clear. I got out of the car. There was nothing there. Not even any coconut trees, just low scrub, thick and wiry. I looked over and saw Perry standing on the other side of the car. 'This is it. This is where it all happened. Ground Zero,' he said. 'Beautiful, isn't it?'

This was where the two balloon-suspended airbursts, Grapple Z 'Pennant' and Grapple Z 'Burgee', had been detonated. It was also the peninsula off which the other four thermonuclear bombs had been dropped, officially five miles from the shore on which we were standing. I remembered Paul Ahpoy telling me about the time he drove down here with a group of other Fijians after one of the tests. The undergrowth was scorched and when he'd kicked a stone it had disintegrated into dust, crumbling over the toe of his boot.

On the drive down to the end of the island we'd briefly stopped at one of the last pieces of Grapple debris; a rusted hollow steel cube half-embedded in a sand dune. This was a forward measuring and observation post and one of the closest manned positions to the blast. It was in a cube like this that Air Commodore Oulton had chosen to observe Britain's first megaton H-bomb. Peter Jones, who would later become head of the Atomic Weapons Research Establishment at Aldermaston, had bored a tiny hole in the wall facing the explosion and placed a white screen on the wall opposite. In this way the shelter was turned into a giant pinhole camera. When Grapple X detonated, the group of soldiers and scientists inside that cube had been able to watch the explosion and mushroom cloud inverted on the white screen on the far wall of the shelter.

I looked up into the clear sky. Up there, fifty years ago, the view of the same explosion from the RAF Valiant that dropped the bomb must have been spectacular. Before I'd come to Christmas I'd heard a recording of the Grapple X drop. The tension in the bomb aimer's voice had been palpable. I'd never heard a 'now' so inhabit the essence of itself as the 'Now!' that followed his 'Steady, steady, steady…' It was as if, at that moment, the word became the bomb, slowly turning out of its cradle to fall and spin through the air below.

Having released the bomb, 'Blue Danube', the Valiant would have lifted, suddenly lighter, with just fifty-three seconds to complete a 1.8 G 140-degree roll escape manoeuvre. Flying with their flash-screens down, and away from the blast area, the crew would have seen nothing of those first crucial seconds when the bomb erupted into a fireball more than a mile across and over one million degrees Centigrade at its core. Only when the mushroom cloud was already climbing higher than their plane was the crew able to turn the bomber around to see a towering cloud of fire and gas, shot with red and orange flame, ice caps forming on its uppermost reaches. Elsewhere in the skies above Christmas, six RAF Canberra 'sniffer planes' would have already been flying towards that same cloud, preparing to collect samples of atomic dust on their wing tips to take back to the Britain for testing. Down on the island itself, meanwhile, Oulton had decided to leave the shelter to 'get some first-hand experience of the blast wave'. He wasn't to be disappointed. When the shock wave arrived, it blew him and his colleague off their feet, 'like scraps of straw in a gale'. At that same moment, where Perry and I stood on the south-eastern point, the blinded birds would have begun their screaming.

Many of the consequences that emanated in the wake of the shock wave of Britain's first megaton H-bomb were well defined. The immediate outrage of other nations such as Japan, Ceylon and India;

the repositioning of Britain on the chessboard of world politics; the birth of Campaign for Nuclear Disarmament; the US government's amendment of the McMahon Act to allow nuclear collaboration between the United Kingdom and the United States once more (with Christmas Island turned over to the United States for more nuclear testing in return). Other consequences of the Grapple tests have been less clear, the veterans' claims against the British government of exposure to ionizing radiation being the most significant. The landscape of this ongoing dispute through which I'd travelled both to and within Christmas Island was not simply formed by contested evidence. It was also a dispute of contested histories. Blurred by extreme secrecy during the tests and eroded by the action of time on memory since, there are some striking contradictions between the official and unofficial records as to exactly what happened on that strip of land in the central Pacific between November 1957 and September 1958.

As Perry and I drove back north again that evening, I became acutely aware of the balance of these differing histories. Having just stood at Ground Zero, having met veterans and read the official accounts, I felt somehow at the fulcrum of that balance; in some way obliged to choose on which side to place the weight of my opinion.

The British government has always maintained that safety was paramount in the planning of the Grapple tests. All personnel would be stationed more than twenty miles from the detonation, out of range of the dangerous initial radiation produced by the blast. The risk of any secondary exposure to ionizing radiation, through contact with radioactive material, had been greatly reduced by the choice of 'clean' high-atmospheric airbursts. As Oulton's booklet had stated: 'A burst at ground or sea level will not be included in Operation Grapple.'

There was no official medical survey of returning veterans after the tests, but since 1988 there have been three epidemiological studies conducted by the National Radiological Protection Board. Individual cases for compensation have been taken as far as the

European Court of Human Rights. None of the conclusions of the NRPB studies provided a firm link between participation in the tests and increased levels of mortality and incidence of cancer (although the third study did acknowledge 'some evidence of a raised risk of leukaemia among test participants relative to controls'). The individual cases, meanwhile, were all defeated in the courts. 'In view of all the evidence,' a House of Commons report concluded in April 2003, 'there are no grounds for compensation to be paid to British nuclear test veterans.'

Faced with this official account of Grapple, I found myself wondering if there had been two possible cases of contamination on Christmas Island. The first was that of ionizing radiation, as claimed by the Grapple veterans. The second was that of the very claim itself. For if the veterans' claim couldn't be proved, wasn't it possible that in spreading their concerns to the Fijian veterans and the inhabitants of Christmas Island they had spread unnecessary and painful doubt, casting 'normal' deaths and illnesses within the scope of an avoidable accident? Had I also been contaminated with this doubt? Seeing cover-ups or mistakes where there were none? Chasing the tail of an old non-story while Kiribati and Christmas faced up to the 'real' challenges of the twenty-first century: global warming, overcrowding, king tides, HIV and child prostitution?

The evidence suggesting that this might not be the case is the evidence stacked against the official history of the tests. This consists largely of anecdotal accounts from personal narratives: the letters of bereaved wives, sisters and children convinced that exposure to ionizing radiation at Christmas Island played some part in the death of their husband, brother or father; the medical histories of skin diseases, cataracts, leukaemia, multiple myeloma, miscarriages, sterility, hair loss, infant mortality and birth defects. The memories and eyewitness accounts speak of a very different Grapple experience to the one described in the official records: one of lax or non-existent safety procedures, of induced psychological disorders among the men, of panic and confusion after the tests. At times these accounts have been supported by what would appear to be incriminating documents. One of the most quoted of these is a paper entitled 'Atomic Weapons Trials' written by the Defence Research Policy Committee to the Chiefs of Staff Committee in May 1953 which states:

> The Army must discover the detailed effects of various types of exposure on equipment, stores and men with and without various types of protection.

Then there is the October 1957 memo from the RAF nuclear Task Force Commander in Australia:

> Aircraft of the No. 76 Squadron flying to Christmas Island and stopping at Nadi [in Fiji] and Canton may be radioactive internally...the fact that an engine may be 'hot' should be concealed from the Nadi authorities unless they ask.

Over my week on Christmas Island it was these divergent and contradictory accounts that increasingly intrigued me. Two particular areas of contradiction between the official and unofficial narratives seemed especially significant. The first was the detonation height and distance of Grapple Y, at three megatons Britain's largest ever H-bomb. The second was a question of rain. With Grapple Y there was simply disagreement. With the rain there appeared to be a complete contradiction: one of existence versus omission.

None of the official accounts of the Grapple Y detonation on April 28, 1958 mentions any incidence of rain following the explosion. Group Captain Kenneth Hubbard, squadron leader of the Valiant bombers, observed the explosion from the ground. In his memoir he gives a detailed description of the detonation of Grapple Y:

> The weapon detonated as planned some 53 sec after release, which meant an altitude of 8,000 ft above sea level... The fireball appeared

as a huge red and orange cauldron of fantastic energy, which gave the impression of revolving. As it did so, it emerged at its apex into a stream of orange-coloured cloud mass moving upwards all the time, and as it ascended the colour changed to white. Then somewhere in the region of 50,000 ft it curved and fanned out from its centre making a cap similar to the top of a mushroom.

The Ministry of Defence report on Grapple Y was written by Group Captain W E Townsend:

> The Task Force Commander ordered the next one as a live drop and the countdown proceeded until the round was released at 1005 hours and burst at 8,000 ft above Ground Zero, fifty-seven seconds later... It was learned this was a 'clean bomb'. The airburst precluded any water or dust being drawn up from the surface which may give possible radioactive fallout and it was not anticipated that any fallout from this bomb would occur.

Lorna Arnold is British nuclear historian. In both her books, Britain, Australia and the Bomb and Britain and the H-Bomb, she draws on the official accounts of Grapple Y. Although she quotes Oulton stating in his final report that 'immediately after the shot the weather had deteriorated', she too makes no specific mention of any rainfall after the detonation. Many of those stationed on Christmas Island during Grapple Y, however, do.

> The ball grew and grew, sending up a huge jagged column, the top of which formed into a giant mushroom cloud, which bellowed towards us, obliterating the sky. Someone nearby said: 'Christ, what have they done to us?' It then rained down on us and most of us got soaked. *Roy Dunstan, Grapple veteran, diary entry.*

> We were watching the black cloud and smoke from the blast which was drifting towards us. When it came overhead, I felt something like a light shower falling on me. I thought it was rain. My husband stood under a lifeboat so he was protected from the light shower. *Mrs Sui*

> *Kiritome, who observed Grapple Y from the deck of a Navy frigate.*
>
> Was there rain? Yes, sometimes, usually for an hour afterwards. *Tonga Fou.*
>
> We would go out and wash in the rain. We thought, hey, a free shower, eh? They told us not to eat the fish for three days afterwards. *Paul Ahpoy.*
>
> The explosion set off a line of thunderstorms, below which we were forced to return to Christmas Island. There was torrential rain, which entered the unpressurised aircraft like a sieve, turning the only detector, a small rudimentary device on the captain's lapel, immediately the wrong colour. *Captain W G Stewart, co-pilot of an RAF Shackleton during Grapple Y.*

The official records of the detonation of Grapple Y all make specific mention of the fact that the bomb was detonated at the planned 8,000 feet (even though Hubbard says it exploded fifty-three seconds after leaving the aircraft, while Townsend states it was fifty-seven seconds). This, it was felt, was a high enough airburst to avoid the contamination of material that occurs during a ground- or sea-level explosion. Many eyewitnesses of Grapple Y, however, believe the bomb detonated at a much lower height. Veterans, both at the time and since, have frequently referred to the 'bomb that went wrong'. According to Tom Birch, one of those veterans, 'immediately after the detonation there was panic among the boffins'. Paul Ahpoy told me that 'all the engines on the landing craft were running' in preparation for an evacuation. Major James Carman, another veteran speaking on a 1990 Channel Four *Dispatches* documentary about Operation Grapple, confirmed that 'general opinion was that someone had got the sums wrong'.

The safety limit for the tests had been set at two megatons. Grapple Y had measured three megatons. It was certainly more powerful than intended, but had something else also gone wrong in the delivery and detonation of the weapon? Captain W G Stewart, the co-pilot of a Shackleton during Grapple Y, was interviewed by journalist Eamonn O'Neill for Ken McGinley's book *No Risk Involved*:

> O'Neill: At what height would you say that particular device was detonated at?
> Stewart: It went off at 800 ft. Yes, it was definitely 800 ft.
> O'Neill: Are you certain it might not have been higher…several thousand feet for example?
> Stewart: No. It was definitely under one thousand feet.
> O'Neill: An official government report on that blast puts the height at 8,000 ft, what is your reaction to that?
> Stewart: No… that's wrong. It was much, much lower than that. Definitely under 1,000 ft.

Stewart's claim was further supported in the *Dispatches* documentary. One of the men interviewed about Grapple Y was Dr John Large, an independent nuclear consultant. Like Stewart, he was convinced Grapple Y had exploded lower than the other air-dropped detonations. The evidence for his claim lay in the stem of Grapple Y's mushroom cloud, what veteran Roy Dunstan had described in his diary as the 'huge jagged column'. Holding the official photograph of Grapple Y's mushroom cloud to the camera, Dr Large traced the striated edge of the cloud's stem with his finger. Such striations, he explained, like the teeth of a double-edged saw when compared to the smooth stems of the other atmospheric mushroom clouds, could mean only one thing: heavy debris, such as seawater or soil, had somehow been drawn into the cloud. The only way this could have happened was if the detonation was at a much lower altitude than 8,000 ft. If this was true, then had the Grapple Task Force literally been 'hoisted by their own petard'? Had Oulton's successful completion of his original brief – to 'drop a bomb in the South Pacific and take a picture of it with a Brownie camera' – also provided the proof that a 'dirty' detonation of the very type his booklet assured would not occur during Grapple had in fact happened?

Perry and I finished our road trip that day watching the sun set while we drank a couple of cans of lager beside the 'Bathing Lagoon' in the north of the island. I remembered the photos I'd seen of soldiers and sailors here during Operation Grapple. Black-and-white images of diving contests, swimming races and even games of water polo. The lagoons, with their offer of both fishing and swimming, had been one of the main areas of recreation for the men stationed here. Back then shark nets had been erected in some of the lagoons, but I wondered if, after Grapple Y, these waters hadn't contained a more lethal and invisible danger than any shark. If the alternative history of Grapple Y was to be believed then a rainstorm so soon after a detonation was likely to have been irradiated. Similarly, if seawater had been contaminated during a low-altitude detonation, then how safe had it been to eat the fish and crabs caught around the island? The longest-lasting radiation particle following a nuclear explosion is plutonium. More or less harmless outside the body, plutonium can be lethal when ingested. I thought of all the fresh fish Paul Ahpoy had said the Fijians used to catch, the salt water showers, that sign outside a tent at Main Camp: FISSION CHIPS.

Sitting there at the bathing lagoon I realised that the balance of disputed histories I'd been aware of during the drive north was more a narrative of imbalance (of grossly mismatched juxtapositions). The intimate decay of an individual's body against the public agenda of world politics; the advanced theories of nuclear physics against an island whose language didn't even have words to contain the ideas for radiation or shock wave; the knowledge gained over the course of the Grapple tests against the doubt seeded in the minds of its veterans; the detailed analysis of each explosion against the failure to survey the men who had witnessed them; the histories of nations and their legacies against the histories of individuals and their offspring.

On returning to Britain it was clear to me that even if the disputed histories of Operation Grapple were to be agreed on, even if the Ministry of Defence were to acknowledge the hot rain or the low-altitude detonation, the Fijian, New Zealand and UK veterans stood little chance of proving their claims of radiation exposure on Christmas Island. This was mainly because while a cancer can be diagnosed, its cause cannot. There is no specific radiogenic cancer, and as the veterans grow older it could be argued they would have suffered from cataracts or leukaemia anyway. It was partly for this reason that the epidemiological studies of the NRPB proved so inconclusive. Even if they had suggested a slightly increased chance of leukaemia following participation in Grapple, they could not provide what the British government required for a compensation claim to be considered valid: a guarantee that such participation would lead to the cancer. The veterans of Christmas Island, it seemed, would have to suffer not only their illnesses, but also the ongoing uncertainty about what may have caused them. Even if they firmly believed they knew that cause, they would still be denied recognition and the accompanying compensation.

I had forgotten, however, about the Massey University study that Paul Ahpoy and Tekoti Rotan had told me about in Suva. I was reminded of it when my attention was drawn to the following question in the House of Commons:

> *13 June 2007. Dr Ian Gibson (Norwich, North) (Lab)*: I would like to point out to the Prime Minister that there is a group that represents British nuclear test veterans, including those who worked on Christmas Island. Some startling work from New Zealand shows that genetic abnormalities are associated with the brave men and women who stared into the face of atomic bombs. Does the Prime Minister agree that we ought to help the people from our country who went out there and served for us?

The next day I emailed Dr Al Rowland, the author of the report. When he replied he attached the full results of his report, including the overview of the study:

> This report presents the findings of three assays performed to assess the genetic status of those New Zealand military personnel who participated in Operation Grapple in 1957–58. Two of the assays: the G2 assay and the micronucleus (MN) assay show no difference between the veterans and the matched controls, which suggests that DNA repair mechanisms in the veterans are not deficient.
>
> The results reported here using the mFISH assay, however, show elevated translocation frequencies in peripheral blood lymphocytes of New Zealand nuclear test veterans 50 years after the Operation Grapple series of nuclear tests. The difference between the veterans and the matched controls with this particular assay is highly significant. The total translocation frequency is 3 times higher in the veterans than the controls who showed normal background frequencies for men of this age group. This result is indicative of the veterans having incurred long-term genetic damage as a consequence of performing their duties relating to Operation Grapple.
>
> A careful comparison of the veterans and the controls for possible confounding factors, together with a close analysis of the scientific literature in related studies, leads us to a probable defining cause for the chromosome anomalies observed. Ionizing radiation is known to be a potent inducer of chromosome translocations. We submit the view that the cause of the elevated translocation frequencies observed in the veterans is most likely attributable to radiation exposure.

Here, it seemed, was another kind of history: the history of an individual's genetics. The existence of such a history meant a crucial switch in the focus of the Grapple debate, from proving the cause of radiation or the incidence of a cancer in a group of men to being able to determine whether an individual had, fifty years ago, been exposed to radiation. The narrative of this genetic history was written in an indelible script, what Dr Rowland referred to as 'a unique permanent signature in the genome'. Was it possible that the veterans' story was one that would be bound by the limits of science? Having believed themselves harmed by some of the most advanced technology of the 1950s, the opportunity of achieving recognition for their beliefs was now being presented to them through some of the most advanced science of the twenty-first century.

The Grapple veterans are still, however, a long way from the end of their journey, and for some that end may be the discovery that they were not, in fact, exposed to any ionizing radiation on Christmas Island. But the report's closing lines still read, for me, as a quiet validation; an answer, at last, to all those piled-up beige files of returned questionnaires in a basement in Suva, to the personal testaments of Christmas Island veterans, to the letters of bereaved wives and children, to Tonga Fou's 'I wonder, I just wonder'.

> We submit the view that the probable cause of the veterans' elevated translocation frequencies is radiation exposure. This view is supported by the observation of a comparatively high dicentric chromosome score in the veterans, which is characteristic of radiation exposure.
>
> The findings presented here are based on only 50 veterans from New Zealand who took part in Operation Grapple. We would encourage those in authority to initiate research to corroborate our findings by conducting a similar study on British and Fijian personnel who also took part in Operation Grapple. ■

MEMOIR

THIS IS NOT ABOUT ME

Janice Galloway

My mother thought I was the menopause. She came to terms with the fact that I wasn't in Buckreddan Maternity Home in Kilwinning, because that was where women went. In those days, the medical profession gave out the impression of no choice. Labour meant Buckreddan: QED. That the name *maternity home* suggested duress and distress was probably not intentional, but the suggestion was there nonetheless. I was sixteen before I found out what Buckreddan looked like, by catching sight of the name on a placard as I shot by on a bus. Red Victorian sandstone, almost a hotel. I had always imagined a poorhouse, women in rows in narrow single beds with thin sheets, the occasional nurse with an origami hat like Florence Nightingale. I had always imagined grey, cold, stern. Now I saw the real thing, it looked fine. I tried instead to picture its ranks of babies, me among them somewhere, but couldn't. All I could muster was the sound of them, crying. I couldn't picture the absurdly named delivery suites, since I had no idea what delivery was or what such a suite might contain. But I could imagine bottles. That was what we got then; we got powdered milk – formula – in bottles.

They tried to make us breastfeed, my mother said, and it was horrible. I told them I was too old, but the Sister didn't care. It's for baby, she said. *Baby*. As though you knew any different.

It was only when her attempts led to baby throwing up enough blood to coat her top sheets, twice, that she was let stop.

I told them, she said. You canny do that sort of thing when you're forty. Anyway, you did fine on the bottle.

Speeding towards Troon on a corporation bus, I pictured the insipid green wards and the Big Ward Sister not taking no for an answer and the red Victorian sandstone that bound them in. I pictured my mother, a small head afloat on a sea of white cotton, a red tide of blood oozing towards her like lava. I pictured the ranks of bottles revolving on a metal trolley, fresh, white and full of reconstituted powder that had once been the produce of larger, abler animals. What I couldn't picture was me, the little vampire in the midst of the melodrama, the source of all that worry. Nothing I did could conjure a creature as dependent and irretentive as a baby.

That's how come you've a delicate stomach, my mother said. *You had a Bad Start.*

Every time she said this, there was a pause. Every time, I knew what was next.

If I'd known you were coming, she'd say eventually, *if I'd found out. Things would have been different.*

I had no reason to doubt her meaning or that her meaning was less than sincere. Things would have been different. Decades on, when my mother was delirious and thinking she was going to die, she let slip she'd miscarried at least another twice after me. There should have been, God help us, more. Maybe I'd put her on her guard, seized all the chances and left my found-out, flushed-out little siblings with none. Maybe, on the other hand, her body had made those decisions alone. It was never clear, never clarified, never referred to again. I was, as my sister reminded me every day of my childhood, bloody lucky to be there at all. If she'd kent you were coming, she'd say. Nobody needed to say the rest.

It is 1955. She is approaching forty and he is fifty.

There's a wooden sideboard, a walk-in larder and a big Ulster sink. The smaller sink is in commission too because washing takes up lots of sinks. Lots of sinks and the wringer that needs fixing and too many buckets of water and the bloody leaky hose that's perished down one side and the whole of Friday. She works in her husband's shop on weekends and during the week when he can't be bothered. She has a feeling it's shut more often than not when her back is turned because it's right next to Massie's bar, which is no help to anybody. Women aren't allowed in Massie's and it makes her furious for no good reason. It's not as though she wants to go in, it's the prohibition. She goes to the Labour Club and the bowling club and it's warm. People play accordions and sing. It's company. Massie's isn't about company. It's about men boozing their money away and making Davie Massie rich, nothing else. Going past it on the way to the train station, the stink of piss and spilled alcohol make her gag, so she crosses the road to avoid it and it chases her, like drain emissions. Even thinking about it now, she realizes, is making her queasy. Queasy or not, there's the washing to do and it's Friday. Outside it's snowing, but that's neither here nor there. Needs must and the devil is always bloody driving.

She's had heartburn since she got up, heartburn, sciatica and this other indigestion pain somewhere near her kidneys. Something they ate last night, maybe. Her head hurts under the scarf she tied like a turban to keep the perm crisp, and the heat in here doesn't help. It's racking. Under the lid of the tub, though, everything's twisting together nicely, getting clean. She pokes a towel with a wooden stick she's been told not to use because it might catch in the drum, but old habits and so on. And the steam comes up, a rush that flushes her face and all the way to the base of her neck, chasing an unexpected trail of sweat down her back. The pain is suddenly horrible, like a fist. Maybe she has a migraine coming. She closes her eyes, looks down as the flush of warmth drives right past her belly and opens them again to see the Hoover sign wavering. And water.

Her feet, now she moves her toes in the slippers, are wet. Her skirt, too; a brownish puddle on the lino, now she looks, seeping between the joins. This bloody machine. Again. There was something wrong with the damn thing from the first day. To be fair, he'd at least bought the thing. It was the only one in the street. Her eyes are watering now, the way they do more often these days. It's the Change, her mother said. Change of Life. That'll bloody sort you out. The thickening at her waistline, the weight in her chest. This was what happens. You turned into an older woman, and that was you, finished. Nobody had any time for you then.

The water keeping coming makes her not want to think any more. She bends to the pile of dirty stuff to fish out a towel, leans into wiping up the puddle, squelching in her stocking soles, and feels dizzy, helpless. The Change. She has twinges in her knees and ankles, flushing in her face, varicose veins and what were called restless legs? Restless legs sound like something people who spent too much time on their feet get, people who are always that bit out of breath from running to keep up with something they can't quite pin down. Restless legs sound like just the kind of thing she would get. Snow changes to hail behind the window, makes a noise like rattling and suddenly it dawns on her. This water, this flood. It's her. Dull-getting-worse pain rocks her back and belly, echoing around her like the rings of Saturn, a big stone thrown in slow motion into a deep, deep well. The water is, she begins to grasp it now, whether she wants to or not: the water is all hers.

It was too late. She was pushing forty, had a daughter who was pregnant herself. She had a nice house, a cat and a washing machine of sorts to care for. But it happened.

It was my fault she stayed, she said, but she had stayed for nearly nineteen years already so I never really took that one on. I know I was responsible for other things. For pain, certainly. For worry and increased fear of what staying with him might do. For things going wrong and her life turning into something so different she sometimes tried to end it. But her being with my father in the first place was not my fault. God knew what plans she had before her waters broke. Whatever, they were away. Gone with the tide and the tangle and the hissing razor shells. Not knowing what was hitting her till the last, through the rage of an unexpected, unpremeditated, unplanned and unwished-for labour, she was a mother all over again.

Late baby, winter baby. Mistake. At least their sex lives were in decent fettle.

She must have mopped up the puddle, taking her time. Nobody else would. Maybe she cried. The washing machine worked fine for another three years, no hitches. After that, we were somewhere else and she was back to wooden poles and boiling water, a scrubbing board, a brush.

If I'd kent, she'd say, her eyes narrowing. If I'd only bloody known.

This is my earliest memory. I am on the floor with my arms stretched out, trestle-style, rising from the rug. And out of nowhere, out of the order, there is nothing but fingers. My fingers, hurting. They buckle and sear like burning. When I turn towards the pain, I see half my hand, the rest disappearing under something black. It's the heel of my father's shoe. He's standing on my hand. There is a sensation of rushing in my head then my mother howling, and the rustle of cloth too loud and too near. Someone says *shhhh* not like the sea. *Shhhhh. Shhhhh.* And awful screaming that must be me.

I have other memories, other pictures of my hands under my father's shoes, the busting sensation all along the arm that went with it. But this is the earliest. Soon, I can add the surprise of random cigarette burns, falling unexpectedly, sudden shocks with no remembered cause. I remember hurrying under the table to get out of the way and something heavy landing above me, the sensation of never being entirely off-guard. And sunlight. Someone opening a curtain to let the sun come streaming, blinding, in.

My father, everyone knew it, was clumsy. Not all the time, but often enough for it to be a fact. As though we had poltergeists or Cornish pixies, our lives were full of accidents, things not attributable or admitted at all. Yet they happened. They happened all the time.

He came home any time of day with a stumble in his step, his voice awkward, his hands not able for his shoelaces. And when he did, afternoon or not, it was time for me to go to bed. *He was in no fit state*, my mother said. *Off you pop.*

In bed, there were no distractions. Even if I couldn't hear them, I knew they were there, through the wall, arguing. Sooner or later, something would smash.

It broke, she'd say when I found pieces, untidied-up fragments, wondered what had happened. *Watch you don't cut your fingers.*

That was it. Despite the prickle in the spine, like the cracked edge of crockery against tooth enamel, an instinct not all was as it should be, it was the stuff's fault. It just broke. *Butterfingers.*

Nothing was permanent, nothing calm. He lost money, found strangers and brought them home, ruthlessly jovial in his own kitchen, men you never saw again yet who sat at the table and got me to fetch them a glass, a cigarette, matches; men who wanted to know if my mother was in. And when the noise got too much, she would appear, fully dressed because there was a guest of sorts whether she knew them or not, ready to scoop me up for bed as though the thought just occurred and she happened to be passing. But everyone knew it hadn't. The men might look temporarily sheepish, but they didn't shift. Who shifted was her. And it was when she shifted, turning to go out with me safe under one arm, that the sniping started.

We didny get you out your bed, eh? Me and my friends here? She kept walking. *You'll be wanting to get us something to eat?*

As though a fight, a confrontation with her discomfort, was what he wanted more than anything else in the world before it slipped beyond his reach. Things, it was understood as we left the room, the laughter, the slink of glass, might get broken. Other times, come home without company, he'd spend ages sitting on the hall carpet with his back to the wall, letting my mother coax him to be. *Take your shoes off, Eddie, let me loosen the laces. Come on, I'll get your shoes off. You sit down and I'll help you with these shoes. Eddie, Eddie, Eddie.*

This was our family, our routine.

Shhh, she'd say. He's asleep with his eyes open again. It was morning, her face shock-white from daylight as she opened the curtains. Don't go in the living room yet and wake him up.

That was the important thing to bear in mind. *Shhh.*

I learned to stay by doors and windows, things that opened. I kept my eyes keen, watching for clues. But our chairs still broke and our picture frames cracked all the same. Once, he threw my trike against the outside wall, and my mother sat down next to it, its bashed mudguard and fallen-off screws, and just stared, not at him, but at the pieces, as though the trike had exploded of its own accord. It wasn't him. It was things that did it. Things, and us, were in a conspiracy against him. That he tried now and then to be someone else, slipping his fingers behind my ears to find pennies, or stringing a little paper Charlie Chaplin doll between two chair backs to make it dance, made me nervous. *Dance, Charlie, dance*, he'd say, and the paper cane would turn, Charlie's barely unfolded legs jerking in time. And he'd look at me. I knew why. I was supposed to smile. I was meant to show I was happy as a June bug with my life and everything in it. But it wasn't true. I hated it but I did not hate him. I did not hate her. I did not hate anybody. I just wished it was different. Soon enough, it was.

It was a Friday night, late, and the stew wasn't ready. I don't know why we were eating at bedtime, but we were. I was in pyjamas, and outside was dark enough to make the windows act as mirrors. I remember getting off the settee, holding a spoon up to hide the reflection of my face in the glass, then heading down the hallway, following the smell of cooking to the kitchen. Stewing steak takes a long time, she said. You'll not make it any quicker by looking at it. On you go and play at something. But there was nobody to play with and anyway, I wanted to be with her, in with the steam and the sense of something magic happening, a mess of different things turning into decent food. When it was ready, she was going to blow on it till it cooled and we'd eat together, up late just the two of us in our night things, conniving.

It's not ready, she said. I told you already, you silly thing. Away and play. I must have gone back to the living room eventually, because that's where I was when the front door opened. And in he came.

In my memory, it opens like a horror film, like a gun going off with smoke furling in its wake. Maybe it was foggy, maybe just his breath coming in from the cold. At any rate, the door opened and he lurched into the hall, leaving it bouncing on the hinges behind him, the whole of the dark outside rushing in like water. And there I was in my night things, holding a spoon, staring.

What are you looking at?

He was sweaty and slack-skinned. He snapped his fingers to make me look at his eyes and I wouldn't, so he gave me up as a bad job and turned back up the hallway. There was always something more alluring elsewhere. Tonight, he could smell it. He thumped his shoulder on the hall-stand, trailing all four and a half yards to the kitchen, growling starting in the back of his throat. I realized she didn't even know he was coming. When he reached the kitchen, I heard her *O* of surprise. There was the dry scuffle of hands, rubbing.

The questions were stuff I'd heard before. Why was she cooking at this time of night? Who was it for? They were the kinds of questions he asked when he was in this mood, the kind that didn't want answers. Then he did the not-questions. She knew full well he didn't want stew. Who told her to cook stew? It wasn't for him so who was it for? He knew how much stewing steak cost. He was going like a train when she cut in.

Jesus Eddie, she said, *don't start. Don't start.*

Her voice hung alone for a moment before he made up his mind. He cranked up the volume and started the whole thing again.

It was me, not her, that chose what to do next. It was the crack in her voice, his pushing like a wall against it, that did it. I ran towards the kitchen light and my father inside it, filling the space. Not knowing what to do, I did something anyway. I spoke at his back.

Mum, I said. It sounded clean, like a triangle. My voice. Not his name, hers. Mum.

He looked over his shoulder, tilting off-beam just enough for me to see her face, for her to see mine. Seizing the chance, she pointed straight at me.

Look what you're doing, she said. She was shaking. *It's for her. Who do you bloody think it's for?*

Something shadowed his face, so brief it was almost not there at all. Then, light-switch sober and without stumbling, he went to the back door and clicked the latch. Night sucked into the warm room, a draught banging the front door, at the other end of the hallway, shut. Slowly, he crossed the kitchen and reached for the pot on the cooker, lifting it in one hand. It stayed there, balanced on the moment as though he was trying to guess its weight. Then he walked to the door with it, reached back, swung, and opened his hand. The pot lifted, turned on the air like a seagull and kept going, out of sight over the washing lines. We all watched the time it had taken to make and the money it cost to buy, the good thing it should have been, disappearing into space. There was a soft thud, like an animal, as it landed out somewhere in the tangle of weeds beyond the garden wall, and a whistling noise in my ears.

That was for us, she said. *Us*. Her voice was stuck in her throat.

Not just you.

There was a long silence, dead slow, while things chose which way they would fall.

Well, he said. It's not for fucking anybody now. Is it?

And he didn't smile, exactly, but he looked okay. Calmer. Business concluded, he left the kitchen to the sound of his own feet on the lino and she tidied up. Nobody cried. I waited on at the open door, my toes freezing, looking out beyond next door's garden. The stars were showing over the pigeon loft and our window was light-filled boxes on the grass. I was working something out as I stood there, nobody moving me on, my mouth hanging open wide enough to catch flies. He had done it on purpose. I thought about the pot, the food inside. He knew it was ours and he'd thrown it away. He had known full well.

Started, things slide fast. The tiniest of realizations can tip life sideways, serve up a last straw. I have a very clear memory indeed of ours.

She's in front of the mirror, singing *If I were the only girl in the world and you were the only boy*, and fetching stuff from the hall cupboard one piece at a time: a cardigan, a rainmate, a scarf. Going out takes time if it's to be done right. And she does things right. Spare rainmate, purse, black nylon gloves. I'm put together already in a navy coat. Inside my gloves the finger spaces tug wavy knitting against my nails. Already it's misty outside, the kind of weather that shows breath. *A Garden of Eden just built for two*. She snips up the lock and hums the rest. Only one more thing to fetch now and we're off. *Stay*, she says. *Just you wait right there and we'll away to your granny's. She wanted me to bring her—*

But I don't hear what it is my granny wanted us to bring, because she's out of earshot already, veering into the kitchen to fetch it. Out of earshot for speaking, anyway. Wherever she is in the house, you can hear her singing.

I'm in a line of shut doors. A dark hump moves in the bottom corner of the mirror and I know it's me. I reach up on the tips of my shoes to try and see a whole face, and I do. Right behind me, the energy of him suddenly everywhere, my father comes through the front door. Only a glimpse of her emerges from the kitchen before I'm tipping sideways and before I know it, I'm not waiting in the hall any more, I'm in the living room and the key is turning out there, shutting me in.

Eddie, she says, from the other side. The handle rattles and stops suddenly. *Eddie. We're just going to my mother's. Open this door.*

Then the whole thing goes too fast. There's thudding, which means he is out there with her, and my mother raising her voice, saying no. The handle slips against the wool of my glove when I try it from my side, but it doesn't budge. Only two things are clear: I am not leaving and she is not getting in. Her voice escalates but he is silent. He says nothing at all. The gloves are tied at the cuff and tight, so hard to shift I hardly try, and there's nothing to do but watch the shutness of the door, listen to the noises behind it, things I can't see, changing. A few dull thumps and her saying no, and a single roar. His. The front door batters shut and there's silence for a whole moment. Then he comes in, alone. He's in a suit, the tie squint and crushed, his eyes not fixed on any one thing. He glances out of the window, shuts the living-room door behind him and locks us both inside. I watch the key turn, the string through its eye slipping inside the blackness of his pocket, and wait.

Mummy's away out, he says.

Her footsteps, the points of her heels, like running or walking on the spot, click over outside.

You've to stay in with me. I watch the place where the key went. You've to stay with me and play a game. He takes his jacket off, straightening the tie, pulling himself, piece by piece, together. *Sit*, he says. He says it the way you talk to a dog you didn't trust. We're playing a game while she's away.

My coat is still buttoned to the neck. We were going out and now we're not and these clothes are not right for inside. His face isn't right either. I only know my eyes have drifted to the door when he catches it, snaps his fingers.

There's nothing out there, he says. *Now sit. Sit there when I tell you.* He points at the settee. *Just bloody sit.*

So I sit. I sit right on the edge and my feet leave the floor and nothing feels solid. Nothing feels safe. He waits staring right at me till he's sure, then walks slowly to the tallboy and rummages in the bottom drawer just as the noise starts. Like a wall falling, the suddenness of it a shock right down to the bone. It takes a moment to realize it's the window, shuddering fit to break. Over the top edge of the settee, her hands come into view, making marks on the glass. My mother is outside her own home, battering her fists against the window so hard the frame flakes paint. But he doesn't turn round. He doesn't even look up, just goes on fishing in the drawer. I look at her face, at his.

Open the door. She's just a wean, Eddie. Open the door.

It's as much a howl as anything, her eyes melted into black creases and that's all I see because he snaps his fingers again, knowing I'll turn away from her, that I'll turn towards him. And there he is, my father, laying out a chequered board on the side table. He picks up a stack of counters in one hand, letting them fit snug. Then slowly, one after another, he sets them down in their rightful places. The set of his body and face say nothing unusual is happening in the room or the space around us at all. But she's still behind me, still getting louder. It makes no sense he can't see. Whether he can or not, he doesn't. And for now, for this moment, I know something. There is what is real and what people can force you to pretend is real, and pretending is the wrong one. I don't know that in as many words, but I know it in my fingers. They're stiff, rusted up with refusal. Not for long, though, nothing that can't be undone. And he knows how. He looks up, puts one last red button dead centre in its square, and stares. The window rattles and she shouts his name, his name like nails down a blackboard, his name. He doesn't even flicker, just keeps looking. And what he's looking at is me. We have the same eyes. Everybody says so. Just the same. They lock now, point to point, and the look wants to break me clean down the middle.

Me first, he says. He slides the playing piece back and forth, playing, while she shouts one last time. Then there's a slithering noise, something heavy slumping hard down on to the path. We both hear it but what he does is he makes his move. One square. And pushes the board towards me.

Now you, he says, calm, clear. I do nothing. *We're playing*, he says, *you and me. See? Now it's you.*

He lifts the hand I know is mine, pulls the ties and slips off my glove in one easy move. Carefully, he places my fingertips firmly on the nearest piece, a dead ivory circle.

Now, he says. *Play.*

Outside, my mother moans like a seal. His eyes rivet on the board so he can't see mine filling up, making the whole room quiver. Even so, the piece starts to shift.

I'm warning you, he says. His jaw clicks.

And I choose. Knowing this is the wrong thing, that this is all the wrong thing, I play.

I don't remember what happened after that. She must have given up and walked to her mother's with no bag, no key, not sure if she'd get back in the same night, the next, ever. But she did. She would have needed to knock, but he would have let her in. Eventually.

Three days later, all the stock in the outhouse behind the shop burned down. The shop nearly went up with it. He'd gone in drunk and dropped a fag on the floor. It was autumn and the place was full of fireworks. Only little boxes, but still. My mother saw the display it made, pretty golden sparks over the roofs of other houses, not knowing what it was as she came back home off a bus from Kitty's.

Every bloody penny, she said, snapping her fingers, *bang*.

Nothing was insured, of course. He didn't believe in insurance.

He said insurance was for mugs. Instead, he took what was left of the housekeeping from the tin in the pantry and consoled himself as he saw best fit. Given time to herself, my mother made a decision. We all found out what it was soon enough.

I have no memory of the move. It occurred to me years later that maybe he had sensed it coming, that fear was why he had shut us together. That he was clinging, trying to terrify one or other of us into stasis, obedience, God help us, affection. On the other hand, maybe not. Whatever the intention, if there was any at all, all he had done was make things pressing. She might have gone to her mother's, her sister's, to all sorts of places if it hadn't been for me. I am under no illusion it was a choice. There was nowhere to take us, but we had to be together. There was nowhere to take us, but we had to go.

She must have gone round, asking. Maybe she went to the doctor to ask for pills *for nerves,* as people did then, and her situation had emerged. Maybe she cried. More likely she didn't. She did not cry easily. But however the conversation turned, Dr Hart, normally a smug and self-contained bastard, said the surgery had a box room. It was over the very building in which they sat and it would keep the rain off. It cost next to nothing, which was more than she had at the time, but she could, he supposed, clean the surgery instead. Work, thank God. Work. She'd been a domestic and a clippie and a shop-keeper's assistant. She'd had a washing machine of her own. Now she got a box room and tuppence to get by on and she took it with open arms. If she wept at all, it would have been then, but she'd have waited till she was outside. She'd have held her back stiff and got out with her face intact as far as she could. The revelation of weakness, in her experience, could do terrible, terrible things.

Over the heads of Dr Hart, Dr Caroll and Dr Deans, then; over the heads of the sniffing, spitting, gurgling, limping, seeping hordes downstairs in the dungeon of the waiting room, we waited too. And when they were gone, when the big outside door was shut over, she came into her own. Fag ash, fallen hair and cast-off tissues, kidney bowls and carpets and big glass jars. Racks of jars. She had to promise to keep me quiet, of course, especially during surgery hours. But I was good at being quiet. It was something at which I excelled. We could get by.

In some ways the move was easy: just clothes and toys enough for one case. Not so much as a kettle. Rose said Eddie wasn't well and needed looking after and she was a bad wife for letting him down, but she knew that already. It was a horrible choice, certainly, but not a hard one. She'd put in twenty-two years already. After all that time, it must have seemed unlikely that more would make anything any better. Rose was his sister, doing what a sister would. Or maybe she just resented being dumped with his care.

Maybe she can do a better job, my mother said. Maybe she can just do the bloody looking after herself.

Nobody got the address to begin with, just in case, and even I knew why. We lost the trike. Some time between Christmas and the New Year, we lost a lot of things. What we acquired was a box room above the doctor's surgery, a two-ring hob and a sink behind a curtain, a divan settee, no toilet. My mother stood at the window of the attic and wept, then chose to look on the bright side.

Oh well, she said. Things can always get worse, she said. We're not dead yet. I remember her stretching her neck, her hand lifting to cross her chest as though checking a heartbeat. Just to check. ■

CONTRIBUTORS

Brian Alfred's paintings on page sixty are taken from his book, *Millions Now Living Will Never Die!!!* (Haunch of Venison). The portraits are, from left to right on each row: Alice Coltrane, Alvar Aalto, Roy Lichtenstein, Hunter S Thompson, Inka Essenhigh, Jack Kerouac, Billie Holiday, Syd Barrett, Ol' Dirty Bastard, Jean-Luc Godard, Muddy Waters and Serge Gainsbourg.

Douglas Coupland is a Canadian author and artist whose visual work often explores the links between text and the made object. His most recent novel is *The Gum Thief*.

Nick Danziger has published four books and has made award-winning documentaries. His photographs have been exhibited internationally.

Louise Dean was awarded the 2004 Betty Trask Prize for her debut novel, *Becoming Strangers*. Her third novel, *The Idea of Love*, will be published by Penguin in summer 2008.

Gautier Deblonde's work has been exhibited at the National Portrait Gallery and Tate Britain. 'The Arctic' is taken from a larger project, *True North*, which will be published in 2009.

Joshua Ferris's first novel, *Then We Came to the End*, was a finalist for the National Book Award in 2007. He is at work on a new novel.

Ruth Franklin is a senior editor at the *New Republic*. She is working on a collection of essays about the literature of the Holocaust.

Janice Galloway last appeared in *Granta* 76. 'This is Not About Me' is from a work-in-progress of the same title, to be published by Granta Books. She lives in Glasgow.

Lavinia Greenlaw's poem, 'The Joy of Difficulty', appeared in *Granta* 100. She has published three collections of poetry, two novels and, most recently, a memoir, *The Importance of Music to Girls*. She lives in London.

SOCIETY OF AUTHORS

The Betty Trask Awards 2008

Annual awards totalling up to £25,000 for first novels by young authors. Candidates must be Commonwealth citizens and under the age of 35. The novel must be a first novel by one author, published in the UK in 2007 or unpublished, and of a traditional or romantic nature.

Closing dates:
30 April 2008 and 30 September 2008

For full details and entry form write with SAE to:

Awards Secretary, The Society of Authors, 84 Drayton Gardens, London SW10 9SB,
or
email: info@societyofauthors.org
website: www.societyofauthors.org

ROYAL LITERARY FUND

FINANCIAL ASSISTANCE FOR WRITERS

The Royal Literary Fund

Grants and Pensions are available to published authors of several works who are in financial difficulties due to personal or professional setbacks.

Applications are considered in confidence by the General Committee every month.

For further details please contact:
Eileen Gunn, General Secretary
The Royal Literary Fund
3 Johnson's Court,
London EC4A 3EA
Tel 0207 353 7159
Email: egunnrlf@globalnet.co.uk
website www.rlf.org.uk
Registered Charity No 219952

POETRY BOOK SOCIETY

The Poetry Book Society

A Book Club For Poetry Lovers

Join the PBS for the best new poetry published each quarter, plus reviews and comprehensive listings in the *Bulletin* and discounts on every poetry book you buy.

Take out a membership before 31st July to receive Christopher Logue's *War Music* and a £10 poetry book voucher **free**. Call **020 7833 9247** or email **info@poetrybooks.co.uk**

Call or email for a free trial issue of the *Bulletin* and to find out more about membership packages for individuals, libraries, students and schools.

CORVO BOOKS

'Falling in love with a piano is a *coup de foudre* and like all great amours it changes our lives.'

Two centuries of musical lives connect in Madeline Goold's biography of her square piano.

Mr Langshaw's Square Piano
£13.99 Hardback 0954325591
www.corvobooks.com

CORVO

Andrew Hussey is Dean of the University of London Institute in Paris. His most recent book is *Paris: The Secret History* and he is currently working on a cultural history of France and Islam.

Akash Kapur is working on a book about Indian modernity, to be published by Riverhead in 2009.

Tim Lott's books include the novel, *White City Blue*, and a memoir, *The Special Relationship*, which will be published by Simon & Schuster in 2009. He appeared in *Granta* 62 with 'The Separated'.

Robert Macfarlane's *Mountains of the Mind* won the 2003 *Guardian* First Book Award. He is a Fellow of Emmanuel College, Cambridge, and the author, most recently, of *The Wild Places*. He was previously published in *Granta* 90.

Hilary Mantel has published nine novels, a book of short stories and a memoir. Her latest novel is *Beyond Black* and her next, about Thomas Cromwell, will be called *Wolf Hall*.

Rick Moody is the author of three short-story collections, a memoir and four novels. One of these, *The Ice Storm*, was made into a Hollywood film directed by Ang Lee. He is at work on a new novel.

Annie Proulx won the 1994 Pulitzer Prize for her novel *The Shipping News*. Her new book of stories will be published this year by Fourth Estate and Scribner.

Xan Rice is the East Africa correspondent of the *Guardian*. He lives in Nairobi.

Robin Robertson has published three books of poetry: *A Painted Field*, *Slow Air* and *Swithering* (which won the 2006 Forward Prize for Best Collection). His translation of *Medea* has just been published.

Owen Sheers is currently a Dorothy and Lewis B Cullman Fellow at the New York Public Library. His books include a novel, *Resistance*, and a collection of poetry, *Skirrid Hill*.

Contributing Editors
Diana Athill, Jonathan Derbyshire, Simon Gray, Sophie Harrison, Isabel Hilton, Andrew Holgate, Blake Morrison, Philip Oltermann, John Ryle, Sukhdev Sandhu, Lucretia Stewart.

hampsteadtheatre
13 to 24 May
stockholm by Bryony Lavery
30 May to 21 June
fast labour
by Steve Waters
26 June to 26 July
on the rocks
a new comedy by
Amy Rosenthal
Tickets from £14
020 7722 9301
www.hampsteadtheatre.com
Swiss Cottage, Exit 2

WAR & PEACE
SHARED EXPERIENCE
Adapted by Helen Edmundson from the novel by Tolstoy
'REMARKABLE... UNMISSABLE... TRIUMPHANT'
Daily Telegraph
10 April - 11 May
hampsteadtheatre
Tickets 020 7722 9301
Online booking www.hampsteadtheatre.com
www.sharedexperience.org.uk
ARTS COUNCIL ENGLAND

DONMAR®
5 JUNE - 2 AUGUST
The Donmar presents the first major London revival in thirty years of Enid Bagnold's remarkable dark comedy.
Cast includes
Margaret Tyzack
Penelope Wilton
Director
Michael Grandage
THE CHALK GARDEN
BOX OFFICE 0870 060 6624 NO BKG FEE
EARLHAM ST, SEVEN DIALS, LONDON WC2 www.donmarwarehouse.com
PRINCIPAL SPONSOR BARCLAYS CAPITAL
ARTS COUNCIL ENGLAND